FOOD LOVERS'
GUIDE TO
PITTSBURGH

Help Us Keep This Guide Up to Date

We would love to hear from you concerning your experiences with this guide and how you feel it could be improved and kept up to date. Please send your comments and suggestions to:

editorial@GlobePequot.com

Thanks for your input, and happy travels!

FOOD LOVERS' SERIES

FOOD LOVERS'
GUIDE TO®
PITTSBURGH

The Best Restaurants, Markets
& Local Culinary Offerings

2nd Edition

Sarah Sudar, Julia Gongaware,
Amanda McFadden & Laura Zorch

gpp

Guilford, Connecticut

Editor: Tracee Williams
Project editor: Lynn Zelem
Layout artist: Mary Ballachino
Text design: Sheryl Kober
Illustrations by Jill Butler with additional art by Carleen Moira Powell and
    MaryAnn Dubé

Maps: Alena Joy Pearce © Morris Book Publishing, LLC

ISSN 2328-8094
ISBN 978-1-4930-0644-1

Printed in the United States of America

All the information in this guidebook is subject to change. We recommend that you call ahead to obtain current information before traveling.

Thank you to everyone who makes Pittsburgh awesome!

Contents

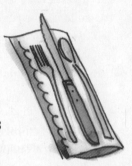

Recipes, 205

Appendices, 225

Index, 240

About the Authors

Julia Gongaware is an accomplished eater and holds a master's degree in journalism and mass communication. When she's not searching for her next great food adventure, which in her case usually involves a cheeseburger, she's researching social media trends for the health care industry. She resides in the heart of Pittsburgh's Little Italy.

Amanda McFadden has a lifelong goal to eat her way across the continental United States, and she's making good progress. That being said, Pittsburgh is still one of her favorite spots to do just about anything, especially eat. When Mandy isn't stuffing her face with the city's best pizza, she is scouting out her next travel destination and working as a digital marketer for one of the world's largest advertising agencies. Mandy resides in Brighton Heights and can usually be found with an ice cream cone in hand.

Sarah Sudar is passionate about two food groups, desserts and french fries, and is obsessed with savoring a cup of coffee after dinner along with a large slice of chocolate cake. She received a master's degree in journalism and mass communication (where she became besties with Julia) and is happy to report that she is actually using her degree wisely by writing this book (and a few others). When she isn't writing about food, she can be found window-shopping for designer handbags and pinning recipes she will probably never make on Pinterest.

Laura Zorch has never met a sugary treat she didn't like. Fact: Her body is composed of 80 percent water and 20 percent cake. Laura holds a master's degree in arts management from Carnegie Mellon University, which helps in her day job as an arts administrator.

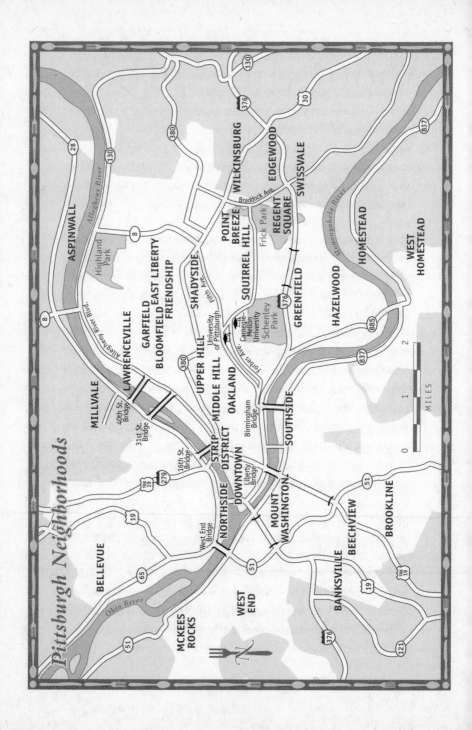

Pittsburgh Neighborhoods

Introduction

This just in: Pittsburgh is all kinds of awesome. This once beleaguered steel town has transformed into a place that people are talking about—in only the best ways possible. The city's technology, health care, education, arts, and music scenes are continuously evolving with every passing year. The cuisine is also evolving within our fair city. Pittsburgh restaurant legends have laid a solid culinary foundation, encouraging a continuous stream of newbies to take risks applauded by stomachs everywhere! Creativity and sustainability are on the rise, but most importantly, the Pittsburgh food scene has remained unpretentious and relatable, just like the people. The variety available runs the gamut of cuisine, flavor, and price, allowing both novice and expert foodies to experience culinary bliss.

Pittsburgh has become more than a city with a rich blue-collar, sports-loving history. It has matured and become a destination that attracts people from far-off lands while wholeheartedly embracing its own. It's our favorite place and hopefully soon to be yours, n'at.

How to Use This Book

Have you ever traveled to a new city and tried to pack the very best it has to offer into your agenda only to find out it wasn't actually the best? We're here to give you the scoop on all things food in Pittsburgh and offer our local insight so you can focus on the important stuff, like lifting a fork to your mouth.

We divided the city of Pittsburgh into regions based on their proximity to Downtown. Downtown is the central hub of our city since that's where many 'Burghers work, attend sporting events, and go to fancy performances at the theaters. From Downtown, we venture around the city to neighborhoods in the North, South, East, and West. We then head into the suburbs because there is some pretty tasty food way outside the city limits. In each of these sections, you will find some of the following:

Foodie Faves

These are our favorite restaurants, the places you can often find us dining in and recommending to friends, family, and strangers.

Landmarks

The places that make up the fabric of our city. If you want an authentic Pittsburgh culinary experience, hit up any Landmark we have listed.

Specialty Stores, Markets & Producers

The go-to places for produce, baked goods, and specialty products. They are located beyond the Strip District, Pittsburgh's most well known neighborhood for specialty food markets, and we'll help you find them.

In addition, we have included the following to help satisfy your hunger:

Bakeries

Pittsburgh is packed with excellent baked goods. We'll give you the rundown on where to find some of the best doughnuts, pies, cookies, cakes, and breads around town.

Local Drink Scene

Pittsburgh has myriad local distilleries producing beer, wine, cider, liquor, and even seltzer water. Nothing goes better with local fare than locally made refreshments.

Recipes

In case you want to cook like the pros, we have a selection of recipes from our favorite restaurants, created by the geniuses inside the kitchens.

Price Code

Our price guide is according to the average price per entree at each restaurant.

$	less than $10
$$	$10 to $20
$$$	$20 to $30
$$$$	more than $30

Getting Around Town

The city of Pittsburgh is made up of 90 neighborhoods, each filled with so many nooks and crannies that it could take a lifetime to see them all. Our solution: If you're only visiting for a short time, get lost with the help of our book. After stuffing your face, take time to explore the neighborhood. If you do, you'll get to experience the true fabric of Pittsburgh through our charming architectural wonders, our eclectic specialty shops, and our locals! Stop by one of the restaurants, bars, or specialty shops we mention and chances are you'll run into someone who lives right around the corner. And we bet he or she will give you the history of the neighborhood, Pittsburgh, and show you a Steelers tattoo whether you ask to see it or not.

To get to the many neighborhoods mentioned in this book, there are a variety of modes of transportation. The Golden Triangle, also known as Downtown, is the core of the city. It's booming with life during the week and is one of the easiest locations to find several modes of transportation to get you around the city. Downtown itself can easily be tackled by foot, bike, or pedicab. Plus, the Strip District, Station Square, and the North Shore are all within walking distance. To see what's on the other side of the Monongahela River, catch the T or walk over the Smithfield Street Bridge (it's the blue one) to the South Side and take one of the two inclines, the Duquesne Incline or the Monongahela Incline, up to Mount Washington even if it's only for the view. The T can also take you to the North Shore as an alternative to walking over the Allegheny River on one of the Three Sisters bridges. Catch the North Shore Connector at Gateway Station Downtown and ride to your choice of two stations near PNC Park, Heinz Field, and Rivers Casino.

Pittsburgh isn't laid out on a grid system like most cities. We do things our own way here with an abundance of one-way streets, tunnels, and bridges. If you're looking for a mode of transportation that quickly climbs all of our hills and eases navigation frustration, we suggest taking the Port Authority of Allegheny County buses to the neighborhood destinations we've recommended. Buses are available for neighborhoods including, but not limited to, Bloomfield, Downtown, Highland Park, Lawrenceville, Mount Washington, Oakland, Point Breeze, Regent Square, Shadyside, South Side, and Squirrel Hill. Information on accessing public transportation can be found at the Port Authority website: portauthority.org.

If you have a hankering for some fresh air or just want to experience the city from a different perspective, we suggest renting a bike. Countless trails run through the city, but the Three Rivers Heritage Trail (friendsoftheriverfront .org) runs for over 20 miles alongside all three Pittsburgh rivers (the Allegheny, Monongahela, and Ohio) and can take you to many of the neighborhoods mentioned in this book. Plus, a few hours of pedaling will surely work up an appetite! For more information on all things two-wheeled, visit bikepgh.org.

Keeping Up with Food News

Looking for more local flavor? Pittsburgh media loves to eat, and there is plenty of information to be had. Here are some of our favorite reads:

Edible Allegheny, **edibleallegheny.com.** *Edible Allegheny* is a magazine dedicated to seasonal, local food and local agriculture. The magazine has featured stories, a dining guide, recipes, and a calendar of events. The calendar of events is important to view if you are looking for a food-related activity to try out while in town. This magazine shouts out local food bloggers and social media users that you need to know in the "Online Dish" feature in each issue. There are many local food bloggers reviewing restaurants and testing recipes, and we love that this magazine is lets the locals know about them.

Pittsburgh City Paper, **pghcitypaper.com.** Free paper here! This alternative weekly newspaper hits street boxes all over the city and online every Wednesday. It delivers a hearty dose of music, culture, and regional news with a zesty tongue. The newspaper is the go-to resource for foodies because of its large listing of local restaurants complete with restaurant reviews. Be sure to check out the "On the Side" feature that offers a quick glimpse into a variety of food-related subjects. For happenings in the local craft brew and spirits scene, the column "On the Rocks" has you covered. If you don't have time to pick up a free paper, no worries. Download the app "CP HAPPS" for free in the App Store or on Google Play to have instant access to what's going on in Pittsburgh, including local food events, live music, theatre performances, and art openings.

Pittsburgh Magazine, **pittsburghmagazine.com.** This monthly magazine is the go-to publication for everything happening in Pittsburgh. Besides letting you know what performances are coming to the Cultural District Downtown, the magazine offers up the latest news about what's happening in the Pittsburgh culinary scene. In the "Taste" section of the magazine, the food editor shows off recent meals in the "What We're Eating" column. In "Dish," a restaurant is reviewed each month, followed by an interview with the chef. Additional content is located online at *Pittsburgh Magazine*'s website, including a restaurant finder that allows you to locate a specific restaurant depending on neighborhood and cuisine type. Also, a listing of the latest tweets from many of the local food trucks is curated so you know where they are parked and what they are serving.

***Pittsburgh Post-Gazette*, post-gazette.com.** Every Thursday, the Food and Restaurants sections of the newspaper and website receive a major update. And every Thursday morning, our eyes are reading both. The "Little Bites" section will fill you in on the upcoming happenings and specials at local restaurants. In "Munch," PG staffers highlight a trip to a new restaurant each week, letting readers know what are some of the best spots to visit around town. If you are looking for more in-depth restaurant reviews highlighting food, atmosphere, and service, be sure to follow featured stories by resident dining critics. For more food news from the PG, be sure to visit the blog, PG Plate, at pgplate.com.

Pop City, popcitymedia.com. Pop City is a weekly e-newsletter that focuses on the latest business development, technology, arts, and innovation news in the city. Oftentimes, there is mention of local restaurants opening up or articles about really cool Pittsburghers that are worth reading. You will fall in love with the city a bit more every time you read the e-newsletter. We warn you, Pittsburgh passion is contagious.

***TABLE Magazine*, tablemagazine.com.** One of Western Pennsylvania's premier food and lifestyle publications, *TABLE Magazine* can be found at grocery stores and markets across the city. This quarterly

EATPGH

Sometimes a little idea can change your life. And, a little idea that crept up in 2009 to explore Pittsburgh, eat everything we could, and share our stories with anyone who would listen has proved to be an extraordinary life changer for us.

We, the gals writing this book, are eatPGH, and our small idea is now big. For the past several years, we have written about our culinary adventures, telling Pittsburghers where and what to eat. We dish about dining out, we share recipes, and we let you know what food, beer, wine, and booze events you have to hit up. You can find us at eatPGH.com, where we let you know all about everything that is delicious.

And, we haven't put our pencils down or our appetites away since we had that idea oh so long ago. In fact, we are now culinary event wizards as well as food writers. Want to eat outside in the heart of Downtown Pittsburgh? We got you. We host an Urban Supper dinner party series that takes the city's greatest fare to the streets. Want to eat with your neighbors and strangers? We have that covered, too. We host meet and eats and progressive meals. We are here to celebrate all that is great about Pittsburgh, with you. Join us for a meal, plan your next dining excursion at eatPGH.com, or tweet us to get a restaurant recommendation.

We know Pittsburgh. We love the direction Pittsburgh is headed. We plan to help the city reach the next level of culinary awesomeness.

Visit us at eatPGH.com, fan us on Facebook at facebook .com/eatPGH, and follow us on Twitter and Instagram @eatPGH.

magazine explores culturally rich topics ranging from what's happening in the restaurants of our vibrant culinary scene and on the local farms, to showcasing new ways to entertain in your home and incorporating the right foods and wellness activities into your lifestyle. The "Grow" section will take you on a journey into gardening. In "Crush," you will learn what's happening in the world of wine. And in "Good Taste," you will be taken into the word of branding, both in home design and in your wardrobe. We pen a column in each issue, so be sure to pick up the latest edition.

Visit Pittsburgh, visitpittsburgh.com. Visit Pittsburgh is the tourism promotion agency for Allegheny County and the surrounding areas. It has a wealth of knowledge about what's going on in and around Pittsburgh. You can find where to stay, eat, and what to do while you are here all at this one-stop website. When venturing to a new city, you should always have a good map. Visit Pittsburgh's website has a rad interactive map of Pittsburgh that is worth checking out. The Visit Pittsburgh staff is active on Twitter (@vstpgh is the main account) and always eager to answer your questions and tell you the cool things about the city.

Festivals & Events

Since Pittsburgh is a melting pot of cultures, the city hosts a variety of ethnic food festivals and food events. Whether eating gyros at one of the Greek food festivals, learning how to step dance at the annual Irish festival, drinking craft beer amongst reclaimed building materials at the Steel City Big Pour, or becoming a fine spirits connoisseur at the Pittsburgh Whiskey & Fine Spirits Festival, there is practically a different food-related

event or cultural celebration each month. Here is a list of some of our favorite festivals and events to attend.

January

Pittsburgh Restaurant Week, pittsburghrestaurantweek .com. Held twice a year, in January and August, Pittsburgh Restaurant Week offers up the chance to dine at many local restaurants while taking advantage of special menus, prix-fixe options, and discount pricing. These specials and discounts are posted on Pittsburgh Restaurant Week's website prior to the week, allowing you to eye up all of the restaurants you want to visit. We suggest you cram in as many as you can, as these prices and specials rarely happen. Be sure to make reservations because tables fill up fast!

February

South Side Soup Contest, southsidesoup.com. In February, Pittsburghers bundle up in their parkas, boots, mittens, and hats, and head to the South Side for the annual South Side Soup Contest. A ticket to this "soup crawl" gets you samplings of the best soups from participating eateries and the chance to be a judge for the best bowl. Be sure to get your tickets early because even though it's cold out, this soup crawl is a sellout. Walk from bar to restaurant to pub and get your soup on. There are usually 20-something soups to try so keep your feet moving if you plan on making it through all of them.

March

Pittsburgh Fish Frys. During the Lenten season in Pittsburgh, many of the locals flock to fish frys held at churches and other organizations. At these fish frys, you can find fish sandwiches, fish dinners, fried shrimp, chowder, macaroni and cheese, coleslaw, french fries, and much more, all for a relatively low cost. Of course, there are a lot of tasty fish sandwiches at restaurants and bars, but during Lent, you should try to get to a fish fry. Since there are so many fish frys held around town during Lent, we simply cannot pick a favorite because they are each worth a try at least once. For an extensive guide of fish frys, the local television news station KDKA puts together a thorough list each year at pittsburgh.cbslocal.com.

Farm-to-Table Conference, farmtotablepa.com/conference. It's all about healthy food at this conference. Aimed at helping consumers lead healthier lifestyles and learn about fresh food origins, the Farm-to-Table Conference offers cooking demonstrations, presentations, and a hall of vendors. Attendees have the opportunity to meet food writers, wellness professionals, dieticians, farm owners, and many more individuals. At the conclusion of the conference on Friday evening, an intimate local food tasting takes place, bringing together exhibitors and like-minded locavores to enjoy samples of local food, wine, and beer.

April

GoodTaste! Pittsburgh, goodtastepittsburgh.com. If you are looking for the largest food and cooking extravaganza in Western Pennsylvania, you found it at GoodTaste! Pittsburgh. This annual cooking event features live demonstrations, cook-offs, and samplings from local restaurants. In addition, there are cooking workshops, foodie goods available for purchase, free product samples (be sure to get your reusable tote bags ready for the goodies), and a wine and spirits tasting area. Looking for more food and fun? GoodTaste! Pittsburgh also holds an event in June called "Hometown Homegrown" at the Heinz History Center, where the neighborhoods of Pittsburgh are celebrated through food, and the Pittsburgh Brew n' Chew, a beer festival, food show, and game-playing event in January. See website for more information.

May

Saint Nicholas Greek Food Festival, stnickspgh.org. Each spring, Saint Nicholas Greek Orthodox Cathedral in Oakland hosts one of the larger Greek food festivals in the area. The smell of gyros fills the Oakland air, bringing out students and residents to the cathedral. Outside the cathedral, tents are set up to seat diners. Inside the church's large hall, the food line is typically long, filled with people all waiting their turn for *moussaka*, lamb *souvlakia*, and *spanakopita*. An insider's note: Since the lines can be very long, preorder your Greek meal online or via fax. See website for details.

Pittsburgh Folk Festival, pghfolkfest.org. The Pittsburgh Folk Festival celebrates the diversity of cultures that make up the Pittsburgh region. At the Folk Festival, you can see dance performances from a variety of ethnic dance troupes and dine on food from practically all over the world. Get a little bit of India, a little bit of Croatia, and a little bit of the Philippines, among other ethnic fare from about 30 different cultures, all on one plate. Feel free to dance in the crowd of people when you hear a folk song you like. If you'd like to learn a folk dance, there are free lessons too! In addition to dancing and food, there are educational exhibits and an international marketplace.

Pittsburgh Wine Festival, pittsburghwinefestival .com. If you love a glass of wine, then this is the festival for you. Held every May at Heinz Field, the Pittsburgh Wine Festival has two tastings. The VIP Tasting features wines that are unavailable in the Grand Tasting, and the crowd is smaller, allowing you more one-on-one time to talk wine with the experts. The Grand Tasting follows and typically attracts over 2,500 people. Wines from all over the world are available for sampling, along with food and entertainment.

June

Pittsburgh Magazine Best Restaurants Party, pittsburgh magazine.com. Each year, *Pittsburgh Magazine* gathers Pittsburgh's best restaurants and throws one large party, appropriately called the Best Restaurants Party. The party is typically sold out, so be sure to get your tickets early! This is a way to sample some of Pittsburgh's most delicious plates. Over 60 restaurants are on display, offering sample after sample after sample of their noteworthy cuisines. Be sure to go on an empty stomach because the samples are filling and will leave you wanting seconds, thirds, and fourths.

July

Slovenefest, slovenefest.com. Western Pennsylvania has a large contingent of Slovenians. So much so that the Slovenian National Benefit Society (SNPJ) makes its home here in Enon Valley, Lawrence County. Once a year, in mid-July, the SNPJ throws Slovenefest—a food, music, and culture extravaganza—at its headquarter location. If button box bands, awesome Slovenian doughnuts, and polka dancing are your flavor, get in on the Slovenefest action! Everyone is welcome.

August

Bloomfield Little Italy Days, littleitalydays.com. Traces of Italy are always present throughout the neighborhood of Bloomfield, but each August the area explodes with Italian heritage. A parade winds through the streets, traditional Italian music is played, and food vendors line Liberty

Avenue during this family-friendly 4-day festival. You can even watch a few games of bocce while you nosh on a sampling of deep-fried risotto balls and Italian hot sausage.

McKeesport International Village, mckeesportinternational village.com. For over 50 years, the City of McKeesport has been celebrating the diversity of Pittsburgh cultures and ethnic groups by turning a neighborhood park into an international village, complete with food, entertainment, and neighborhood camaraderie. Ethnic fare cooked by patrons from cultural organizations and church groups representing Serbian, Lebanese, Slovak, Chinese, African-American, and a variety of other nationalities is at your disposal for eating. Though there is a small fee charged for admission into the International Village, parking is free. Be sure not to leave your appetite in the car.

Savor Pittsburgh, savorpgh.com. Every August, over 1,500 people attend Savor Pittsburgh. This culinary competition includes samplings from over 25 local restaurants who battle with each other to receive "Best Appetizer," "Best Entree," "Best Dessert," and the ultimate bragging rights, "Dish of the Year." Throughout the night, guests enjoy top-shelf cocktails, live music, and dancing. All proceeds from the event benefit premature research conducted by the Magee-Womens Research Institute and Foundation.

September

Coors Light Kickoff and Rib Festival, heinzfieldribfest .com. The Annual Coors Light Kickoff and Rib Festival is our city's celebration of the start of the Steelers football season. Rib vendors from around the nation venture to Pittsburgh with their racks, smokers, and sauces ready to take on hungry Pittsburghers of all ages. Admission is free, and activities, games, and entertainment are available for the entire family.

Oktoberfest at Penn Brewery, penn brew.com. Can't make it to Munich? Try Penn Brewery for your Oktoberfest-ing! The event takes place over two weekends in September. Whichever weekend you choose, you can enjoy house-made seasonal craft brews, live music, and some of the best German food in the city. Nothing says Oktoberfest better than pretzels, 'kraut, and beer! Penn Brewery looks out for the vegetarians as well, offering meatless sloppy joes because, to veggie lovers, 'wursts are the worst.

Pittsburgh Irish Festival, pghirishfest.org. Since 1991, the Pittsburgh Irish Festival has been dedicated to generating awareness of Irish heritage in Pittsburgh. The festival runs for three days (the weekend after Labor Day) and features live music and dancing, shopping, educational activities, Irish bingo, and, of course, delicious food. Who doesn't love dauber bingo and food? We do! Irish specialties are obviously on the menu, including sausages, corned beef and cabbage, boxty pancakes, potato soup, desserts, and much more. Definitely a taste of Ireland in the 'Burgh.

Pittsburgh Lebanese Food Festival, pghlebanesefestival .com. The Pittsburgh Lebanese Food Festival is a three-day weekend at Our Lady of Victory Maronite Catholic Church in Carnegie. Dine in or take out tons of Lebanese specialties like kibbee, lamb, grape leaves, spinach and feta pies, falafel, tabouli, and hummus. Hungry yet? Orders can be placed in advance online if you are hungry and in a hurry.

Steel City Big Pour, constructionjunction.org/pages/bigpour. Held each year at Construction Junction, the city's coolest place to find reclaimed bathtubs, shelving, and mantels, the Steel City Big Pour is the must-attend craft beer event in the city. Get tickets early—it sells out fast. Tickets include regular admission (gets you all the local craft beer samples you can handle) and designated driver (gets you all the locally made nonalcoholic drinks you can handle). There's also a reuse enthusiast ticket that includes admission, a t-shirt, and donation to Construction Junction. Proceeds from sales go toward supporting Construction Junction's mission of conservation through the reuse of reclaimed building materials. Inside this huge party, you get access to craft beer samples, food from local eateries, live art and music, raffles, and a good-ole' time with tons of Pittsburghers. If you are drinking, be sure to try the Steel City Big Pour specialty brew, which is made every year by East End Brewing Company.

October

Pittsburgh Whiskey & Fine Spirits Festival, pittsburgh whiskeyfestival.com.
A festival for the spirits, and we ain't talking about the boogity-boo kind here. The annual Pittsburgh Whiskey & Fine Spirits Festival is for spirits connoisseurs who want to sample cordials, gin, rum, tequila, scotch, vodka, and, of course, whiskey from around the world. Attendees ranging from novices to experts pack Rivers Casino to sample hundreds of fine spirits alongside an assortment of food. If you are a novice and want to learn how to become a scotch drinker or want to add whiskey connoisseur to your resume, attend this event.

December

Lawrenceville Joy of Cookies Cookie Tour, lvpgh.com/ cookietour.
Free things fill our heart with joy. So do cookies. Enter Lawrenceville Joy of Cookies Cookie Tour. The Lawrenceville Joy of Cookies Cookie Tour is a free event held for four days (Thursday through Sunday) during the first weekend in December that helps boost the neighborhood's economy. The purpose is to host an "un-mall" experience, urging shoppers to support local, independent businesses. The tour consists of galleries, shops, restaurants, bakeries, and other businesses

in Lawrenceville and an official map is drawn up each year. You can visit over 30 businesses on the map at your convenience, collecting free samples of cookies and cookie recipes along the way. In addition to the cookie tour, there is a cookie mall bake sale, typically on the Saturday of the weekend tour. Proceeds from the bake sale are donated to local community organizations.

The Nationality Rooms Holiday Open House, pitt .edu/~natrooms. Every winter, the Nationality Rooms at the University of Pittsburgh hold a Holiday Open House. Admission to the event is free, and you can tour all 29 Nationality Rooms inside the Cathedral of Learning. During this open house, each Nationality Room is decorated in the holiday traditions of each room's heritage. Be sure to stop by the Early American Room on the third floor of the Cathedral because it is said to be haunted. Spooky! Live performances by ethnic dance troupes, ethnic food, and a global marketplace are also set up during this event in the Commons Room of the Cathedral. A definite go-to event if you are looking to learn more about a variety of ethnic cultures (and feast on some tasty delights) all in one place.

Downtown Pittsburgh & Station Square

Downtown Pittsburgh, like the rest of the city, is in the midst of a renaissance. While it may be running a couple of paces behind some of the area's more vibrant, populous boroughs, "Dahntahn" is second to none in culture and unique eateries.

Much of Downtown's resurgence as a solid place to dine relates directly to the influence of The Pittsburgh Cultural Trust. The Trust began transforming dilapidated buildings in the late 1980s. Now, these spaces like the Benedum Center, O'Reilly Theater, Harris Theater, and Heinz Hall bring crowds Downtown in droves for entertainment. The Trust's galleries, Wood Street Galleries, Space, 707 and 709, and Future Tenant, facilitate cutting-edge art experiences in a neighborhood once filled with adult video stores. With the additions of the Toonseum and the Arcade Comedy Theater, Downtown has become a cultural oasis. It comes as no surprise that the Downtown Cultural District restaurants would be equally as impressive. The District boasts dining spots that thrill theatergoers, art aficionados, and anyone with a rumble in their bellies.

Renovations to Market Square and Point State Park add to the dining ease of Downtown with locales that offer outdoor seating in warmer

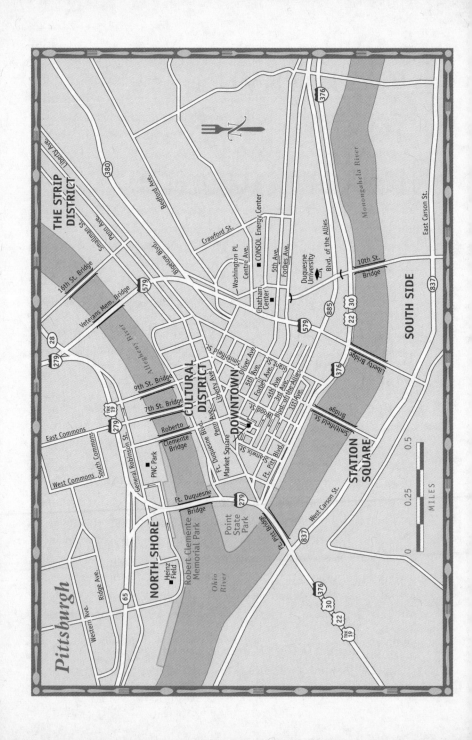

months and friendly neighborhood haunts. Downtown's neighbor across the Monongahela River, Station Square, a riverfront entertainment mecca, features mainly big-box dining establishments, but a few gems are worth the short walk over the seriously beautiful (and blue) Smithfield Street Bridge.

While you may hear that traveling to Downtown is like scaling Mt. Everest (it takes both skill and practice), that is more myth than fact. Downtown is drivable and bike friendly, parking is plentiful and cheap after 5 p.m., and you will most likely run into Pennsylvania's state flower (the construction cone) only once or twice. Don't let a little navigation stand between you and a taste of the 'Burgh's Golden Triangle.

Foodie Faves

The Apollo Cafe, **429 Forbes Ave., Pittsburgh, PA 15219; (412) 471-3033; apollocafepittsburgh.com; Mediterranean; $.** Walking into The Apollo Cafe is like walking into Grandma's house. The quirky interior is old-school and welcoming, and the food stays in line with that at-home feel. Since 1988, The Apollo Cafe has served the Downtown lunch crowds an eclectic mix of Mediterranean grub and comforting, hearty soups and sandwiches. A full breakfast menu is also available for early birds. From grilled cheese to grape leaves, this sweet cafe has something for everyone. And everyone—yes, everyone—loves the soups. These rich bowls are almost legendary, especially the tomato basil. It is one-of-a-kind with tiny dough balls in every bite. After your first taste, you will be lining up at least once per week to get your fill. Coincidently, getting in line is actually your first step at Apollo upon entering. Hungry crowds queue at the start of the cold bar, complete with hummus, broccoli salad, and a smattering of hot items (like that infamous soup). Grab a red tray, order your meal and sides, and slide that tray down the railing. Before you pay, you will be greeted with a selection of baked goods (try the brownie!). Make sure your wallet is full of cash; this is a no-credit-card joint. An ATM is on-site if you are in a pinch.

Blue Line Grille, 1014 5th Ave., Pittsburgh, PA 15219; (412) 281-2583; bluelinegrille.com; Sports Bar; $$. If you are looking for a pit stop before a Pens game at CONSOL Energy Center, Blue Line Grille is just your spot. This sports bar is located directly across the street from CONSOL (how convenient) and serves up some high-quality bar food snacks. You won't find any sad frozen potato skins or fried mozzarella sticks here. What you will find are Doc's Nachos: tortilla chips smothered in a housemade beer cheese and melted shredded cheese topped with jalapeños, tomatoes, and black olives, and drizzled with a scallion cream sauce. Definitely not some sad chips with questionable orange cheese. The menu is also filled with fresh salads, build-your-own burgers and pizzas, and wings. And what's a sports bar without drinks? There are plenty of bottles and drafts, but if you want to ensure a Pens' win, try one of the Pens-themed signature cocktails, such as the 71 Malkin's Moscow Mule made with Absolut Orient Apple, lime juice, and ginger beer. It's served in a copper mug with a hockey stick stirrer for good measure.

Bluebird Kitchen, 221 Forbes Ave., Pittsburgh, PA 15222; (412) 642-4414; bluebirdkitchen.com; Breakfast & Lunch; $. Amidst a sea of sit-down restaurants and fast-food joints sits Bluebird Kitchen in a location prime for Downtown patrons. Breakfast and lunch are served to-go style from this cool cafe. If you have a bit of time, pull up a stool along the counter that overlooks Forbes Avenue. Fare ranges from hot coffee and warm pastries in the morning to fresh salads and inventive sandwiches in the afternoon. Bluebird keeps fan favorites on the menu year-round, like the chicken salad croissant and the tuna nicoise salad, but churns out seasonal sides, daily soups, and a monthly salad selection to please everyone's ever-changing taste buds. Desserts and sugary morning-time snacks abound and are a perfect supplement to business meetings, so thank goodness for the catering menu! Offerings change daily so there's always a reason to stop in. Additional location: Downtown, 11 Stanwix St., Pittsburgh, PA 15222; (412) 281-4422.

Braddock's Pittsburgh Brasserie, 107 6th St., Pittsburgh, PA, 15222; (412) 992-2005; braddocksrestaurant.com; American; $$$. Braddock's Pittsburgh Brasserie, located in The Renaissance Hotel Pittsburgh, is a fine place to grab a cocktail or enjoy a great meal before a theater show in Pittsburgh's Cultural District. The restaurant is located next to Byham Theater near the Allegheny River. By far, the best item on the menu are the braised short rib pierogies with creamed leeks in "I think I've died and gone to heaven" pan juices. You will want multiple orders because no one at your table will want to share after they have their first bite. Besides the pierogies, Braddock's serves breakfast, lunch, and dinner entrees that are reminiscent of American comfort food, but with a modern flare. If you make it past the appetizers of pierogies or grilled Strip District kielbasa with sauerkraut and assorted mustards, you can't go wrong with the crab cakes or the house-made potato gnocchi and lobster. See Executive Chef Jason Shaffer's recipe for Short Rib Pierogies on p. 218.

Butcher and the Rye, 212 6th St., Pittsburgh, PA 15222; (412) 391-2752; butcherandtherye.com; New American; $$$. A painted mural of a butchered rabbit. A display of meat cleavers. An antler chandelier. It is all about the details at Butcher and the Rye. The so-hip-you-could-cry interior makes a serious visual impact. The wall of whiskey behind the downstairs bar also adds to the super-hot aesthetic. The upstairs bar, or the Rye in Butcher and the Rye, is on equal footing in terms of sexiness. Red and black graphic leather chairs and vintage-inspired light fixtures bring a classic cool to the second floor, which serves housemade bitters from the long bar. The bar staff here is beyond fantastic, even gaining a nod from the James Beard Foundation. When you drink at Butcher and the Rye, you are guaranteed a decent cocktail. The food here is no slouch either. Chef Richard DeShantz knows what is up and certainly knows his meats. Small plates for sharing dominate the menu with offerings like pig candy (pork belly, apple kimchee, and miso caramel) and dry aged tartare. Richness extends to the main dishes and desserts (we see you, deep-fried brownie). With a great menu, excellent drinks, and the crazy cool atmosphere, Butcher and the Rye is the perfect place to see and be seen.

Chinatown Inn, 520 3rd Ave., Pittsburgh PA 15219; (412) 261-1292; chinatowninn.net; Chinese; $$. We've heard many a tale be told of Pittsburgh's once thriving Chinatown. Today, all that's left is one little restaurant with a big reputation, Chinatown Inn. The restaurant has ample seating, but since the food is straight out of tasty town, there's almost always a lunchtime line. The service is fast and friendly, though, so don't let a little wait deter you. At Chinatown Inn you can score yourself a lunch combo with beef, poultry, or seafood. Vegetarian? They've got you covered. One of our favorite combos is General Tso's tofu served with fried rice and a spring roll. The portions are the perfect size, which will leave you with just enough room to polish off a fortune cookie and a cup of tea before you leave. Here's another selling point—free lot parking Mon through Fri after 6 p.m. for dinner.

Craftwork Kitchen, Concourse Level, 600 Grant St., Pittsburgh, PA 15219; (412) 979-4754; craftworkcatering.com; Sandwiches; $. Don't let the ironic signs and WrestleMania figurines fool you; the food served at Craftwork Kitchen is far from laughable. Hoagies, fries, and loaded nachos are available during the summer when the guys are on the U.S. Steel Tower plaza. If you're around on a Friday, relieve your 9-to-5 lunchtime blues with a handcrafted burger during Burger Friday. The Paula Meen, Blue Man Group, or Garden Gnome are all choices that will keep you grinning from the first to last bite. The fun doesn't stop when the weather turns cold. Sandwiches, soups, salads, and sides are available during the winter when Craftwork goes inside the building. Try the chorizo meatball hoagie, porkgasm, or *bánh mì* sandwich, and don't forget to add the White Lightning chili. All sandwiches are big enough to share, but with the kind of flavor they deliver, that's not likely to happen.

Diamond Market Bar & Grill, 430 Market Sq., Pittsburgh, PA 15222; (412) 325-2000; diamondmarketgrill.com; American; $$. Thanks to the owners of Primanti Bros., Diamond Market Bar & Grill is serving up delightful dishes in the heart of Market Square. Pittsburgh-made potato and feta pierogies served with cabbage and olive sour cream; macaroni and cheese made with cheddar, gruyère, and pepper jack cheeses; and Iron City mussels served in a sauce made from Iron City beer are just some of the noteworthy appetizers on the menu. We recommend you bring a big appetite when you come to visit because you'll be greeted with barbecue sandwiches of hand-pulled pork, hand-pulled chicken, and beef brisket; Angus burgers; and hot turkey sandwiches. To complement whichever sandwich you choose, you can order fresh-cut fries with a variety of toppings, like cheese curds and gravy, or sweet potato wedges seasoned with brown sugar, cinnamon, and cayenne pepper. House-made soups, handspun milk shakes, and apple and cabbage slaw round out a unique yet down-home menu that gets four thumbs up from us.

Ephesus Pizza, 219 4th Ave., Pittsburgh, PA 15222; (412) 552-9020; ephesuspizza.com; Pizza; $$. Pittsburgh is home to like a billion pizza places. Each serves up slices with a certain style. Since 2001, Ephesus Pizza's style has been loading toppings upon toppings on a doughy bed of seasoned crust with a Mediterranean and Turkish twist. While there is something to be said for plain cheese, at Ephesus there is something to be said for cheese pizza with a couple of extra toppings. Go for the

Greek pizza topped with gyro meat, tomato, onion, black olives, and feta, mozzarella, and provolone cheeses with white sauce. Or the Ratatouille pizza graced with grilled eggplant, red and yellow peppers, zucchini, caramelized onions, mozzarella and provolone cheeses, with red sauce and topped with goat cheese. These pies come in a personal size so if you have trouble deciding, you can try a few! Additional location: 616 Lincoln Ave., Bellevue, PA 15202; (412) 776-7660.

Franktuary, 325 Oliver Ave., Pittsburgh, PA 15222; (412) 288-0322; franktuary.com; Hot Dogs; $. Imagine, if you will, a gourmet hot doggery that resides in the basement of a church. It's a reality if you live in Pittsburgh! At Franktuary, you can get your dogs plain or dressed up, all beef or veggie, and with a side of pickles or pierogies. If it's your first time visiting, we say go for the Pittsburgh dog, with a smooshed pierogie and coleslaw, and the Buffalo dog, with Frank's Buffalo Wing Sauce and bleu cheese dressing, two of our favorites. Stop by the Butler Street location in Lawrenceville for Tuesday trivia, or head to Sunday brunch for a religious experience, or any day of the week for a craft cocktail to pair with your hot dog. You can also find Franktuary rolling around via bicycle, delivering dogs Downtown, and, best of all, it has a food truck that roams the city looking for hungry folks to feed! As one of their many taglines exclaims, "Franks be to God!" Additional location: Lawrenceville, 3810 Butler St., Pittsburgh, PA 15201; (412) 586-7224. See Owner Megan Lindsey's recipe for Sweet Onion Sauce on p. 222.

Grit & Grace, 535 Liberty Ave., Pittsburgh, PA 15222; (412) 281-4748; gritandgracepgh.com; Asian Fusion; $$$. When you think late-night bites, greasy burgers and nachos often come to mind. Grit & Grace is out to turn that greasy notion on its head. Inspired by his Asian-American upbringing, Chef-Owner Brian Pekarcik has created a menu featuring contrasting flavors blended together to create perfect harmony. Grab a table (if you can) or make a new friend at the communal table or long modern bar. Once you're settled, start your meal with a few select bites from the dim sum tray. The dim sum menu changes on the regular, but try the pork belly with orange, chili, garlic, and ginger, and the scallop ceviche with lobster gelee, lime, and red pepper, if they're available. Once you're done snacking, order the steamed bun with house-made mortadella, coriander mustard, and bread-and-butter pickles. You'll never crave your mom's fried bologna sandwich again. If you're still hungry, try the braised goat or seared hanger steak. See Brian Pekarcik's recipe for Roasted Carrots, Fresh Cheese, Toasted Edamame, Little Gems Lettuce, & Chili Vinaigrette on p. 216.

Habitat Restaurant, 510 Market St., Pittsburgh, PA 15222; (412) 773-8848; habitatrestaurant.com; International; $$$$. Habitat Restaurant brings a level of sophistication to Market Square. The locally sourced restaurant is on the second floor of the swanky Fairmont Hotel. Grab a seat by the window and watch passersby on the street below or pull up a chair by the kitchen and watch the sous chef put the finishing touches on dishes like the curried butternut squash soup and the roasted beets and organic goat cheese salad made with local wildflower honey, cracked pepper, and coriander. Servers carry unique silver amphibian pitchers for water and present exquisitely prepared appetizers, entrees, and desserts. If you visit Habitat for lunch, a must order is the Executive Express, a platter with the soup, salad, sandwich, and dessert of the day. See Pastry Chef James Wroblewski's recipe for Carrot Cake with Cream Cheese Icing and Caramel Sauce on p. 210.

Istanbul Grille, Concourse Level, 600 Grant St., Pittsburgh, PA 15219; (412) 999-0841; istanbulgrille.com; Mediterranean; $. Head inside the U.S. Steel Tower for a lunch you won't soon forget. There, a small lunch counter filled with traditional Turkish fare will be your midday saving grace. Step up to the counter and tell the guy smiling at you (his name is Josh, by the way) that you're a first-timer. He'll walk you through the choices and load up your plate in the process. Start by choosing a vegetarian or meat plate. Then you'll get a hearty scoop of the dressed salad with either white sauce or hot sauce. Once you do that it's pretty much a cafeteria-style free-for-all. Choose from a variety of Turkish favorites like tabbouleh, baba ganoush, hummus, grape leaves, and bulgur rice, all of which will be heaped so high it could feed two people. Be sure to bring at least $10 with you. Istanbul is cash only. Or maybe free if you show Josh and his food some love.

Las Velas Mexican Restaurant, 21 Market Sq., Pittsburgh, PA 15222; (412) 251-0031; lasvelasmex.com; Mexican; $$. Margarita-o-clock starts at approximately 5 p.m., Mon through Fri at Las Velas Mexican Restaurant in Market Square. It features fresh-made sangria and margaritas and offers a variety of half off cantina fare sure to make your hour even happier. Poblano dip served with hand-cut chips; *flautas* stuffed with chicken, peppers, cheese, and more; and *sopecitos,* four to an order and topped with either chicken, steak, chorizo, or carnitas are just a few of the options available. If happy hour isn't your style, swing by early for lunch or late for dinner. We suggest the *tacos del paisa*, otherwise known as fish tacos, good at any time of day. Three tacos come loaded with freshly breaded tilapia, shredded cabbage, pico de gallo, and a creamy chipotle sauce. And let's not forget about the side of rice and beans.

Market Street Deli Co. and Market Street Grill, 2 PPG Place, Pittsburgh, PA 15222; (412) 471-5851; marketstreetdeli.com; Deli; $. If you're in the market for a fresh and hearty Downtown lunch, Market Street Deli Co. and Market Street Grill is the ticket. Reminiscent of a deli or grill found in many New York City neighborhoods, Market Street serves up fast and inexpensive lunches so you can get back to your busy schedule. The daily specials can range from a buffalo chicken wrap to classic deli sandwiches like the Reuben or club. What makes this deli different than your average run-of-the-mill sandwich shop? Its homemade Parmesan potato chips and their piping hot, homemade soups. If your palate is craving something fried or grilled, simply peek around the deli counter and order a loaded cheeseburger and fries from the grill. You'll be in and out in no time.

Meat & Potatoes, 649 Penn Ave., Pittsburgh, PA 15222; (412) 325-7007; meatandpotatoespgh.com; Gastropub; $$–$$$. Meat and potatoes? Yes, please! The simplest of American eats gets a hip upgrade at one of the hottest spots in the Cultural District foodscape. Chef Richard DeShantz opened the gastropub in 2011, and the space has been packed ever since. Meat and potatoes are not the only thing on the menu, but carnivores will be delighted with the many meat-heavy options. Standout dinner entrees include the bolognese pappardelle with pancetta, short rib, and pork shoulder and the 34-ounce rib eye for two or for a very hungry one. This joint provides some 1930s atmosphere to go along with your meal; we're just glad it is no longer Prohibition. Brunch is also served on Saturday and Sunday, complete with all-you-can-drink Bloody Marys at the bar! See Meat & Potatoes's recipe for Chicken Potpie on p. 212.

Nine on Nine, 900 Penn Ave., Pittsburgh, PA 15222; (412) 338-6463; nineonninepgh.com; American; $$$$ (Bar Nine: $$). If you are looking for a restaurant with a romantic atmosphere and tasty food, then Nine on Nine is the place to go when Downtown. The intimate dining room serves elegant hot and cold starters and entrees, complete with a Theatre Menu and a Chef's Tasting. *Note:* Reservations are strongly recommended for the dining room on weekends and during evening theater performances. In the dining room, the risotto made with wild mushrooms and white truffle oil is the perfect starter. For an entree, try the prime strip with smoked hominy grits. If you can't get reservations in the dining room, the adjacent Bar Nine is just as fantastic. The bar has its own small, more casual menu consisting of refined bar food, including beef sliders, tacos, and lobster macaroni and cheese. Though the prices may be a bit expensive, the atmosphere, food, and drinks are definitely worth every penny.

Our Daily Bread, 320 6th Ave., Pittsburgh, PA 15222; (412) 471-3436; ourdailybreadpgh.org; Cafeteria; $. Not all church basements are created equal, and Our Daily Bread, located on the ground floor of the First Presbyterian Church of Pittsburgh, is proof. The no-frills cafeteria will leave both your belly and wallet full and has been a warm helping hand in the Downtown community since 1932. It's just like your high school cafeteria only with way less drama and a greater sense of community. Rows of tables filled with a diverse crowd line the old basketball court. Home-style cooked meals like meat loaf with mashed potatoes, burgundy beef over noodles, and fish with macaroni and cheese are sure to warm you up on cold Pittsburgh days. Each day home-made soup like wedding and chicken rice are available as well as a salad bar to accompany your meal. You pay by weight, but most of the hearty lunch options end up under $6, a price we can all be thankful for these days.

Seviche, 930 Penn Ave., Pittsburgh, PA 15222; (412) 697-3120; seviche.com; Latin American; $$. Named after raw seafood marinated in citrus juices, Seviche brings a vibrant, Latin flavor to Downtown while serving small plates and tasty cocktails to a typically sharp-dressed crowd. The dish to try is obviously the spot's namesake, which you can watch being created at a specialty bar. The seviche is prepared in several forms, from the traditional to the "Fire and Ice" (for those feeling particularly spicy and ready for some habañero action).

For non-seafood fans, the chorizo tacos are a standout on the taco menu. The tacos come two or three per order and though they may be bite-size, they are big on flavor. Be sure to order a drink, such as the Mango Mojito, one of our favorites. And, if you enjoy dancing, join in on salsa dancing fun at Seviche every Monday starting at 9 p.m.

Sienna Mercato, 942 Penn Ave., Pittsburgh, PA 15222; (412) 281-2810; siennapgh.com; Eclectic; $$. Three floors of awesomeness await you at Sienna Mercato. The first floor, Emporio, is the meatball floor. Choose pork, chicken, beef, or vegetarian balls to coat in a variety of sauces like government cheese, chicken gravy, and spicy arribiatta. Meatballs can be ordered as sliders, grinders, on paninis, or bunless. The menu includes more than balls, but you would be wrong to not order at least one. Emporio has a draft list that reads like a novel and other fun beverages such as an iced tea carton and Italian sodas, which are paired nicely with vodka. The second floor, Mezzo, is all about charcuterie and wood-fired pizzas. Get your meat platter on! The third floor, il Tetto (Italian for "rooftop") is the pièce de résistance: a beer and wine bar with a retractable roof. In warm weather, the roof is able to peel back to let the sun or stars shine through. Even if Pittsburgh weather isn't cooperating, the glass roof provides a spectacular view of the cityscape and the sky. There is no other spot in town that can boast of such a remarkable ceiling. Sienna Mercato would make a great meal exploration, navigating your taste buds through all three levels: balls, boards (of meats and cheeses), and breathtaking views.

Sienna Sulla Piazza, 22 Market Sq., Pittsburgh, PA 15222; (412) 281-6363; siennapgh.com; Italian; $$. Inside out and outside in. Sienna Sulla Piazza in Market Square is the perfect spot for outdoor dining, with a seamless flow from inside to outside. In warm months, the front of the restaurant opens out to the sidewalk, allowing for dining al fresco and a lovely view of one of Downtown Pittsburgh's most loved public spaces. When the weather is cold, the inside of Sienna still feels streetlike, with exposed brick and soft lighting. It is a great spot to spend some time: ordering from the long wine list (glass or bottle); indulging in antipasti like mozzarella-stuffed meatballs; and sharing a flatbread with prosciutto and arugula. The pasta selections are rich and satisfying, and the main entrees, or secondi, are beautifully presented whether you choose quail, or salmon, or tenderloin, or . . . anything! Sienna's sister restaurant, **Sienna Mercato** (p. 29), is located in the Cultural District.

Six Penn Kitchen, 146 6th St., Pittsburgh, PA 15222; (412) 566-7366; sixpennkitchen.com; American; $$$. Whether you are looking for a weekend brunch spot before a matinee of the ballet, a casual business dinner, or an after-work happy hour, Six Penn Kitchen is sure to satisfy your cravings. Here, the menu changes frequently but always seems to include a gourmet burger and a variety of entrees, such as the Jamison Farm lamb bolognese, skillet-style rotisserie chicken, and buffalo mac'n cheese. Start your meal off with the complimentary breadbasket, which is stocked with several varieties to please the palate. Be sure to save room for the signature dessert at Six Penn called the "circus," a plate filled with house-made cracker jacks, whoopee pies, cinnamon doughnuts, and fluffy cotton candy. The restaurant has three levels of dining, including two bars, a private dining room on the second floor, and a rooftop lounge with stellar views of the city, especially during Pirates fireworks nights.

The Sonoma Grille, 947 Penn Ave., Pittsburgh, PA 15222; (412) 697-1336; thesonomagrille.com; American; $$$. The Sonoma Grille is a little slice of the West Coast right along Penn Avenue. Stocked with over 1,000 wines, this place makes it easy to get distracted and perhaps drink your meal. But the food should certainly steal some of your attention. The menu of Cali-inspired dishes is built on the strengths of locally sourced ingredients, so it adapts as the seasons change. Start your meal with the wild mushroom naan: mushroom confit with roasted tomatoes, chevre, Kalamata olives, arugula, and cilantro pesto. Entrees range from duck and free-range venison to diver scallops and lamb. Expect to be treated fabulously from start to finish, as the service is as excellent as the roving breadbasket. Sunday at Sonoma features a lively Jazz Brunch with Pittsburgh-area musicians. For a reasonable set price, you get a breakfast cocktail, all the makings of a solid meal, and a live concert. The wine, the atmosphere, and the food could trigger some California dreaming, but the sights and sounds of the 'Burgh will make for a pretty sweet reality.

Sree's Foods, 701 Smithfield St., Pittsburgh, PA 15222; (412) 860-9181; $. Downtown Pittsburgh is filled with countless upscale restaurants but also has a few unassuming spots that could easily be overlooked. Sree's Foods ranks high on the overlooked list. Tucked into an oddly shaped building on a busy corner, Sree's Foods serves authentic Indian cuisine for lunch. For around $5 you can sample various Indian staples like tamarind chicken, spinach black-eyed peas, eggplant curry, and tomato dal. Mrs. Sree prepares all the food, mostly vegan and vegetarian options, daily based on a philosophy she and her late husband, Mr. Sree, incorporate into each dish: that food is life. Their attention to spice and flavor elevates the dishes to the next level and creates that slow, satisfying burn that will keep you craving more.

Stone Neapolitan Pizza, 300 Liberty Ave. #100, Pittsburgh, PA 15222; (412) 904-4531; stonepizzeria.com; Pizza; $. Pizza promised in 90 seconds? Hard to believe, but true nonetheless. Stone Neapolitan Pizza is the first of its kind in Pennsylvania, serving up pies in a matter of minutes. Located on Liberty Avenue in Downtown Pittsburgh, Stone caters to the fast-paced lunchtime crowd of hungry businessgoers. The huge blackboard menu lists out all the options for a quick

lunch, including the House Pies: Margherita, Quattro Formaggi, and Del Cafone. If you are more of the creative type, you can make your own pizza by choosing one (or more) of the many fresh toppings to adorn your stone-fired dough. In true Neapolitan style, the oil and cheese are the heroes and the toppings simply enhance the experience. With all those options, it'll take you longer to decide what to order than it will for your creation to be created!

Storms Restaurant, 429 Fourth Ave., Pittsburgh, PA 15219; (412) 288-4321; stormsrestaurant.com; Italian; $$. Barely noticeable from the street, Storm's Restaurant is one of those "hidden gems" that you only know about because so-and-so's friend's coworker told you that you had to go there. Found basement level of the Pittsburgh Finance Building on Fourth Avenue, Storms serves up classic Pittsburgh Italian food. It is great for a sit-down lunch for business partners or a night out with your family for good eats and good conversation. The low ceilings close you in enough to make your meal feel intimate without being constricting, and the menu has all the classics like chicken picatta, broiled spots, and eggplant parmesan. Entrees are served with a side of pasta or veggie of the day and a soup or salad and fresh bread for everyone! Portions are the perfect size, leaving you with just enough room for a slice of cheesecake or their delightful tiramisu.

Ten Penny, 960 Penn Ave., Pittsburgh, PA 15222; (412) 318-8000; tenpennypgh.com; American; $$$. On the corner of 10th and Penn is the appropriately named spot Ten Penny. The restaurant has an open feel with exposed wood beams, Edison bulbs, and giant floor-to-ceiling windows that open in warm weather. Seating wraps around a large center bar and includes comfy, big booths on the perimeter. If you have a large group, you can reserve the private back room complete with a big, communal table, and your own television if you need to watch a game or a reality show or whatever you are currently digging. Ten Penny has several menus including brunch, lunch, dinner, and late night. There are plenty of plates to share that are worth the order including the crispy brussels sprouts made with a Jack Daniel's balsamic glaze and the mega meatball, which lives up to its name. Lunch is heavy on tasty sandwiches and salads. Dinner ups the ante with fancy selections like veal osso bucco. The drink menu features wines by the bottle or glass, Champagne, and a host of liquor. The dessert menu also features an extensive list of after-dinner liquor options (all of the port!). The real treat? Ten Penny provides still water *or* sparkling water free of charge. That is one sparkling touch of class!

Tic Toc Restaurant, 400 Fifth Ave., Pittsburgh, PA 15219; (412) 232-2307; Diner; $. Tucked into the corner among men's clothing on the first floor of Macy's department store is the Tic Toc Restaurant. It's a hidden Downtown gem and classic Pittsburgh. The menu looks like it hasn't changed since it was first penned, and the same goes for the patrons. If you're mid-shop and have a hankering for a tuna melt or want to reminisce about the good ol' days, Tic Toc will help you in both departments. There's a lunch counter as well as a dining area that's usually full during the lunch rush. The menu features diner standards like meat loaf, open-faced turkey sandwiches, and liver and onions. We suggest the chicken potpie. Large chunks of chicken, peas, and carrots are in a rich creamy sauce and topped with a flaky round of puff pastry. It's accompanied by a spinach salad topped with mandarin oranges and dressed with its signature sesame dressing. Pair that with a classic milk shake or malt, and you have a perfect midday lunch break.

Verde Good Beans, 412 First Ave., Pittsburgh, PA 15219; (412) 523-8885; Breakfast & Lunch; $. The instant you walk into Verde Good Beans on First Avenue, you enter a sort of euphoric state. The decor is happy and homey, and you feel as if you know the staff on a personal level, like you're childhood friends. The menu at this breakfast and lunch spot changes often, so be sure to check Facebook and Twitter to see what the specials are before you pop in. Sustainable, organic foods and local coffees and teas are served. Order up one of the hearty soups or stews and pair it with a create-your-own panini. One of our favorite dishes is their black bean pumpkin soup, which you can enjoy from a tiny bistro table or curled up in an overstuffed chair. Its quirky decor makes us smile almost as much as the fact that they have Mulberry Creamery gelato and about a million specialty smoothie and coffee drinks on the menu.

Winghart's Whiskey & Burger Bar, 5 Market Sq., Pittsburgh, PA 15222; (412) 434-5600; winghartburgers.com; Burgers; $$. Walking into Winghart's in Market Square is kind of like walking into Cheers, where everybody knows your name. Okay, so the Winghart's crew doesn't know our names (yet), but they're great at making you feel welcome. Winghart's offers specialty burgers you'll want to eat for breakfast, lunch, and dinner. Two of our favorite burgers are named after the owner's friends and family, like the Denny Double Blue with bleu cheese dressing and crumbles, and The Shipwreck with brie, caramelized onions, arugula, bacon, and white truffle aioli. The burgers come wrapped in paper and not on a plate, so a bit of messiness is inevitable. There is nothing quite like sitting at the lunch counter enjoying a juicy burger, basket of fries, and a whiskey, beer, or cider from **Arsenal Cider House** (p. 192). If you aren't feeling a burger, the wood-fired pizzas are equally as awesome. Additional locations: See website.

Landmarks

Grand Concourse, 100 W. Station Square Dr., Pittsburgh, PA 15219; (412) 261-1717; muer.com/grand-concourse; Seafood; $$$$ **(Gandy Dancer Saloon: $$).** The Pittsburgh and Lake Erie Railroad

Station was built in 1901. Now, a century and some change later, the trains are long gone but the grandeur of an era gone by remains. Since 1978, the Grand Concourse has occupied this ornate space along the Monongahela River and provided Pittsburghers with the opportunity to marvel at truly remarkable architecture while indulging in classic seafood fare. It is one of the only places in town that offers the option of a freshwater lobster tail as a side dish. Can everyone say "fancy"? The Sunday brunch here is particularly epic with everything from salmon Rockefeller to bananas Foster. Take a date here, cozy up in a plush banquette, and, boy howdy, do you mean business! The Grand Concourse's sister restaurant, the Gandy Dancer Saloon, is right next door. The old-timey railroad feel extends to the Dancer, but the splendor is traded for a more casual quaintness. It is a good spot for a cocktail, saddled up to the polished-wood bar, or for a hardy fish sandwich.

The Original Oyster House, 20 Market Sq., Pittsburgh, PA 15222; (412) 566-7925; originaloysterhousepittsburgh.com; **Seafood; $.** Some bars and restaurants scream Pittsburgh. They're made up of the fabric of what makes Pittsburgh, Pittsburgh. They smell like Pittsburgh. They look like Pittsburgh. And with walls filled with portraits of our city's heroes and flickering Iron City neons, some just give you the true sense of what it's like to be from the 'Burgh. The Original Oyster House in Market Square is one of those places where you can cozy up to the bar, strike up a conversation, and leave with a full belly and a new friend. It was established in 1870 and is Pittsburgh's oldest bar and restaurant. Films have been made here. Important sports figures, entertainers, and politicians have eaten here. And most importantly, giant fish sandwiches that require a special bun are on the menu here. If that doesn't make you want to join the ranks of its thousands of other customers, then maybe its New England clam chowder, Maryland-style crab cakes, baked scrod, or giant collection of Miss America Pageant contestant photographs will.

Sinful Sweets, 901 Penn Ave., Pittsburgh, PA 15222; (412) 235-7865; sinfulsweetsonline.com. If loving chocolate is wrong, we don't want to be right. We will keep on sinnin' with the help of Sinful Sweets on Penn Avenue. The owner, Christopher, a tattooed and seemingly tough (but actually sweet!) gentleman, may bear no likeness to Willy Wonka, but he has a sincere appreciation for all things sugar. He is often behind the counter or manning the chocolate dipping station. The bright pink storefront is packed full of all the good stuff: truffles, chocolate-covered bacon, chocolate-dipped potato chips, ice cream, toffee . . . and the list goes on. A case of freshly made cake pops is worth a look, too. If you are lucky to get there before it sells out, try the chocolate chip cookie dough cake pop. Tastes like cookie dough. It is addicting, rich, and, well, downright sinful. The other pop flavors are inventive and coated with a chocolate candy layer. Everything in store is paid by the pound or ounce, excluding the ice cream, which is pay by the scoop or special concoction. Can't wait to pound that box of treats? Tables by the windows offer a place to house some truffles before making it out of the door. So go ahead and be gluttonous.

The Strip District

Need unlicensed sports apparel? Head to the Strip. Got a hankering for fresh noodles? Get on over to the Strip. Want to people-watch like a pro? Trot on down to the Strip.

Desire a true Pittsburgh experience? You guessed it . . . take a trip to the Strip.

The Strip District is the market-filled area from 11th to 33rd Streets sandwiched between Liberty Avenue and Smallman Street. Once populated with factories manufacturing the likes of steel and glass, this bustling stretch of neighborhood now boasts a diverse and fresh selection of ethnic food and the most original Pittsburgh memorabilia in town. Though you can no longer fulfill an order for steel, you can order up some fresh mozzarella and a football stadium snow globe.

The dining scene here, like the retail, offers a bit of everything. A refined palate will have no trouble finding a restaurant that ticks all the boxes of a good meal. While swanky dinner spots abound, the real stars of the Strip are the "this food is sticking to my ribs" places that have become Pittsburgh institutions. If you don't stand in line outside of a restaurant at least once while visiting the neighborhood, you are doing something wrong.

Just remember to follow the crowds for lunch and then get fancy for the late-night meals. But you should always keep your newly purchased black and gold merchandise at the ready.

Bar Marco, 2216 Penn Ave., Pittsburgh, PA 15222; (412) 471-1900; barmarcopgh.com; Cocktail Bar; $$. Housed in the former No. 7 Engine Co. building, Bar Marco specializes in craft cocktails, unique wines, and flavorful small plates. You will have a hard time ordering off the drink menu because there isn't one. The skilled bartenders will ask you about your flavor preferences and craft a cocktail to your liking. The small plates menu is on constant rotation, but some staples that stay around include the bacon-wrapped dates stuffed with manchego cheese and the Bar Marco burger. If you're looking for a truly unique and memorable dining experience, the 10-seat wine room in Bar Marco's cellar offers an intimate dinner of 8 to 12 courses paired with wines. Be sure to get here on Monday night for "No Menu Monday." Bar Marco opens up the kitchen to local chefs, charity organizations, and anyone who wants to show off their cooking skills for an evening. All food proceeds from the evening go directly to the guest chefs.

Bella Notte Pizza Pasta & More, 1914 Penn Ave., Pittsburgh, PA 15222; (412) 281-4488; Pizza; $$. Bella Notte is just a short walk from numerous cafes, florists, and specialty markets. You can sit inside and watch pizza dough being tossed with care, or, if weather permits, pull up a seat outside and watch the crowds pass by giving your plate googly eyes. The most important detail to your pizza order will be deciding what toppings to get. The topping list is quite long, including pineapple, hot sausage, artichokes, Canadian bacon, and the list goes on. Our topping of choice at Bella Notte is pepperoni, which is shredded and thrown on the pizza, achieved nowhere else. The shredding seems to allow all of the juices to seep out of the pepperoni and onto the pizza, and we love it. In addition to pizza, there are hoagies and salads and more on the menu, but really, it's all about the pizza here.

BREAD AND SALT

Rick Easton sets up shop wherever he's able. Be it the empty lot beside Bar Marco in the Strip District or inside on one of the restaurant's famed No Menu Monday's, be it at Wild Purveyors, the brick-and-mortar farmer's market in Lawrenceville, or at the community bread oven in Braddock with The Brew Gentleman Co., Rick takes to the streets with his carby goodness since he is without a shop of his own. The Pittsburgh restaurant industry has embraced his talents (and his tasty products), and together they have produced event after event, welcoming 'Burghers to enjoy bread in common and uncommon ways.

He has worked alongside some of the best chefs in the city, creating masterpieces like Middle Eastern fare with Root 174's Keith Fuller (p. 126), Pittsburgh-style sammys with Cure's Justin Severino (p. 103), and one-of-a-kind dishes with Justin Steel from Bar Marco (p. 38).

He also keeps busy by slinging pizzettes to passersby. Pizzettes? You mean you've never heard of them? For shame. Single-size pizzas: a spread of sauce, a sprinkling of freshly grated cheese, seasoned to perfection atop a fried slab of dough. Light, fluffy but crispy, and flavorful. He can whip up a mean bagel, loaves of bread that look almost too picturesque to slice, and plenty of sandwich-ready varieties.

The professional artisan bread maker that he is, Rick is as passionate about the process as he is the final product. He has particular blends of flour that he uses for everything he bakes and is striving for perfect flavor across the board. Wheat, an important component of said process, is something he strives to obtain from local farmers, making him all the more okay in our books.

To find out where Rick will be, follow **Bread and Salt** on Facebook at facebook.com/breadandsalt.

Casa Reyna, 2031 Penn Ave., Pittsburgh, PA 15222; (412) 904-1242; reynafoods.com/content/casa-reyna; Mexican; $. The hidden basement restaurant of well-known Pittsburgh Mexican grocer Reyna Foods, Casa Reyna serves up tacos, margaritas, and salsas that will make you want to shake your maracas. The tortillas are made fresh every day, and you can watch the magic happen while you're inside! Start off by ordering the chips and at least two of the salsas, like the tomatillo and mild chipotle salsas. The taco list is almost as extensive as the tequila list. Go for the *al Pastor* (marinated pork with onions and pineapple) or *Barbacoa* (marinated lamb) tacos, made with perfectly seasoned meats and fresh toppings all in traditional Mexican style. Wash down your meal with a shaker full of margarita or a tequila flight. If you're looking to try Reyna's but don't have time to take a seat, the taqueria outside has an assortment of their best dishes that you can buy and eat street side as you explore the Strip District.

Cioppino, 2350 Railroad St., Pittsburgh, PA 15222; (412) 281-6593; cioppinoofpittsburgh.com; Steak House; $$$. Across the street from the Cork Factory Lofts is Cioppino, specializing in seafood and steaks. The main dining room is open, breezy, and filled with rich wood tones. Oversize leather chairs and couches, dark lighting, and the rich smell of cigars make for a relaxing atmosphere in the lounge and cigar bar. Can't decide where to sit? Why not experience all three? Start with a drink in the bar, where you can choose from the extensive domestic and import beer list, martinis, single malts, or cognac. Then enjoy dinner in the main dining area. Starters include shrimp cocktail, lobster risotto, oysters on the half shell, and beef carpaccio. Entrees include seafood options like cioppino, which consists of clams, Dungeness crab, Mediterranean sea bass, mahimahi, mussels, jumbo shrimp, scallops, clams, fennel, and onion, and meat options of filet mignon or New York strip steak. Finish the night with an after-dinner cocktail, a selection of house-made desserts, and a cigar in the cigar bar.

Eleven Contemporary Kitchen, 1150 Smallman St., Pittsburgh, PA 15222; (412) 201-5656; elevenck.com; New American; $$$–$$$$. Eleven Contemporary Kitchen is a member of the big Burrito family of restaurants (see **Mad Mex** [p. 118], **Casbah** [p. 101], **Kaya Island Cuisine** [p. 42], **Soba Lounge** [p. 131], and **Umi** [p. 139]). One of the swankiest big Burrito restaurants is Eleven, which provides an upscale dining experience from its intimate booths to its proclaimed "Contemporary American" cuisine. Waitstaff is assigned to particular tasks, so you will never have an empty water glass or want for bread; the copper menu covers dance under the low light; and the food is presented beautifully with a certain level of comfort cooked right in. Dining at Eleven demands a slower pace and a diner's willingness to feel pampered. While flavorful dishes like the farmhouse chicken resting on a bed of creamy risotto may fill you up, do not skip the sweetness. The banana cream pie, a deconstructed dish with banana pudding, vanilla wafer, and dulche de leche is a game changer in the dessert realm. Treats this miraculously delicious are a rare breed. Just like Eleven.

The Enrico Biscotti Co. and The Enrico Biscotti Cafe, 2022 Penn Ave., Pittsburgh, PA 15222; (412) 281-2602; enricobiscotti.com; Italian; $. "I'll take one of each please!" will be your go-to phrase when ordering at The Enrico Biscotti Co. You will want to devour every pastry you lay your eyes on, including the handmade Italian biscotti, scones, breads, and macaroons. This place literally smells like the inside of an oven, in the most amazing way. Once you have your bags of biscotti and pastries in hand, make an immediate right out of the tiny bakery and walk down the narrow passage to the cafe. Serving lunch 6 days a week (Mon through Sat) from 11 a.m. to 3 p.m., and brunch on Sat from 7 until 11 a.m., Enrico's Cafe offers up rustic Italian dishes all prepared in the open-aired kitchen, including a wood-fired oven for the pizza pies. The beans and greens are a must order, as well as the brick-oven pizzas. The menu changes daily, and special dinners and cooking classes are held often. Check Enrico's website for more details on these special events.

Gaucho Parrilla Argentina, 1607 Penn Ave., Pittsburgh, PA 15222; (412) 709-6622; eatgaucho.com; Latin American; $$. Literally translated to mean "cowboy," Gaucho came onto the Strip District scene and wrangled loyal customers from day one. The wood-fired scent of Argentinean food permeates Penn Avenue as folks enjoy grilled steak, chorizo, corn, chicken, and vegetables all from the comfort of a gorgeous communal table and counter lining the perimeter. When the weather's warm, grab a seat under one of the colorful umbrella tables in the alley next door. Be sure to bring a bottle of your favorite wine as Gaucho is BYOB and invites you to indulge while you feast on empanadas (steak and pepper pastries), *camarones* (grilled shrimp) and *gaucho papas* (roasted potatoes). If the menu, explanatory but mostly foreign, scares you a bit, don't hesitate to ask one of the red handkerchief-wearing gents to help you out. You'll get descriptions, delicious recommendations, and a bit of a history lesson.

Kaya Island Cuisine, 2000 Smallman St., Pittsburgh, PA 15222; (412) 261-6565; bigburrito.com/kaya; International; $$$. Spice is definitely not lacking in any dish you'll find at Kaya. Don't be afraid to mix and match *tropas,* or starters. We recommend the conch hush puppies, the Kaya chips with mango-tomatillo salsa, or the Yucatan hot bean dip. If you are feeling like an entree, order the crispy fish tacos served with Reyna's tortillas. If you're looking for a unique take on a traditional burger, order the Kaya burger, served with a sunny-side up egg, avocado, crispy bacon, Chihuahua cheese, and Kaya's special sauce. Kaya is known for its happy hour, Mon through Fri from 4:30 to 6:30 p.m., with half off draft beers and single serving drinks, and Sunday brunch from 11 a.m. to 4 p.m. If you're in the Strip on a Thursday, head to Kaya for fried chicken night, featuring all-natural and locally raised chickens. Eat up, mon!

La Prima Espresso Bar, 205 21st St., Pittsburgh, PA 15222; (412) 281-1922; laprima.com; Coffee Shop; $. Getting around the Strip super early on Saturday mornings can be quite difficult if you are not an early bird. You will need to be alert as you walk, shop, and carry your loads of goods. To help keep your eyes open during your shopping journey is La Prima, both a neighborhood coffee shop and coffee roaster. Start your morning by ordering up a cappuccino and a thick slice of Sicilian pizza baked by the adjacent Colangelo's Bakery. Sounds like a strange combo, but trust us, it's delicious. At La Prima, not only are quality coffees and espressos crafted, but also the coffee beans are roasted at their roaste in Manchester. Top-notch quality if you ask us. Additional location: Carnegie Mellon University, Wean Hall, 5000 Forbes Ave., Pittsburgh, PA 15213; (412) 268-2000.

Osteria 2350, 2350 Railroad St., Pittsburgh, PA 15222; (412) 281-6595; osteria2350pittsburgh.com; Italian, $. Right next to **Cioppino** (p. 40) is Osteria 2350, both of which are owned and operated by Chef Greg Alauzen. While Cioppino excels at fine dining, Osteria 2350 takes a rustic, home-style approach to Italian classics. The menu features soups, salads, sandwiches, and pasta. And it is an excellent choice for lunch or a laid-back dinner. We enjoy pulling up a burlap-covered chair to the stainless-steel bar for a quick bite. The antipasti plate is always a good option to start and includes Parma Sausage Products prosciutto, salami rustico, sweet sopressata, coppa secca, mozzarella, and aged provolone. If you're in the mood for a sandwich, two good options to consider are the meatball sub, which is large enough for two, or the prosciutto sandwich with fresh mozzarella, roasted peppers, and Parma's prosciutto. While the sandwiches and pizza are always a great choice, the pasta, most of it made in house, is the way to go. Our favorite is the house-made gnocchi baked with parmigiano reggiano and fontina. The gnocchi is delicate and fluffy, and the sweet red sauce and hearty dose of cheese make it our go-to choice for both lunch and dinner.

Penn Avenue Fish Company, 2208 Penn Ave., Pittsburgh, PA 15222; (412) 434-7200; pennavefishcompany.com; Seafood; $–$$. Besides purchasing fresh fish and seafood at the Penn Avenue Fish Company to take home and cook yourself, you can get killer fish sandwiches for lunch. Of course there are a few other places in the Strip where you can get a fish sandwich, but at Penn Avenue Fish Company you can order something more nontraditional. Fish sandwiches come in a plethora of varieties, including salmon, tuna, swordfish, tilapia, and cod. If looking for something lighter, order up a few oysters on the half shell or the Penn Avenue Fish Company summer salad: field greens topped with grilled tuna, tomatoes, celery, dried cranberries, edamame, and kettle-cooked jalapeno potato chips, and drizzled with a creamy housemade vinaigrette. If sushi is more your speed, pull up a seat at the sushi counter and order a few sushi platters and maki combinations. Additional location: Downtown, 308 Forbes Ave., Pittsburgh, PA 15222; (412) 562-1710.

Peppi's Old Tyme Sandwich Shop, 1721 Penn Ave., Pittsburgh, PA 15222; (412) 562-0125; peppisubs.com; Sandwiches; $. Philadelphia may be known for its cheesesteaks, but Pittsburgh can definitely hold its own thanks to Peppi's Old Tyme Sandwich Shop. At Peppi's, you can order up your cheesesteak with chicken, steak, sausage, Italian meats, and even veggies. Whichever way you choose, we recommend ordering your sub with onions and peppers, and don't forget fries on the side. All of their sandwiches are served on locally made Mike & Dave's Italian bread. The most famous item on the menu is the "RoethlisBurger," a hot sausage and beef sandwich topped with scrambled eggs and American cheese. The sandwich is named after Steelers quarterback Ben Roethlisberger and can also be ordered as "The #7." At Peppi's, the workers move fast, and it's amazing to watch them slicing, dicing, frying, and wrapping. It's enough to make you work up an appetite, which is good, considering most of Peppi's subs can feed half of the Pittsburgh Steelers. Additional locations: See website.

Pho Van Vietnamese Noodles & Grill, 2120 Penn Ave., Pittsburgh, PA 15222; (412) 281-7999; phovan.net; Vietnamese; $$. Pho Van offers fresh and fun Vietnamese food. Pho (pronounced "fuh") is a beef and noodle-based dish that is influenced by both Chinese and French cuisine. At Pho Van you can order your noodles with a variety of cuts of beef including tenderloin, brisket, trips, meatballs, or even get pho chicken. Each order of pho is served with sides of basil, bean sprouts, and lime, flavors that all incorporate well with the meat and noodles. If you aren't sure what you want to go for, you can order off the grill. We recommend the rice noodles and grilled shrimp bowl, which is topped with cucumber, carrots, bean sprouts, peanuts, and Pho's homemade chili garlic sauce. It's a great way to experience Vietnamese food without venturing too far out of your comfort zone. We say go "pho" it!

Savoy, 2623 Penn Ave., Pittsburgh, PA 15222; (412) 281-0660; savoypgh.com; Eclectic; $$$. Savoy is crazy, sexy, cool. Upon walking through the front doors, you are immediately hit with the swanky vibe that Savoy is giving off. The interior is modern, sleek, warm, and a bit funky. The large, illuminated first-floor bar top, textured walls, and colorful artwork all serve as backdrops to the elegant white linen tabletops and plush white chairs. And the food is just as impressive. Chef Kevin Watson is cooking up an eclectic array of Mediterranean, Southern, and contemporary styles of food to fill his menus. During dinner, try the fried chicken and waffles served with corn pudding and Pennsylvania maple syrup, a modern take on one of Kevin's childhood favorites. For brunch, you can order off the Sunday's Best menu, which includes a fried green tomato and crab cake benedict and shrimp and grits, or go all in and eat your heart out with the Chef's Table Buffet. And if you want to just chill for happy hour, Savoy has you covered with a second-floor lounge and rooftop patio.

Thin Man Sandwich Shop, 50 21st St., Pittsburgh, PA 15222; (412) 586-7370; thinmansandwichshop.com; Sandwiches; $. Sandwich making is an art form. It takes patience, vision, and skill to craft a sandwich that isn't ordinary. It also takes high-quality, fresh ingredients. When all of those things come together, you get a sandwich fit for a king. And Dan and Sheri Leiphart have done just that at their tiny corner restaurant, Thin Man Sandwich Shop. Indian butter chicken, spicy Vietnamese beef meatballs, and Korean barbecue beef brisket are just a few sandwiches that have graced the menu. A menu dictated by ingredients found in the Strip or at nearby farms. This helps keep things fresh and introduces patrons to new flavors. So pull up a stool and watch as your sandwich is crafted with expertise and care. Want the full Thin Man experience? Go with the namesake, the Thin Man. It's made with chicken liver mousse, local bacon, frisee, and red wine vinaigrette on a baguette. Pair it with a seasonal side like winter squash soup or local greens and a house-infusion made with **Pittsburgh Seltzer Works** seltzer (p. 200).

21st Street Coffee and Tea, 2002 Smallman St., Pittsburgh, PA 15222; (412) 281-0809; 21streetcoffee.com; Coffee Shop; $. A good cup of coffee or tea is a morning essential. Even more essential if you are going shopping for produce before noon. 21st Street handcrafts each cup of coffee and tea to perfection. Intelligentsia coffee beans are used to brew each cup individually, which can take a few more minutes than getting a cup of joe at a standard coffee shop. Be patient and try not to watch the slow drip process, as it won't happen as fast as you may like. Two things you will not find at 21st Street Coffee and Tea are cream and sugar. This place suggests you drink each crafted coffee beverage as prepared. But if you really need a little sweetener in your cappuccino, just ask the barista. In addition to the large seating area, 21st Street Coffee and Tea has a communal workspace on its second-floor loft, complete with desks, chairs, lamps, and wireless access, that can be "rented" out daily, weekly, or monthly. Additional location: Downtown, 225 5th Ave., Pittsburgh, PA 15222; (412) 281-0121.

Landmarks

DeLuca's, 2015 Penn Ave., Pittsburgh, PA 15222; (412) 566-2195; Diner; $. Red and white checkered floors. Green wooden booths from years ago. Grease scents floating through the air from an open kitchen behind the counter. Welcome to DeLuca's, a throwback diner with, what some might argue, Pittsburgh's most perfect breakfast. The menu includes lunch options, but to go to DeLuca's and leave without sampling the morning's best is a crime. The giant, fluffy pancakes are the star of the show at this joint. With a lengthy list of mix-ins like chocolate chips and blueberries, your pancakes can be personalized to your liking. If you have a real sweet tooth, order a pancake (or waffle) sundae, with ice cream and topping combos that will instigate a trip to the dentist. Other solid breakfast items include a big breakfast burrito and omelets that dwarf the plates. Lines form outside every Saturday and Sunday, but don't fear the wait. Once indoors you'll be treated to illogical amounts of food that have been satisfying 'Burghers for decades. Additional location: Robinson Township, 1110 Park Manor Blvd., Pittsburgh, PA 15205; (412) 788-1007.

Klavon's Ice Cream Parlor, 2801 Penn Ave., Pittsburgh, PA 15222; (412) 434-0451; klavonsicecream.com; Ice Cream; $. Step through the doors at 2801 Penn Avenue and, sure enough, you'll be transported through time. Opened as a pharmacy in the 1920s, Klavon's has since been re-imagined as an ice cream parlor complete with original features. A marble counter runs the length of the shop dotted with metal barstools. Wooden booths provide alternative seating across the brown and beige floor. On display are relics from the pharmacy days. All the nostalgia is as delightful as the ice cream and, good golly, the ice cream is a delight! Klavon's offers all the classic sundaes, deliciously thick milk shakes, and floats any ice cream lover could want. The ice cream is imported from Penn State Creamery in State College, Pennsylvania. Flavored whipped cream, created in-house, makes a nice topper to any treat. Service here is top-notch with a truly friendly staff that will make you feel right at home, if home were an early-20th-century drugstore. If you need more sugar as you exit, a plethora of penny candy sits by the cash register ready to be devoured. Klavon's also serves coffee and lunch.

P&G's Pamela's Diner, 60 21st St., Pittsburgh, PA 15222; (412) 281-6366; pamelasdiner.com; Diner; $. P&G's Pamela's Diner is a Pittsburgh classic. For out-of-towners the original Strip District location is a must-try although there are five other equally delightful locations. College students. Families. The after-church crowd. It seems like everyone heads to Pamela's on Saturday and Sunday mornings for the famous crepe-style pancakes. Even President Barack Obama flipped for the flapjacks back in 2008. He enjoyed them so much that the following

Memorial Day those famous breakfast staples were served at the White House for the President, the First Lady, and 80 veterans. After that how could you not want to stop by and see what all the fuss is about? Our go-to dish is the Morning After, which offers up 2 crepe pancakes, eggs, your choice of bacon or sausage, and toast. We admit we almost always go a step further and order a side of the Lyonnaise potatoes and recommend you do the same as the crispy, perfectly seasoned taters complement the crepes in a way that has us going back morning after morning. Additional locations: See website.

Primanti Bros., 46 18th St., Pittsburgh, PA 15222; (412) 263-2142; primantibros.com; Sandwiches; $. The Primanti sandwich is a Pittsburgh staple, and when visiting, you must eat at least one. If you eat more than one in a single day, we won't judge. Started in the early 1930s, Primanti Bros. sold sandwiches to truck drivers delivering goods to the Strip District. Layered on two thick, hand-cut slices of white Italian bread, the Primanti sandwich comes with meat of your choice (capicola, fish, sirloin steak, roast beef, and much more), provolone cheese, fresh-cut french fries, coleslaw, and tomatoes. Onions are extra. One rule of thumb to eating at Primanti Bros.: Order the sandwich as it comes. No substitutions please, or you will be judged. The Strip location is open 24 hours a day, 7 days a week, with other locations throughout Pittsburgh, Florida, and West Virginia. If you make it to one of the suburban locations, try the homemade pizza. Even though you should always get a sandwich at Primanti Bros., the pizza is also quite tasty. Additional locations: See website.

Smallman Street Deli, 2840 Smallman St., Pittsburgh, PA 15222; (412) 434-5800; smallmanstreetdeli.wix.com/smallman streetdeli; Deli; $. Smallman Street Deli is one of those places you get excited to visit. The enormous deli board lists out meats and cheeses galore that you can order and take home with you. You can order homemade soups that change daily (try its famous matzo ball or its hearty chili), or make it a complete meal and pair it with a classic Reuben or Rachel. Our favorite part of the meal has to be its famous crunchy kosher dill pickles. Smallman Street Deli is a family-owned and -operated joint, and they sure do make you feel like family when you show up. We challenge you to not want to go back the next day after you experience a deli the way a deli should be. Additional location: Squirrel Hill, 1912 Murray Ave., Pittsburgh, PA 15217; (412) 421-3354.

Specialty Stores, Markets & Producers

Fort Pitt Candy Co., 1642 Penn Ave., Pittsburgh, PA 15222; (412) 281-9016; fortpittcandy.com. Looking for Nerds? Pop Rocks? Sugar Babies? Or a simple Tootsie Roll? You are going to want to head to the Fort Pitt Candy Co. Upon walking into the dimly lit storefront, you will literally be surrounded from floor to ceiling with candy. So, watch your step as you walk around the sugary confections. With seasonal merchandise and candies reminiscent of childhood, like candy cigarettes and flying saucers (at least from our childhoods), this place is sure to satisfy your sugar craving. Candy can be purchased by the box or individually, depending on how intense your sugar craving might be. In addition to sweets, the Fort Pitt Candy Co. carries snack items, such as chips and pretzels, various tobacco products, and is a spot to play your numbers, aka the Pennsylvania Lottery.

The Leaf & Bean Company, 2200 Penn Ave. #1, Pittsburgh, PA 15222; (412) 434-1480; leafandbean.com. Leaves and beans. Beans and leaves. What a concept for a specialty store. The

Leaf & Bean Company is a one-stop shop for all your fine tobacco and caffeine needs. Its 2 locations, the Strip District and McMurray, offer a place to sit and enjoy a cup of joe while enjoying a smoke with a bud. Even if you aren't one to indulge, you're not going to want to miss a trip to The Leaf & Bean. During the warmer months, the exterior has seats available for sipping and smoking in the sunshine, and when there's a chill in the air, you can take the party inside and enjoy the mellow atmosphere. You'll be surrounded by flea market finds that would make your grandma and hipster neighbor jealous. The Leaf & Bean has its own humidor, rolls cigars in store, features live music on Saturday, and offers free Wi-Fi. Once you've been, you're definitely going to want to become a regular. Additional location: 3525 Washington Rd., McMurray, PA 15317; (412) 942-6670.

Lotus Food Co., 1649 Penn Ave., Pittsburgh, PA 15222; (412) 281-3050. Lotus Food Co. is a large Asian specialty grocer that fantastically offers fresh tofu sold by the block. The space is also well stocked with additional goodness from snacks to frozen and fresh fish to dumplings. Let's say you have a craving for shrimp puffs. Guess what? You can buy them here, along with soybean drinks, fish sauce, and any other Asian condiment that you won't find at your run-of-the-mill grocery spot. On weekends, Lotus is a particularly popular market, so brace yourself for a bit of a crowd. It will help to have a plan as you navigate the aisles, but it is nice to take your time and examine all of the interesting flavors and spices that will make your meal sparkle.

Marty's Market, 2301 Smallman St., Pittsburgh, PA 15222; (412) 586-7177; martysmarket.com. Part high-end grocer, part eatery, and part coffee shop, Marty's Market has it all—even an in-house butcher. The store specializes in local, fresh produce and prides itself in being like a year-round farmers' market. Ask the Marty's staff about where the produce and the meats for butchering are sourced. They will be happy to tell you about the origins of your soon-to-be meal. Need some inspiration to incorporate the local ingredients in your meal planning? Marty's has a full calendar of special events to help patrons appreciate food, including a music series and cooking classes. If eating prepared foods and not preparing food is your jam, visit the cafe for delicious house-made soups and creative sandwiches at lunch. If you are an early bird or a brunch aficionado, the breakfast options are not to be missed. Pancakes with cinnamon butter make a strong case for the best flapjacks in town, and sausage made by Marty's butcher livens up the 'wiches. Some of the best breakfast picks in town pair perfectly with a glass, or a carafe, of fresh-squeezed orange juice, which scores a 10 out of 10 on the thirst-quenching deliciousness scale. From the produce, to the meat, to the meals, quality always takes center stage at Marty's.

Mon Aimee Chocolat, 2101 Penn Ave., Pittsburgh, PA 15222; (412) 395-0022; monaimeechocolat.com. Mon Aimee Chocolat, you say? A specialty shop whose specialty is chocolate, you say? Sign. Us. Up. Mon Aimee Chocolat sells sweet confections from all over the United States as well as 26 countries. You can find chocolate-covered bacon bars, truffles, nostalgic candies like candy cigarettes and Teaberry gum, plus something that makes Mon Aimee famous: its wide variety of malt balls. You will have between 10 and 12 flavors to choose from on any given day. If you are in search of a bit of whimsy, choose one (or more) of its unique chocolate molds in shapes like deviled eggs, frogs, and popsicles. Would you rather slurp your sweets? Mon Aimee has a to-die-for hot chocolate, and on a warm day in the 'Burgh, get a scoop of Capogiro Gelato Artisans' gelato.

Parma Sausage Products, Inc., 1734 Penn Ave., Pittsburgh, PA 15222; (412) 391-4238; **parmasausage.com.** Parma Sausage Products, Inc., is a must-stop in the Strip District for any occasion, on any kind of day. The small family business specializes in Italian pork products. Downstairs is the deli counter, which is filled with friendly faces and delicious meats. Upstairs is where the real magic happens. Here, Parma makes fresh sausage that is hand trimmed, ground, mixed with spices, and stuffed in natural casings; salami and pepperoni that are aged in its custom-built aging room; coppa secca; prosciutto made from fresh Berkshire Pork ham; and pancetta. It's hard to beat fresh anything—let alone fresh meat. So fresh you can taste the quality, care, and commitment Parma puts into each product available. And lucky for you, Parma offers its products online so you can enjoy them in the comfort of your own home if you can't make it to its home in the Strip.

Pennsylvania Macaroni Company, 2010–12 Penn Ave., Pittsburgh, PA 15222; (412) 471-8330; **pennmac.com.** The Pennsylvania Macaroni Company, known to Pittsburghers as "Penn Mac," is the go-to specialty store in the Strip for Italian goods and cheeses. The lively and enormous cheese counter is stocked with over 400 different varieties of artisanal and imported cheeses, such as Danish Havarti with dill, aged Crotonese, and Amish farmers cheese. Maneuvering the cheese counter on a busy Saturday morning can have you waiting awhile, but trust us, it is so worth the wait. Besides cheese, the store has practically any product you may need to cook an Italian feast in the grocery section, including fresh pasta, olive oil, fruits, vegetables, spices, sauces, and loaves upon loaves of **BreadWorks Bakery** bread (p. 181). If you are from out of town and fall in love with the store, you can shop online and sign up online for the Cheese of the Month Club. See website for details.

Pittsburgh Popcorn Company, 209 21st St., Pittsburgh, PA 15222; (412) 281-5200; **pghpopcorn.com.** Reminiscent of a classic boardwalk shop in terms of branding and feel, the Pittsburgh Popcorn Company offers flavorful popcorn that is far from traditional. These popped kernels get extra-special treatment. Everyday offerings include crunchy caramel, sweet and salty kettle, Wisconsin cheddar, and cheddar/caramel mix, among others. Things get really crazy and seriously delicious for the flavors of the week. Thin Mint-flavored popcorn. Buffalo wing-flavored popcorn. Dill pickle-flavored popcorn. Each week brings different choices of way-above-average kernel creations. Popcorn is sold by the bag or tin. The special weekly flavors can sometimes carry a higher price tag, but also a higher payoff on the delightfulness scale. The Pittsburgh Popcorn Company sells its goods online, but the weekly flavors are only found in stores. Other places to get poppin': See website.

Pittsburgh Public Market, 2401 Penn Ave., Pittsburgh, PA 15222; (412) 281-4505; pittsburghpublicmarket.org. Relocated from Smallman Street to Penn Avenue in the Strip District, Pittsburgh Public Market is burgeoning with vendors from all walks of life, selling the freshest of foods to the most inquisitive of Pittsburghers. From Clarion River Organic's produce and East End Brewing Company's beer, the market has something for everyone. Stop for a cup of coffee or fancy topped latte at Caffé D'Amore so you have something to sip on while you weave in and out of the aisles. Take a shopping bag to load up on homemade noodles from Ohio City Pasta, hummus from Najat's Cuisine, and a bottle (or two) of Steuben from Oak Spring Winery. Beyond groceries, the market also hosts vendors selling pottery, woodworks, and soaps, and holds events for locals to come in and enjoy the open space, mingle, drink, and eat, all while shopping!

Prestogeorge Coffee & Tea, 1719 Penn Ave., Pittsburgh, PA 15222; (412) 471-0133; prestogeorge.com. If the coffee and tea don't draw you into Prestogeorge, then the roasted peanuts will. Peanuts are roasted outside the front door in an antique roaster and sold by the brown bagful inside. Just as the shop's name says, coffee and tea are the primary products sold. The walls are stocked with barrels and large glass containers of coffee beans and loose-leaf teas with enough flavors to please all of the coffee and tea lovers in your life. Flavors are seriously out the wazoo. Think Scottish breakfast tea, jasmine flowering tea, sticky bun coffee, and tropical banana nut coffee, just to name a few. If you don't want to carry coffee beans around the Strip with you (because they can be quite heavy), you can order a cup of joe, tea, latte, smoothie, or other specialty coffee drink at the inside coffee bar.

Reyna Foods, 2031 Penn Ave., Pittsburgh, PA 15222; (412) 261-2606; reynafoods.com. Reyna Foods has been supplying Pittsburgh with Latin American and Caribbean food and products for over 20 years. A wholesale supplier and retail store, Reyna Foods carries a wide variety of Latin American brands as well as its own homemade products. Reyna makes blue, white, red, and yellow corn tortilla chips that are available by the bag or in bulk. Also, you can find black and gold chips for all your Pittsburgh sports parties. You can purchase a variety of freshly made salsas, seasonings, empanadas, and tamales as well. In the back of the market, fresh corn and flour tortillas are made daily. When you're done shopping, make a pit stop at the taco stand out front. There, you can get soft corn tortilla tacos made with your choice of meat, topped with sour cream, lettuce, cheese, tomato, onions, and cilantro. We suggest getting at least two tacos, because these babies are so good you'll regret only getting one.

Robert Wholey Market, 1711 Penn Ave., Pittsburgh, PA 15222; (412) 391-3737; wholey.com. Robert Wholey Market is the place to get fresh seafood in Pittsburgh. Though the market also sells fresh meats and poultry, it's all about the seafood here. When walking through the chilled fish market, you will encounter fresh lobsters, cooked and raw shrimp, crabs, oysters, mussels, clams, fish, and much more, all of which are available to take home for your own personal cooking. If cooking seafood isn't your forte, visit Andy's Sushi Bar for some nigiri and maki sushi. Don't like sushi? Stop by the fish kitchen and pick up a fresh breaded fish sandwich, such as the Wholey Whaler (1 pound of fried fish goodness on a bun), crab cakes, or lobster macaroni and cheese, and chow down. Wholey's also has a produce and grocery section (pick up a tub of their homemade peanut butter) and a fudge counter. On the way out, be sure to stop by the huge piggy bank (named Rachel the Pig) and deposit some loose change. All donations go to The Children's Institute of Pittsburgh.

S&D Polish Deli, 2204 Penn Ave., Pittsburgh, PA 15222; (412) 281-2906; sdpolishdeli.com. Pittsburgh is almost synonymous with pierogies. The Eastern European heritage of the 'Burgh is strong, and several places around town bring this culture to our mouths. S&D Polish Deli in the Strip is one of those spots. S&D is a specialty grocer and the perfect place to grab a steaming hot plate of some of the best pierogies, haluszki, and kielbasy in town. The lunch menu, served daily until 3:30 p.m., includes every Polish delight. Mouth culture like whoa. Definitely indulge in a serving of pierogies, if nothing else. These tasty buggers can be ordered with cheddar cheese, farmer cheese, or kraut and mushroom. There is also a pierogi special of the day, which includes an interesting assortment of flavors, like cherry, plum, and sweet cabbage. You can purchase frozen pierogies here as well, or sign up for one of S&D's pierogi making classes and learn how to make the Pittsburgh staples at home! Before you leave, pick up a pound or two of Polish cheeses and meats. The store also keeps Polish traditions alive with products like Easter butter lambs and Oplatki Christmas wafers.

There are plenty of things to delight in at S&D, making it easy to come back again and again.

Sunseri Jimmy & Nino Co., **1901 Penn Ave., Pittsburgh, PA 15222; (412) 255-1100.** A loud mouth, a cigar, and fresh baked bread: three things that make Sunseri Jimmy & Nino Co. a Pittsburgh legend. Take a walk along Penn Avenue in the Strip District and you'll catch whiffs of stogie smoke and the familiar yeasty scent of carbs. You'll also hear "You need the bread!" "Get your bread!" "$5!" Strangely, the combination is enough to give you pause and then you're hooked. The stand in front of the market is open rain or shine and doles out delicious baked goods to passersby in the form of pepperoni rolls and pizza bread, onion bread, and classic Italian bread. All warm. All inexpensive. Inside the shop, you can feast on sandwiches made with said delicious baked goods along with Italian meats, cheeses, and other prepared foods. It's a must-stop along the Strip. Don't worry, they'll reel you in!

North

The North Shore and Northside, accessed quite easily by the Three Sisters Bridges (the three bright yellow bridges that could be triplets), are in close proximity to one another but vastly different. Each distinct area is worth a visit and a long stay.

Heinz Field, PNC Park, the Carnegie Science Center, Rivers Casino, and The Andy Warhol Museum dominate the shore region of the Allegheny and the Ohio Rivers. A riverfront trail provides opportunity for a scenic stroll, especially during active boating seasons. Not surprisingly, the North Shore boasts good locations to catch a bite to eat before catching a foul ball or to hang out and watch any sort of sport on TV.

Just beyond the Shore lies old Allegheny City, or the Northside, one of the most architecturally stunning areas in Pittsburgh. Sections like the Mexican War Streets and Deutschtown are lined with gorgeous row houses and hundreds of years of history. Here, the restaurants are all intimate spaces that fit within the historic surroundings. Food offerings are diverse, creative, and unexpected in the best way possible.

Pittsburgh to the North is more than a collage of old and new; it is a fascinating slice of the city that tastes as good as it looks.

Foodie Faves

Allegheny Sandwich Shoppe, 822 Western Ave., Pittsburgh, PA 15233; (412) 322-4797; Breakfast & Lunch; $. A no-fuss breakfast or lunch is what awaits you at Allegheny Sandwich Shoppe. This small neighborhood restaurant starts serving hungry patrons promptly at 6:30 a.m. French toast, buttermilk pancakes, or Belgian waffles are available, but the egg dishes are the stars. Specialty omelets or breakfast bowls like the meat lovers supreme scrambler made with scrambled eggs, ham, sausage, bacon, potatoes, and cheddar cheese are solid choices. The best part: You get a heaping portion of early morning love for a few bucks and some change. After 11 a.m. lunch is served. Start your meal off with a cup of the soup of the day and follow it up with one of the Shoppe's famous dishes. The carved roast beef sandwich comes with thinly sliced roast beef stacked high on a Kaiser roll and accompanied by thick-cut french fries. Another solid choice is the Dagwood. This two-hand sandwich complete with roast beef, smoked turkey, Virginia baked ham, and bacon is stuffed between three slices of marble rye. Additional locations: Downtown: 542 Forbes Ave., Pittsburgh, PA 15219; (412) 553-6700; and 440 Ross St., Pittsburgh, PA 15219; (412) 393-0940.

Benjamin's Western Avenue Burger Bar, 900 Western Ave., Pittsburgh, PA 15233; (412) 224-2163; benjaminspgh.com; Burgers; $$. Burgers are the name of the game at Benjamin's Western Avenue Burger Bar. Yes, it offers a few other options, but why go to a "burger bar" for a salad? Start your burger adventure by choosing a single or double patty. Benjamin's uses a blend of sirloin, brisket, and short rib for a moist and flavorful burger that will be cooked to your liking on a flat cooktop. Vegetarians also have reason to celebrate. Benjamin's offers a veggie burger made with chickpeas, roasted sweet potatoes, poblano peppers, caramelized onions, and fresh herbs. Next,

GUS AND YIAYIA

Gus and Yiayia's nostalgic shaved ice cart is a Pittsburgh staple if ever there was one. For literally longer than anyone can remember (they've been there since 1934!), the orange buggy has been a permanent fixture on Pittsburgh's Northside. Parked right outside Allegheny Commons West Park, you can't help but notice the rainbow-colored umbrellas all but flagging you over. Upon closer inspection, you'll be treated to a friendly smile and three menu options. Ice ball. Buttered popcorn. Peanuts still nestled in their salty little shell.

Let's start with the ice ball. This classic cool-down is composed of a ball straight up shaved from a block of ice right in front of your eyes. It is plopped into a little paper cup and drowned in your choice of what seems like a trillion syrup flavors, which are all lined up in rows, making their home in the middle of the cart. If a trillion flavors gives you heart palpitations, don't worry, they encourage you to mix it up a bit. One of our favorite combinations is cherry and root beer. Ice ball sizes range from small to medium to large so you're covered depending on your snack budget, appetite for syrupy goodness, and need for something to give you a break from the hot summer heat in the 'Burgh.

If you need something to cut your sugar shock, you're in luck because the same cart that is chock-full of sweet is also chock-full of savory. Freshly popped corn is visible through the windows of one side of the cart and is scooped into a paper bag for you to enjoy (for less than $2!). Roasted peanuts round out the offerings, again scooped fresh from the cart and into your waiting hands.

Gus and Yiayia's is a slice of innocence that tends to bring people of all ages together if only for a fleeting moment. One trip will be sure to bring back summer nostalgia of running out into the street as a kid with a handful of change and a knowing smile, about to buy a memory!

pick a topping combination. Choices range from the Benjamin's Basic Burger with lettuce, tomato, onion, and choice of cheese to rosemary-balsamic goat cheese and green apple. We're especially partial to the buffalo sauce, bleu cheese, and romaine lettuce combo. Finally, pick a side. Choose from home fries, potato salad, curried cabbage coleslaw, and several more options to round out your entree.

Carmi Family Restaurant, 917 Western Ave., Pittsburgh, PA 15233; (412) 231-0100; carmirestaurant.com; Southern; $–$$. Carmi Family Restaurant is our favorite Southern restaurant on the Northside. Housed in what used to be an Irish-themed bar, Carmi has decor that could suggest a leprechaun is lurking around the corner. No bother though, as this borrowed ambiance really enhances the charm of the place. Plus, you will absolutely feel lucky once your food arrives and you experience Southern cooking at its finest. Order the chicken and waffles—the fried chicken is seasoned to perfection and crisp as can be. The baked macaroni and cheese will make you rue the day you ever ate the boxed variety. And the chicken and dumpling soup is comfort in a cup! It certainly helps that the service here is beyond outstanding. The waitstaff is attentive, but not intrusive, and incredibly friendly. You will feel like part of the family the moment you sit down. Maybe that leprechaun needs a roommate? See Owner Carleen Kenney's recipe for Candied Yams on p. 208.

El Burro Comedor, 1108 Federal St., Pittsburgh, PA 15212; (412) 904-3451; elburropgh.com; Mexican; $. Southern California imports, Owners Wes DeRounard and Derrek Burrell, opened up El Burro Comedor in 2012 hoping to re-create some of their San Diego taco memories. The teeny-tiny storefront on Federal offers some of the 'Burgh's best tacos and burritos. San Diego would be proud. A painted menu on the back wall gets the tummy rumbling with an array of tacos, burritos, salsas, and more. The tacos are served hard, soft, or rolled. Carnitas and chorizo are our go-to taco picks. These babies are perfect in pairs or threes—don't order just one! The burritos are *muy gigante y muy delicioso*. Try the chile relleno for a little bit of a kick and a surprising crunch. Do you want fries in your burrito? We sure do. If so, order the California burrito, complete with *carne asada* and french fries. No meat for you? That's totally cool. Vegans can get their taqueria fill here too; the menu always includes a vegan option or two. The small space offers several bar stools to enjoy your tasty picks inside. The food is also super portable, so if the weather is nice, take your picks to the park across the street. El Burro also delivers.

James Street Gastropub and Speakeasy, 422 Foreland St., Pittsburgh, PA 15212; (412) 904-3335; jamesstreetgastropub.com; Gastropub; $. With 3 floors, 15 taps, and many live events during the week, James Street Gastropub and Speakeasy in the Northside serves up more than just food and booze. Trivia, jazz, and blues can all be enjoyed in the basement speakeasy. You can catch a game sitting bar side on the first floor and order a beer from their seemingly endless list of brews. In the third-floor ballroom, pick a partner and dance the night away. Burgers, Cajun fare, and classic Pittsburgh chicken salads are offered alongside oysters, pierogies, and wings, making it the perfect place for a night out to enjoy game playing, game watching, or toe-tapping. It helps that James Street is open late on weekdays and even later on weekends, making it an after-party type of place for when you know the night just isn't ready to be over.

Legends of the North Shore, 500 E. North Ave., Pittsburgh, PA 15212; (412) 321-8000; legendsatthenorthshore.com; Italian; $$. Legends of the North Shore is worth a trip if only for the homemade focaccia that makes its way to each table to start the meal. These crispy, nicely seasoned carb sticks are perhaps what put the "legend" in Legends. And even though the bar is set high from the get-go, you won't be disappointed with what comes next. Legends offers comforting Italian favorites, crafted lovingly in the open kitchen swallowing half the cozy restaurant space. Homemade spaghetti noodles smothered in "Mama's Gravy" (Legend's own chunky tomato marinara) and topped with a giant meatball that falls apart at the touch of a fork, is a classic, and perfect, choice for lunch or dinner. If pasta just won't do, a portion of the menu is dedicated to sandwiches prepared with rustic Italian flair. Prepare to be floored by combos like zucchini and goat cheese (again, on that legendary focaccia). Legends has promotional deals often. Don't forget your wine; Legends is BYOB.

Lola Bistro, 1100 Galveston Ave., Pittsburgh, PA 15233; (412) 322-1106; lola-bistro.com; Eclectic; $$$. Tucked away in Allegheny West is the tiny, charming Lola Bistro. The cozy interior space with tin ceilings has enough room for about 25 diners. On some weekday evenings you may even be the only patron(s)! This intimate feeling makes Lola Bistro a good spot for a nice date or a place to catch up with long-lost friends. You will be served by one of the owners, Yelena, and her husband, Michael, who cooks in the back. A small menu has a diverse offering of from-scratch starters and entrees; a little chalkboard by the door reports the daily specials. While the menu changes, a staple is the *Pelmeni*, or Siberian dumplings. Soft dough is filled with a mixture of lamb and beef, topped with a dill sour cream. We also recommend trying one of the pasta entrees. The noodles, like everything else on the menu, are made in-house and are perfectly prepared. Dishes are not huge but are rich on flavor. Each plate is satisfying and lives up to the comfort food designation that graces the top of the menus. Lola Bistro is BYOB with a corkage and six-pack fee.

Monterey Pub, 1227 Monterey St., Pittsburgh, PA 15212; (412) 322-6535; montereypub.com; Irish; $$. Nestled amongst row houses in the historic Mexican War Streets district, Monterey Pub is a warm, neighborhood joint with traditional bar food as well as distinctive Irish dishes. You can seat yourself along the bar in a cozy, wooden booth, or head to the (slightly) larger dining area in the back, complete with fireplace. The decor here makes certain that you are aware of the Guinness on tap. This brew also makes a good showing in the absolutely delicious Irish fare offered on the menu. Try the pub-style shepherd's pie, an outstanding taste of Ireland with a layer of Guinness-marinated shredded meat, vegetables, and cheddar-topped mashed potatoes. Other Irish tastes include bangers and mash and fish-and-chips. Be sure to ask about the desserts of the day. The homemade concoctions like chocolate butter cake are sweet meal endings and will allow you to linger a little longer in the charming surrounds.

Nicky's Thai Kitchen, 856 Western Ave., Pittsburgh, PA 15233; (412) 321-8424; nickysthaikitchen.com; Thai; $$. Nicky's Thai Kitchen is small. Like 18 tables small. And it's loud. It gets significantly larger and quieter in the warmer months though when the back patio opens up. Despite the cramped quarters, Pittsburghers still flock to this Northside staple for quality Thai cuisine. The menu is extensive, and even standard Thai dishes like Phad Thai and green curry are special here. It also offers chef specials like a sweet and tangy shrimp red chili and *gaprow lad kao*, or stir-fried meat (pork, chicken, or beef) in a spicy brown sauce with bell pepper, basil, and a fried egg on top for good measure. Jasmine rice accompanies dishes, but opt for the nuttier brown rice for a small up-charge. As far as appetizers, fresh spring rolls come sliced and oozing with color, and the crab rangoons come delicately crisp and served with an intoxicating pineapple sauce. Nicky's is BYOB. We recommend making a reservation for weekends unless you want to spend time gazing into the eyes of the large Garuda statue in the entrance. Additional location: Downtown, 903 Penn Ave., Pittsburgh, PA 15222; (412) 471-8424.

Landmarks

Max's Allegheny Tavern, 537 Suismon St., Pittsburgh, PA 15212; (412) 231-1899; maxsalleghenytavern.com; German; $$. If you are looking for authentic German fare, head to Max's Allegheny Tavern, the site of a former hotel in the early 1900s and a well-known speakeasy during Prohibition. Whether enjoying a few brews during happy hour or a full meal in one of the dining rooms, you must try the Bavarian soft pretzels, which come three per order. These deep-fried goodies are accompanied by a side of honey mustard sauce, and you can even order them stuffed with cheese. As for German fare, it may be hard to pinpoint what exactly you want on the extensive menu. Have no fear! Get your fill of wursts and other German delicacies with the Max's Sampler Platter, in which you can choose three of Max's entrees, ranging from bratwurst and kielbasa to various schnitzels and roasted pork. Be sure to save room for dessert because 1) there should always be room, and 2) Max's has apple strudel, served with or without vanilla ice cream.

The Park House, 403 E. Ohio St., Pittsburgh, PA 15212; (412) 224-2273; parkhousepgh.com; Neighborhood Bar; $. The Park House is touted as Pittsburgh's oldest tavern (apparently, The Park House was one of the 'Burgh's first licensed bars at the completion of Prohibition). The building dates back to 1889, and not much has changed decor wise so it seems. Rich, dark wood paneling and the narrow space create a warm atmosphere. You'll feel even more welcome as you help yourself to all the free popcorn and peanuts you can handle. Try not to fill up on the snacks; the food at The Park House is not the typical bar fare. Really delicious hummus, falafel, and grilled lamb pita give the menu a Middle Eastern tilt. It is a great and delightful departure from barroom standards. Make sure to ask about the special, as it could be something crazy awesome like a peanut butter and bacon sandwich. The Park House also has a nice selection of craft beers on draft, live music multiple days a week, and always a Wednesday night bluegrass jam.

Specialty Stores, Markets & Producers

Tom Friday's Market, 3639 California Ave., Pittsburgh, PA 15212; (412) 766-4500; tomfridaysmarket.com. A Brighton Heights neighborhood staple for over 50 years, Tom Friday's Market is part deli, part butcher, and part grocer. One of the last of its kind within Pittsburgh city limits, Tom Friday's has fresh hanging cuts of meat, reminiscent of the good old days when you could walk down the street and purchase a fresh cut for dinner. Beef, pork, poultry, sausage . . . you name it and you can likely find it at Friday's. You can also shop frozen meats, fresh produce, and cheese and deli selections of the local variety, like Islay's and SilverStar meats. The customers are loyal, the service is friendly, and the convenience factor alone is something they can hang their hats on. All housed within a small corner shop, the quaint Tom Friday's is a must-see for a taste of the good old days.

South & West

Pittsburgh's South Side has stunning Victorian row houses, and Mount Washington has magnificent views. The South is also home to many 'Burghers in the residential neighborhoods of Banksville, Beechview, and Brookline. A trip over the West End Bridge will take you to the tiny village of the West End, where you can visit art galleries and feast on some tasty treats.

The South Side is bursting at the seams with hidden gems in the old architecture, like small storefront restaurants, happening boutiques, and parlors of the tattoo variety. You have probably heard some crazy-time stories about this section of the 'Burgh. Most of them are probably true. East Carson Street runs through the heart of the South Side flats and is home to the most bars on one street, in Pittsburgh proper. While the conditions of the sidewalks on a Sunday morning can often be suspect, the South Side is one of the most enchanting areas to get a bite to eat. Restaurants here are intimate, by virtue of their architectural location, and eclectic in choice. You can find any flavor you desire and then pop around the corner for a cocktail.

Mount Washington is a short trip up a tall hill by car or, more purely Pittsburgh, by incline. While the area is mainly residential, the neighborhood has the best views of the city, and restaurants have capitalized. Romance hovers in the air here, as it is hard to not be totally taken with the 'Burgh and its sparkling lights below.

Acacia, 2108 E. Carson St., Pittsburgh, PA 15203; (412) 488-1800; acaciacocktails.com; Cocktail Bar; $$. Don't get discouraged if you walk past the door to Acacia a few times. The entrance is meant to blend in with its surroundings. Old newspapers and boards cover the windows, and the only hint that there's life behind the door is the soft hum of jazz music. But don't be afraid. Push the door open and leave the bustle of Carson Street behind—the 1920s are waiting. The speakeasy-style bar features handcrafted classic cocktails and a highly curated beer list. Bourbon, whiskey, and countless other spirits make your libation options almost endless. So take a risk and veer from your typical cocktail order. Your dapper bartender has an encyclopedic knowledge of classic cocktails. Once your drink is finished being shaken or stirred, you'll be rewarded with a cocktail made specifically to your liking. Acacia doesn't currently offer food, but that shouldn't stop you from enjoying an after-dinner drink or a nightcap.

Beehive Coffeehouse & Dessertery, 1327 E. Carson St., Pittsburgh, PA 15203; (412) 488-4483; beehivebuzz.com; Coffee Shop; $. Beehive Coffeehouse is by far one of the coolest and quirkiest places you may ever come across. Repurposed and recycled items have been transformed from trash into treasure and have found new homes on the walls of the Beehive as funk-a-delic art. Once you place an order for one of its famous hand-squeezed lemonades, specialty teas, or a classic latte and a sweet treat, grab a seat at one of the many tables with mismatched chairs and funky lamps. The Beehive has free Wi-Fi so if you get hungry while surfing the web, order one of its specialty sandwiches, wraps, soft pretzels, or soups. You can also enjoy live music while sipping on a coffee cocktail, beer float, or liquor milk shake. Literally, a place for everyone, Beehive is a great stop for when you simply can't decide where to park it for a few hours.

Beto's Pizza, 1473 Banksville Rd., Pittsburgh, PA 15216; (412) 561-0121; Pizza; $. At Beto's, you are either going to absolutely fall madly in love with its thick, square-cut pizza slices, or you will never ever want to eat a slice of it again. Why? The toppings are cold. Yes, cold. Cold cheese, cold banana peppers. Cold. The thick square crusts are crispy, piping hot, and topped with crushed tomato sauce and cold toppings of your choice. You may think it's very weird (we did), but the pizza is seriously excellent. You can order in and take a seat in the small dine-in room or take the pizza to go. No matter where you choose to eat your cold-topping pizza, the line to order will be long and most likely out the door. Pizza is ordered by the slice with toppings at an additional charge. The toppings are piled so high, you might just breathe an olive up your nose when you take a bite. Besides pizza, Beto's also serves up hoagies, sandwiches, salads, and a long list of fried side dishes.

Big Dog Coffee, 2717 Sarah St., Pittsburgh, PA 15203; (412) 586-7306; bigdogcoffee.net; Coffee Shop; $. Neighborhood coffee shops are just as prevalent as neighborhood bars in Pittsburgh. They're in most neighborhoods, tucked among row houses and store-lined streets. The best ones provide more than just coffee and snacks. They provide a creative space for learning and dreaming like only a coffee house can. Originally a bakery, Big Dog Coffee, off East Carson Street, has all the charm you'd expect from a building that's been around since 1889. A fireplace, two bay window nooks, a twinkling chandelier, and a large built-in wooden bar make the inside feel more like a cozy house than a coffee shop. Big Dog serves Intelligentsia Coffee products made by baristas that know how to make a great cup of joe. From lattes, mochas, espresso, tea, and more, Big Dog has all the coffee shop basics covered. To accompany its tasty robust coffee, Big Dog serves pies, cookies, and breads from local pastry chefs; homemade soups; gelato

THE PIG & TRUFFLE COOKERY SCHOOL

Chances are you might need a cooking lesson if you are reading this book all about dining out. Luckily, Chef Lisa Hyde Grosz at The Pig & Truffle Cookery School can help you out. Located on an historical estate in Greensburg (about 30 miles from Downtown), The Pig & Truffle offers private cooking lessons for 2 to 12 people and private dinners for 6 to 12 people.

Typical cooking classes are 3 hours long, in which Chef Hyde Grosz offers you a 5-course meal, teaching you how to make three of the courses. Each cooking lesson costs about $110 and includes corkage fees, a recipe book for you to take home, and of course, eating the fruits of your labor. Sure, you can pay that much in a restaurant on three courses and drinks, but trust, us, this will be much more fun. Classes and course offerings change monthly, focusing on seasonal ingredients, and can be customized depending on your taste.

The Pig and Truffle, named after Chef Hyde Grosz's love of English Pub names, is located in the guest house on the Grosz estate. When you enter, you are immediately greeted by Chef Hyde Grosz and welcomed to the party with dance music, setting the tone for a fun evening ahead. A cocktail and chef's starter, such as oysters

from **Mercurio's** (p. 117) in Shadyside, and organic oatmeal with lots of fix-ins'.

Cambod-Ican Kitchen, 1701 E. Carson St., Pittsburgh, PA 15203; (412) 381-6199; cambodicankitchen.com; Cambodian; $. Character: Not all restaurants have it, but the ones that do leave a lasting impression long beyond their food. Cambod-Ican has character and tons of it. What was once a tiny street truck sandwiched between two buildings in the South Side has become a full-fledged restaurant. Some remnants of the street vendor life remains: handwritten menus

Rockefeller or manchego cheese and figs, will also greet you. During the lesson, Chef Hyde Grosz shows you how to prepare an appetizer, entree with side dish, and dessert. Along the way, she encourages you to use your senses, tasting, touching, and smelling the ingredients that make up the dishes. You will also notice that Chef Hyde Grosz doesn't hold back in the kitchen, giving some instructions in French or dropping a profane word here and there. Don't be alarmed, it's all about the experience; an experience of what it's like to work in a real kitchen. She also shares her real-life kitchen experiences with you, telling stories of her cooking adventures in South Florida and Oxford, England, and offering up cooking tips for you to take home and use when you re-create her recipes or any you are attempting to make.

Chef Hyde Grosz is vibrant, spunky, and crazy passionate about cooking. You enter her kitchen as a stranger, but leave as part of a newfound family. Attending a cooking lesson at The Pig & Truffle will have you learning, laughing, and making new friends.

Visit **The Pig & Truffle Cookery School** at 202B Millersdale Rd., Greensburg, PA 15601; (724) 522-5354; pigandtruffle.com.

and humorous notes that line the walls, a friendly and speedy staff, and a window to place your order. Upon inspection of the menu you'll see it holds several items with high regard. The fried wontons are a favorite, and the shish kabob platter comes with two "world-famous" chicken kabobs, rice, and Cambod-Ican's special "Moon" sauce. You'll probably want to order extra "Moon" sauce. Trust us. If you're in the mood for a little spice, try the curried vegetable bowl with a bevy of fresh vegetables and your choice of meat. Don't forget to send a friend to the bathroom while you're there. We know it sounds weird, but it will provide a hearty chuckle when you see the bathroom keys.

Carson Street Deli and Craft Beer Bar, 1507 E. Carson St., Pittsburgh, PA 15203; (412) 381-5335; carsonstreetdeliand craftbeer.com; Deli; $$. The Donnie Brasco at Carson Street Deli is one of our favorite sandwiches in the 'Burgh, forget about it. For less than a 10 spot you get buffalo chicken, hot pepper cheese, banana pepper rings, lettuce, red onion, tomato, and egg salad piled high on fresh baked BreadWorks Italian bread drenched in bleu cheese dressing. Okay, you can order ranch if you're one of those people, but we recommend its more delicious counterpart. Carson Street Deli has a ridiculous number of other delightful sandwich combinations including the Balboa, a French baguette filled with imported Genoa salami, sopressata, prosciutto, hard salami, spicy capicola, provolone, oil and oregano, and roasted red peppers. Or you can build a sandwich and eat a legacy that is all your own. One of the best delis in Pittsburgh, Carson Street Deli also boasts over 300 craft beers that you can crack open whilst in the deli or beer garden, or mix and match a six-pack and take home with you.

Casa Rasta, 2056 Broadway Ave., Pittsburgh, PA 15216; (412) 344-4700; casarastapgh.com; Caribbean; $–$$. If you are looking for some of the most delicious tacos north of the border, head to Casa Rasta in Beechview. You might miss this place when you first drive down Broadway Avenue, but once you try the tacos, you'll never miss this place again. Actually, you'll be coming back on the regular. Here, the tacos are served in two warm corn tortillas stuffed with flavorful fillings. We recommend ordering at least two or three, depending on how hungry you are. Some of our favorites include the *al Pastor* (roasted pork, pineapple, raw onion, and cilantro drizzled with an avocado cream sauce) and the *carne de birria* (shredded beef topped with raw onion, cilantro, and a chocolate chili sauce). In addition to tacos, these fillings can also be served up as burritos, tortas, tostadas, and quesadillas. Not only do we love the tacos, but we also love that Casa Rasta's menu has plenty of vegetarian and vegan items to choose from, including the quinoa and cilantro soup, jambalaya, fajitas, and Jamaican jerk tofu. Be sure to get your taco fix Mon through Sat, because Casta Rasta is closed on Sun.

Crested Duck Charcuterie, 1603 Broadway Ave., Pittsburgh, PA 15216; (412) 892-9983; crestedduck.com; New American; $$. Executive Chef Kevin Costa is creating some of the best charcuterie in town. So much so, many local restaurants, such as **Meat & Potatoes** (p. 27), **Spoon** (p. 133), and **E2** (p. 105) are serving up his aged meat products. At his intimate and romantic restaurant in Beechview, Kevin is showcasing his charcuterie along with duck confit crepes, duck liver and honey mousse, crispy pork belly, and bistro steaks. Start your dinner off here with the pickle plate (pickled green tomatoes, beets, ginger carrots, peppered okra, and spears), and of course, charcuterie. Kevin shows off his impressive talent on his charcuterie board, presenting his Penn Avenue salami with fennel, garlic, and pink pepper, duck mortadella with pistachios, goose speck, and sweet coppa alongside spicy grain mustard and walnut pesto. Next, order one of Kevin's hot plates, such as the spicy meatballs: delicate, yet hearty meatballs made with beef, pork, bacon, and aged ham served atop a bed of arugula pesto and topped with shaved toma celena cheese. The Crested Duck restaurant is BYOB and open for dinner Thurs through Sat.

Dish Osteria and Bar, 128 S. 17th St., Pittsburgh, PA 15203; (412) 390-2012; dishosteria.com; Italian; $$$. Tucked away off the main path of East Carson Street, you will find Dish Osteria and Bar located on the first floor of an old house. The bar has a South Side neighborhood feel, but with a touch of European flair. Don't let the homey exterior fool you. Inside is a lively bar and a small, intimate dining room with amazing Italian food. Dishes are prepared in the small kitchen and consist of antipasti, handmade pasta dishes, and main entrees of fresh seafood and steak. We suggest pulling up a seat at the bar and ordering a cocktail or glass of wine and a few plates, such as the *melanzane grigliate e mozzarella di bufala*, grilled eggplant and buffalo mozzarella, and the *rigatoni alla scamorza*, rigatoni tossed in a cream sauce with smoked mozzarella, prosciutto, pistachios, parmiggiano reggiano, and fresh black pepper. We are always big fans of ordering what's on the daily special menu, so be sure to ask what the chef is cooking up special the evening you go. For a more intimate experience, possibly with a date you want to impress, be sure to call ahead and make a reservation for the dining room.

Double Wide Grill, 2339 E. Carson St., Pittsburgh, PA 15203; (412) 390-1111; doublewidegrill.com; Barbecue; $$. Once a gas station, Double Wide Grill specializes in barbecue and vegetarian diner food. Its character shines through in both its decor and menu. A large vintage pickup truck sits above the full-size bar, where you can enjoy one of the 40-plus drafts. One of the most creative food features at Double Wide is the "Build Your Own TV Dinner" option. Choose from "On Tráys" including a Delmonico steak, hot and sweet pineapple chicken, and coconut rum tilapia, and sides like cheddar grits, coleslaw, or vegan shoestring fries. You can also get several varieties of wood-grilled burgers like the breakfast burger, your choice of burger (beef, turkey, chicken breast, lentil, or portobello) on thick Texas toast and finished with bacon, a fried egg, and cheddar cheese, and barbecue like ribs, brisket, or pulled pork. Double Wide is also one of the few locations along East Carson Street with a large outdoor patio, so be sure to visit during the summer months and join in a game of cornhole. Additional location: 100 Adams Shoppes, Mars, PA 16046; (724) 553-5212.

Fiori's Pizzaria, 103 Capital Ave., Pittsburgh, PA 15226; (412) 343-7788; fiorispizzaria.com; Pizza; $. Fiori's is a Pittsburgh pizza staple. The small shop cranks out pies like it's their job. Oh, well, we guess it is! Call in an order for pickup or take one of the few seats for a dine-in experience. Either way, you're going to fall in love with the cheesy goodness that is placed before you. Something that makes a slice of Fiori's different from other slices is the sweet sauce. We like ours loaded up with pepperoni, black olives, and hot pepper rings. Starving and sometimes slightly drunk Pittsburghers load up on Fiori's pie plus sides of onion rings, buffalo wings, etc., after a night out at the bar. They're open late, and we mean late, especially on the weekends. So when those late-night pizza cravings hit, you know where to go! Additional location: 3801 Washington Rd., McMurray, PA 15317; (724) 941-5910.

Ibiza Tapas & Wine Bar, 2224 E. Carson St., Pittsburgh, PA 15203; (412) 325-2227; ibizatapaspgh.com; Spanish; $$–$$$. Ibiza is known for making tasty tapas and some of the best sangrias in town. When making a reservation, be sure to request seating on the back patio. At night, the patio is lit only with candlelight and the light that comes in from the floor-to-ceiling window dividing the inside restaurant from the outside. On a breezy, warm summer night, it's quite a romantic spot in the 'Burgh. The menu is seasonal, and the tapas reflect flavors from across the globe, mostly hitting Spanish notes. We suggest ordering many of the hot and cold tapas plates such as the hot mini crabcakes with blood orange, honey, and caramel, the assorted cold cheeses with candied fruit, and a pitcher of sangria to share with your dinner guests. The tapas plates come out as prepared, so there is no rush when dining here. Also, don't worry about finding parking in the South Side because Ibiza has valet.

Isabela on Grandview, 1318 Grandview Ave., Pittsburgh, PA 15211; (412) 431-5882; isabelaongrandview.com; International; $$$$. Isabela on Grandview is an intimate restaurant with ridiculously expansive views of Pittsburgh. With seating upstairs for about 2 dozen, and windows for days, no diner will be in want for the show-stopping scene of the Golden Triangle and our dazzling cityscape. Equally as enthralling is the open kitchen in the back of the dining room. A prix-fixe Chef Tasting Menu of 5 courses is offered every day for diners who want to get a good sample of the elegant fare. Steak here is a good bet, but more interesting flavor combinations like tuna and tangerine can make appearances on the menu as well. You will be treated like a rock star from the moment you arrive until the moment you leave. Chances are you'll even get a photo snapped by the owner, George Merrick, as he makes his rounds. Your smile will come easy, thanks to the good meal, excellent service, and one heck of a backdrop.

La Tavola Italiana, 1 Boggs Ave., Pittsburgh, PA 15211; (412) 481-3336; latavolaitalianarestaurant.com; Italian; $$$. High atop scenic Mount Washington sits La Tavola Italiana. If you're looking for a quick Italian dinner, this is not the spot. Life slows once you're seated as La Tavola's seasoned waitstaff recites the specials of the day. For the main course the menu covers all the basics: traditional pasta dishes, chicken, veal, seafood, and steak. We suggest a chef's special: tortellini with giant lumps of crab meat and shrimp bathed in a spicy yet not overpowering roasted red pepper cream sauce. Whichever dish you choose comes with a salad lightly tossed in the house dressing and accompanied by crunchy garlic bread. Since you're not being rushed out the door, you'll have room for one of the homemade desserts like cannoli or tiramisu. La Tavola is BYOB so bring a bottle of wine (or two) and enjoy a relaxing homemade Italian dinner.

Las Palmas Carniceria, 700 Brookline Blvd., Pittsburgh, PA 15226; (412) 344-1131; Mexican; $. Few foods taste as delightful as foods you buy off the street. Street food isn't plentiful in Pittsburgh, but Las Palmas, with two locations, is a favorite for college kids who are looking for a good, inexpensive meal and for folks looking for authenticity in their Mexican cuisine. You can fill your fresh, warm corn tortillas with an array of meats from seasoned chicken to ground beef, steak, and chorizo. Cilantro, onions, and salsas are available to top the tasty pockets. Those offerings change on a daily basis so it's recommended to try a few at a time while you get the chance. At $2 a taco, you have little to lose. Both locations are set up outside markets where you can find traditional beverages, pico de gallo, and even stacks of fresh tortillas to take with you. Additional location: Oakland, 326 Atwood St., Pittsburgh, PA 15213; (412) 682-1115.

The Library, 2302 E. Carson St., Pittsburgh, PA 15203; (412) 381-0517; thelibrary-pgh.com; **Neighborhood Bar; $$.** Best known for their happy hour specials, The Library offers half off appetizers and has sides under $5 so you can try the Arabian Nights (Cajun black bean and chickpea hummus served with pita and veggies) and the Marco Polo (a freshly baked pepperoni roll served with housemade pizza sauce), all for less than the cost of a hardback book. If you opt for a sandwich or wrap, we suggest the sweet potato fries on the side, and to help combat the fear of a pending book report, grab a drink. The specialty cocktails have literary references as well, like James & the Giant Peach (Long Island made with Peach Pinnacle), plus beer and wine. The Library has indoor and outdoor dining, and we promise you won't be sssssh'd.

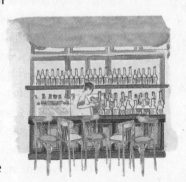

Mallorca Restaurant, 2228 E. Carson St., Pittsburgh, PA 15203; (412) 488-1818; mallorcarestaurantpgh.com; **Spanish; $$$.** Mallorca serves traditional Spanish cuisine in the heart of the South Side. The cozy, main dining area is reminiscent of a library, but instead of books, wine lines the shelves. Candlelit tables set the mood, even during the afternoon. A second dining room is a little lighter in atmosphere. The hosts, wearing suits, offer service with a smile and an appropriate "señor" or "señorita" greeting. The menu heavily favors seafood, with shrimp, lobster, and clams as specialties. The *paella valencia* is a traditional dish with Spanish sausage, rice, chicken, and the aforementioned seafood. For non-sea-excavated food, try the *pollo Mallorca*, chicken stuffed with spinach, pine nuts, and raisins in a creamy red sauce. Every table receives a plate of crisp vegetables, rice, and thick-cut potato chips to share. Eating everything from your packed plate will be an impossibility, and taking a siesta after will be a necessity.

Mario's South Side Saloon, 1510-1514 E. Carson St., Pittsburgh, PA 15203; (412) 381-5610; mariospgh.com; Sports Bar; $. In the South Side and want to watch a football game? You can go to any of the bars, but Mario's is always a good call. Mario's attracts a crowd of all ages: college kids looking for beer specials and cable television to watch a football game to their parents looking for the same thing. Who doesn't love a beer special and a football game? Among your drafts and bottles of beers is a menu of delicious bar food, including pastas, ribs, sandwiches, and burgers. And of course, traditional Pittsburgh bar food like Yinzerogies (potato and cheese stuffed pierogies) and buffalo chicken dip. If you really want to become a Yinzer, try our city's brew, an Iron City, or I.C. Light if you are watching your calories. If you don't like drinking beer, you can still order an Iron City, but in your sandwich. The Iron City Reuben has all the traditional fixings of a Reuben, but what makes this sandwich unique is that the sauerkraut is marinated in the beer. Additional location: Shadyside, 5442 Walnut St., Pittsburgh, PA 15232; (412) 681-3713.

Mike & Tony's Gyros, 1414 E. Carson St., Pittsburgh, PA 15203; (412) 431-2299; mikeandtonysgyros.com; Mediterranean; $. In Pittsburgh, the bars close at 2 a.m. And if you find yourself in a South Side bar when the lights are turned on, you probably need to know what to do next. Answer: You find yourself some late-night grub. There are a few quality post-drinking places to eat in the South Side, and Mike & Tony's is one of the crowded eateries where Pittsburghers line up. Open until 3 a.m. Tues through Sat, Mike & Tony's is just the place to get a nice greasy meal to cure an unwanted hangover. A gyro special, gyro sandwich with a side of french fries and a fountain drink, will hit just the right spot. If not, Mike & Tony's offers other Greek specialties, including souvlaki, Greek salads, spinach pies, and baklava. And if you're looking just for a plate of french fries and cheese, you can get that here too. Mike & Tony's has two additional locations in Downtown and Bridgeville. See website for specific locations and menus.

Nakama Japanese Steakhouse and Sushi Bar, 1611 E. Carson St., Pittsburgh, PA 15203; (412) 381-6000; eatatnakama .com; Japanese (Hibachi: $$$–$$$$; Sushi: $–$$). If you want to eat and drink where all the cool kids do, then trendy Nakama is the spot. Since its opening in 2003, Nakama has been packed with patrons, and the popularity doesn't seem to be quieting down anytime soon. You can enjoy sit-down hibachi in the back of the restaurant, where the chefs are always eager to please while they flip their spatulas cooking scallops, filet mignon, and sesame chicken. If you are just looking for sushi, the small sushi bar in the front is the perfect spot to post up and watch your meal made in front of you. Just want to grab a drink? The large bar overlooking East Carson Street is always a hot spot among patrons. Reservations are a definite must if you want to sit hibachi style, and there are a variety of specials offered during the week. See website for all the details.

OTB Bicycle Cafe, 2518 E. Carson St., Pittsburgh, PA 15203; (412) 381-3698; otbbicyclecafe.com; Neighborhood Bar; $$. OTB

Bicycle Cafe is a bike-friendly bar and restaurant. OTB is the place to go if you are looking for quirky menu items, or if you have a fierce craving for a burger slathered in peanut butter. Yes, you read that right. That would be The Dirt Rag Delight, a half-pound burger with lots of bacon, American cheese, dill pickles, and a healthy serving of Wholey's homemade peanut butter. It's delish. Just trust us, okay? All the menu items are cleverly named after bike parts or bike lingo, like the Clipless Pedal, sesame-encrusted ahi tuna, and the Tandem, an old-fashioned grilled cheese sandwich paired with a bowl of tomato soup. You can have your pick of burgers, paninis, salads, and it's a bar after all, so lots and lots of beer. It might be enough to even make you want to take a bike ride afterward. Additional location: North Park Boathouse, 10301 Pearce Mill Rd., McCandless Township, PA 15101; (724) 940-5000.

Piper's Pub, 1828 E. Carson St., Pittsburgh, PA 15203; (412) 381-3977; piperspub.com; **International; $$.** In Pittsburgh, we love the Steelers and we love watching them even more. It is a given that any time a game is on, bars all over the city are broadcasting. Piper's Pub loves football too, but this place really loves the kind of football that we call soccer in America. Piper's is Pittsburgh's place to get traditional fare from across the pond in the British Isles and the place to watch football games from across the Atlantic. The place even opens up in the early morning hours if soccer games are on the telly. The menu is filled with curry and chips, bangers, corned beef and cabbage, shepherd's pie, Guinness stew, and fish-and-chips. And on Sunday a special entree called "Sunday Supper" is added to the menu. To wash down your meal, you must try one of Piper's scotches or a draft from the beer list. Be sure to check out brunch on Saturday and Sunday.

Pizza Sola, 1417 E. Carson St., Pittsburgh, PA 15203; (412) 481-3888; pizzasola.com; **Pizza; $.** If you find yourself wandering along

East Carson Street after a long night of bar-hopping, Pizza Sola should be one of your final destinations. Don't let the long serpentine line snaking its way out of the door deter you. A giant slice of New York–style pizza is exactly what you need. Once you make it to the counter comes the tricky part: What pizza to enjoy? Yes, Pizza Sola has other menu items, but its pizza is belle of the ball. Each pie is hand-tossed and topped with its own homemade tomato sauce and mozzarella. You can also choose from a variety of classic and gourmet toppings to create your own pizza or choose from red sauce, white sauce, or "always famous pizza" premade options by either the slice or whole pie. And don't forget to add a locally made Red Ribbon flavored pop to your order. Once you've paid, grab a stool, several napkins, and take in the sounds and shenanigans of the South Side at night. Additional locations: See website.

The Pub Chip Shop, **1830 E. Carson St., Pittsburgh, PA 15203; (412) 381-2447; thepubchipshop.com; International; $.** Need a taste of the United Kingdom? The Pub Chip Shop has you covered. The sister spot of Piper's Pub, The Pub Chip Shop is Pittsburgh's answer to the kebab trucks and chip shops dotting the likes of London and Edinburgh. Open late—2 a.m. on weekends—it is one of the only places in town to get a good meal or snack after a few brews. Savory pies and fish-and-chips (french fries) are the staples here. While the menu trends English, some Pittsburgh pops up in the pierogi savory pie and pasty. Along with fish and pies, The Pub Chip Shop also offers baps (sandwiches). Put some jolly-old adventure into your mouth and try one of the menu specialties like the scotch egg: a fried, sausage-encased, hard-boiled egg. Sides include soups, coleslaw, macaroni and cheese with Welsh cheddar, and mushy peas. Wash the British fare down with a deep-fried Mars bar, a gooey, rich dessert fit for a queen or king of indulgent snacks. Note that there is not a lot of seating at the communal tables inside, so you may want or need to grab and go.

Redbeard's Bar & Grill, 201 Shiloh St., Pittsburgh, PA 15211; (412) 431-3730; redbeardspgh.com; Neighborhood Bar; $$. Redbeard's Bar & Grill is an authentic Pittsburgh neighborhood bar. The walls are lined with murals of Pittsburgh sports heroes and signed jerseys of current superstars. The folks on the barstools are regulars. And the good times are yours to be had. It might look cramped from the outside, but once inside it opens up and offers three areas to sit: the bar, dining room, or patio (there is a heated tent for the winter months). With 14 high-def TVs, it's the perfect spot up on the Mount (that's Mount Washington for you non-locals) to watch a Steelers or Penguins game. The menu is largely standard bar food with a few hidden gems like deep-fried pickles and green beans with a spicy pepper coating. Tuesday nights are all about tacos and Wednesday nights are all about wings at Redbeard's, so be sure to stop by early on either night to grab a table. Additional location: Downtown, 144 6th St., Pittsburgh, PA 15222; (412) 261-2324.

17th Street Cafe, 75 S. 17th St., Pittsburgh, PA 15203; (412) 381-4566; 17thstreetcafe.com; Italian; $$. 17th Street Cafe off East Carson Street feels like home. The quaint restaurant is as cozy and warm as the owner himself, who often visits tables to say hello. The menu consists of mostly Italian favorites with a 17th Street Cafe twist. Starters like greens and beans can be spiced up a bit by adding portobello mushrooms and asiago cheese. Main courses include dishes like wild mushroom ravioli, stuffed with woody crimini mushrooms and drizzled with truffle oil, and seared duck breast served with a grainy mustard demi-glaze, sun-dried cranberries, and mushroom risotto. Pay attention to the specials of the day because they are equal parts comfort and unique flavor combinations. The main attraction and a must-try are the asiago cheese-stuffed pillows. These can be substituted for any of the pasta dishes, and we recommend doing so. The pillows are so delicate and packed with flavor that they'll instantly push your dish to the next level. We especially enjoy them with pesto, which is a rich green color and has a hearty fresh flavor.

Shiloh Grill, 123 Shiloh St., Pittsburgh, PA 15211; (412) 431-4000; theshilohgrill.com; Neighborhood Bar; $$. Personality must run in the family because the "older sister" of **Harris Grill** (p. 109) in Shadyside has just as much spunk and sarcastic attitude as its younger sibling. Open weekdays at 4 p.m. and Saturday at 11:30 a.m., Shiloh has a small dining area and bar as well as a deck for warmer non-raining Pittsburgh days or nights. Good luck with that last part. Shiloh Grill offers a similar drink and food menu as Harris Grill, just in a more majestically elevated location. Order up Polish Church Basement Pierogies or the Thanksgiving in Blawnox burger. Shiloh also has a Sunday brunch buffet starting promptly at 10 a.m. The prix-fixe menu with "over one million different things" includes a frozen mimosa or a Bloody Mary as the perfect cure for those hangover blues. In addition to the buffet choices, omelets are also available for brunch. And don't forget, Tuesday is Bacon Night here too!

Slice on Broadway, 2128 Broadway Ave., Pittsburgh, PA 15216; (412) 531-1068; sliceonbroadway.com; Pizza; $$. Home of the Ginormous pie, Slice on Broadway in Pittsburgh's South Hills is best known for the toppings, toppings, toppings to choose from. It's a picky eater's dream, building your own pizza from the dough up. First up is selecting a sauce: red, white, or green. Yes, green sauce. A basil pesto whipped up with garlic and extra-virgin olive oil. Next up, toss on some meats and veggies. Meat options range from meatballs to sopressata while veggies get fancy with sundried tomatoes and artichoke hearts. The combinations are endless when you add in the cheeses that range from goat cheese to crumbled feta. A few tables dot the sidewalk during the warmer months, and when it's too cold to go out, you can dine in. The curtained windows welcome you and give you the feeling you're tucked into a table at your neighbor's house about to partake in a meal with friends.

The Smiling Moose, 1306 E. Carson St., Pittsburgh, PA 15203; (412) 431-4668; smiling-moose.com; Neighborhood Bar; $$. Maybe best known as a Pittsburgh punk rock hot spot, The Smiling Moose has started flexing its culinary muscles. The downstairs bar looks like it was decorated by a college student, complete with cult movie posters and classic arcade games. The menu on the other hand is far from rebelling with youth angst. It features soups, snacks, salads, sandwiches, and sliders. While menu items like crostini of rosemary and basil, topped with fresh and lively tomato salsa and farmer's cheese, and the grilled cheese sandwich with three cheeses (cheddar, pepper jack, and mozzarella), bacon, and tomato are delicious, the sliders are a must. Choose from options like the Chinese five-spice sliders topped with peanut cilantro and sweet chili mayo or hot pastrami with grilled pepper, kraut pepper jack, and horseradish mayo. Sliders come three to an order and are hopefully accompanied by a flavorful yet light pasta salad with peas, sunflower seeds, and farmer's cheese. Don't forget to add a cup of the soup of the day. It regularly wins the South Side Soup contest. The Smiling Moose also has 20 beers on draft and a cooler full of bottles to go with whatever you choose off the menu. See Owner Mike Scarlatelli's recipe for The Captain Spaulding on p. 209.

Stagioni, 2104 E. Carson St., Pittsburgh, PA 15203; (412) 586-4738; stagionipgh.com; Italian; $$. Stagioni relocated from its tiny storefront in the Bloomfield neighborhood to a charmingly redone, two-floor space on the South Side in 2012. The new location allows for more people to experience the rotating Italian menu full of homemade pastas and additional Italian treats. Waiters are well informed about the entree choices and are happy to explain your options. While the menu changes frequently, one staple is always right on top: Made to Order Mozzarella. Here's the deal: You order the mozzarella; the chefs make it on command. As fresh as it gets, folks, and an easy choice for best dish night in and night out. The mozzarella comes with prosciutto, olives, and roasted red peppers, and is bathed in a light balsamic reduction. Once your mozzarella plate has been licked clean, try the gnocchi dish of the evening. The light and airy (really!) gnocchi is prepared in house, along with the other pastas. As the bustling energy of the South Side zips past the windows, you'll hardly notice; you'll be too busy finding room for dessert and cooing, *"Delizioso!"*

Tartine, 400 S. Main St., Pittsburgh, PA 15220; (412) 921-1600; tartinepgh.com; French; $. A vintage bicycle rests along the entrance railing of Tartine's soft blue exterior, brightening up the main drag of the West End Village. This adorable detail is your first hint that you are about to have a delightful experience inside. And the adorableness does not stop once indoors. There is a good chance you will see a dog (a real dog!) resting underneath a chalkboard welcome sign in the corner. So Parisian! Open daily until 2 p.m., Tartine serves up classic French breakfast and lunch fare that is truly *magnifique*. The small menu is packed with delicious options that make choosing a meal a mouthwatering struggle. Can't decide between the goat cheese quiche with a side of Lyonnaise potatoes and the waffle coated with fruit preserve? You don't have to make that decision—get the waffle on the side! Dishes like the country bread topped with pear, bleu cheese, and walnuts are artfully presented and taste bud approved. No matter your choice, be prepared to be dazzled and enchanted. You will leave Tartine planning your next trip back to this charming bistro, and that trip cannot come soon enough! Tartine is cash only. Make sure to bring enough bills to indulge with a selection from the bakery case.

Waffles INCaffeinated, 2517 E. Carson St., Pittsburgh, PA 15203; (412) 301-1763; Breakfast & Lunch; $. Waffles! Waffles with stuff on them! Waffles INCaffeinated in the South Side has waffles piled high with all of the stuff. Crazy concoctions like The Benny, poached eggs, crab, ham, and hollandaise sauce on a freshly made Belgian waffle, and the Funky Monkey, bananas, peanut butter chiffon, and chocolate fudge drizzle on, you guessed it, a waffle, make this quirky little outpost a fun breakfast and lunch choice. Waffles aren't your jam? Well, maybe you shouldn't be at a place that literally has waffles in the name! Just kidding, you guys! Rest assured that there are other choices for the non-waffle lovers here too. Traditional breakfast goodies including french toast, bacon, omelets, and hash browns keep the breakfast party going. Interesting crepes, salads, and sandwiches round out the tasty menu. Cappuccino and French press coffee will give you a caffeinated zing. All in all, this is a really fun place with great twists on the breakfast and lunch classics. Bring a group of friends so you can order a selection of waffles and share the love. The kiddos will love it here too. Waffles INCaffeinated has a second location in Beaver, 453 Third St., Beaver, PA 15009.

The Zenith, 86 S. 26th St., Pittsburgh, PA 15203; (412) 481-4833; zenithpgh.com; Neighborhood Cafe; $$. Part vegetarian restaurant, part art gallery, part antiques store. The Zenith is a hidden gem on the South Side. Just as eclectic as the antiques store part of the Zenith is the restaurant, complete with mix-matched antique furniture, dishes, and wall art that is all for sale. The Zenith has an extensive menu of teas sold by the pot, and a weekly menu of soups, appetizers, salads, entrees, and sandwiches that will even please meat eaters. The restaurant is open for lunch and dinner on Thursday, Friday, and Saturday, and for brunch on Sunday. Sunday brunch is an interesting offering of ordinary breakfast foods like waffles and eggs paired with a buffet of seasonal salads ranging from pasta to bean. Most notable, though, is the table of pies and bundt cakes. Seconds and thirds encouraged. By far one of the most unique places in the city, The Zenith allows you to fill up your belly with tea and eats, fill your closet with vintage clothing, and fill your house with antique treasures.

Landmarks

Alla Famiglia, 804 E. Warrington Ave., Pittsburgh, PA 15210; (412) 488-1440; allafamiglia.com; Italian; $$$$. Romantic date to impress? Anniversary dinner? Super special occasion? Alla Famiglia is just the place to celebrate. It's that special here. Before we even get to the food, we want to advise you to make a reservation via telephone and ask to be seated in the Cucina dining room, near the open kitchen. Sitting here will allow for a dining experience where you can watch and interact with the chefs preparing your meals, as the smells of simmering sauces and sautéing meats waft through the air. It will probably be difficult to pick what to order, but some of our must-try favorites include the mozzarella cheese-stuffed meatball appetizer laid on a bed of red sauce, and the pasta with cheese, pepper, sea salt, and olive oil tossed tableside in a large cheese wheel. Impressive. Entrees, such as the veal, filet mignon, and lamb, each come with a side salad, pasta course, and a breadbasket complete with spicy "holy oil," cecci bean gusto, and a goat cheese and olive spread. Needless to say, the portions here are generous, so sharing is perfectly acceptable by us! Whatever you order, be sure to save room for the homemade raspberry tiramisu.

Fat Head's Saloon, 1805 E. Carson St., Pittsburgh, PA 15203; (412) 431-7433; fatheadspittsburgh.com; Sandwiches; $. Beer and sandwiches. That's what you are going to get when you go to Fat

Head's. Known for sandwiches as big as your head, aka Headwiches, this landmark is the place to go to in the South Side. 'Burghers and non-'Burghers agree. *Maxim Magazine* voted Fat Head's The Southside Slopes Headwich the #5 best sandwich in the USA! That may be because this Headwich comes with kielbasa, grilled onions, fried pierogies, American cheese, and a zesty horseradish sauce. If you can't finish a Headwich, it's okay because most folks can't conquer it. Other delish options include wings, salads, sandwiches, wraps, and burgers. Whatever you order, you must accompany it with a beer. Fat Head's serves up an impressive beer menu complete with beer from its own brewery in Ohio.

Specialty Stores, Markets & Producers

The Milk Shake Factory by Edward Marc Chocolatier, 1705 E. Carson St., Pittsburgh, PA 15203; (412) 488-1808; **edwardmarc.com.** The Milk Shake Factory? Make that the DREAM factory! The cutest little shop along East Carson Street, The Milk Shake Factory by Edward Marc Chocolatier has a menu of over 55 flavors of milk shakes, an assortment of sundaes, and old-fashioned floats and sodas. Don't see anything you like on the menu? The milk shake magicians will whip you up something wonderful. The best thing about these shakes is the Factory's commitment to hardy milk and real ingredients. If you choose a shake with cake, you better believe you will be drinking up real cake crumbs through your straw! After making the tough flavor choice, enjoy your iced confection at one of the old-fashioned soda shop tables. Old-timey-ness extends throughout this gem, from the tin ceilings to the checkered floor. The Milk Shake Factory by Edward Marc Chocolatier is under the ownership of the Edward Marc Chocolatier, a fourth-generation gourmet chocolate business almost a century strong.

Try to resist the chocolates sold here; it will not happen (nor should it!). See The Milk Shake Factory's recipe for PB & J Milk Shake on p. 215.

Page Dairy Mart, 4600 E. Carson St., Pittsburgh, PA 15210; (412) 431-0600; pagedairymart.net; Ice Cream. Rejoice ice cream lovers: There is a place you can order a sundae and a milk shake—in one! That place: Page Dairy Mart. This roadside wonder features a frosty treat menu of decadent options, including that ice cream sundae/creamy shake combo known as a Southside Shake. Another stand-out? The chocolate chip cookie sundae made with the best cookies in town from **Nancy B's** in Homestead (p. 180). The history of Page Dairy Mart is as rich as the creamy cones. Roundabout 100 years ago, gas to fill up your jalopy was on the menu, not ice cream. Now, cars en masse roll up to Page for cool treats on warm nights, making finding parking an interesting battle that is worth the fight. Page is open seasonally, so check the website and social media outlets to make sure it is serving up the good stuff before you go. You can also expect to wait in quite a line when the weather is fine, so bring your patient pants along with your appetite.

The Pretzel Shop, 2316 E. Carson St., Pittsburgh, PA 15203; (412) 431-2574; thepretzelshop.net. The Pretzel Shop is a cash-only specialty store, open 6 days a week and closed on Sun. The shop sells soft pretzels and caters to college kids, vintage deal seekers, and outdoor enthusiasts who are looking for a quick bite to eat between meals. Pretzel sandwiches are available for breakfast and lunch, and we count them as a meal. For breakfast you can order a sausage, egg, and cheese, and for lunch you have your choice of a pizza pretzel, a ham and cheese pretzel, a chicken salad pretzel, and many, many more. To satisfy your pretzel craving and your sweet tooth, what is better than a twisted mound of salty, carby goodness? We're referring to their cinnamon and sugar pretzel. Pretzels might just become the universal meal.

The Pretzel Shop even shares its twisted knots with local area eateries, so you can find them in a variety of unique dishes throughout the city.

S & S Candy & Cigar Co., 2025 E. Carson St., Pittsburgh, PA 15203; (412) 481-6577; sscandycigar.com. Your sweet tooth will start tingling as soon as you walk into S & S Candy & Cigar Co. Shelves filled with Double Bubble, Skor Bars, Sky Bars, Snickers, Lemonheads, Laffy Taffy, Sixlets, Cowtails, Peppermint Patties, Candy Cigarettes, Sour Patch Kids, Twizzlers, Swedish Fish, Frooties, gum balls, Gummi Bears, and the list goes on. S & S has you covered for just about any kind of candy you can think of new and old. It even has an entire room with candy separated by color, size, and flavor. Only like banana flavored Runts? You can buy a 2-pound bag and indulge your inner diva like Beyonce. Want 27 green gum balls? You can buy 27 green gumballs in small, medium, or large and blow green bubbles till you just can't anymore. Once you come down from your sugar rush, head to the back of the warehouse for a wide variety of tobacco products or to play the lottery.

East

You will see that the East chapter is the largest, and rightfully so. The East boasts thriving communities chock-full of hipsters, academics, artists, and families. Universities, boutiques, galleries, and bars fill the streets. Each neighborhood has a distinct character, from the artful Lawrenceville to the Victorian, swanky Shadyside. There is literally something for everyone in the area, and the dining scene proves equally as fruitful.

It helps that this large cross section of town is experiencing a culinary renaissance. Innovative chefs are bringing their exciting, experimental cuisines to the neighborhoods (East Liberty and Garfield are especially heating up). Restaurants here are revitalizing communities and reinvigorating the Pittsburgh dining scene. New, interesting spots are popping up alongside old favorites, and our tummies could not be more pleased.

Foodie Faves

The Allegheny Wine Mixer, 5226 Butler St., Lawrenceville, Pittsburgh, PA 15201; (412) 252-2337; alleghenywinemixer.com; Wine Bar; $$. Named after the famed "Catalina Wine Mixer" scene in the movie *Step Brothers*, The Allegheny Wine Mixer is giving wine bars a good name. The casual space is far from the stodgy and pretentious wine bars you might be picturing. Paint-by-numbers artwork hang

DJ's Butcher Block

You might not think you need a butcher, but you do. They offer high-quality, local cuts of meat that will leave your favorite chain grocery store weeping. They'll cut the meat in front of you, to your specifications, and even tell you how it should be prepared. Plus, buying from a butcher will help support a local community artisan and significantly up your meat A-game. It's an all-round win. And DJ's Butcher Block is just the place to find your new butcher.

The interior is simple. Two small wire racks are filled with pasta sauce, olives, balsamic vinegar, and homemade jellies. Natural and local eggs from Seibel's Family Farm in Clinton, PA, and local, hormone free whole, skim, 2 percent, and buttermilk from Brunton Dairy in Beaver County are kept cold in a small cooler. But most of that will be easily overlooked by the overflowing display case filled with your future dinner.

Slabs of beef, whole chickens, sausages, and more are waiting to go home with you. Chicken can be purchased whole, ground, or segmented by leg, wing, or breast. All-natural pork can be carved into chops, tenderloin, ribs, or bacon cut to your desired thickness. Purchase a rack, a leg, a loin chop, or ground local lamb. Grass-fed beef can be cut into a New York strip, sirloin, filet mignon, flank, or ground for the best burger of your life. DJ also offers over 10 varieties of fresh specialty sausage (about five varieties rotate daily) including hot and sweet Italian, kielbasa, maple sage breakfast, and chicken chorizo.

Head to **DJ's Butcher Block** at 4623 Liberty Ave., Bloomfield, Pittsburgh PA 15224; Mon through Fri from 10 a.m. to 6 p.m. or Sat from 9 a.m. to 4 p.m. Looking for something special? Give DJ a call at (412) 621-3100 or visit djsbutcherblock.com.

from the walls and 60s garage rock blares from the speakers. It's the kind of place you can wear a t-shirt and jeans while enjoying a $100 bottle of wine. It's also a stomping ground for many in the growing Pittsburgh food community. So you might just run into a few people mentioned in this book. While you might laugh at the name, the knowledge behind the bar is far from funny. Certified Sommelier Jamie Patten leads a team of talented bartenders and manages an ever-growing wine, beer, and cocktail list. AWM also offers a few snacks in the form of creative grilled cheese sandwiches, and of course meat, cheese, and chocolate plates.

Aiello's Pizza, 2112 Murray Ave., Squirrel Hill, Pittsburgh, PA 15217; (412) 521-9973; aiellospizza.com; Pizza; $$. Aiello's has been serving up Italian favorites to the Squirrel Hill neighborhood since 1978. Traditional pasta and deli-style hoagies are on the menu, but the main attraction here is the pizza. The sauce is a bit on the sweet side, the cheese is plentiful, and the crust has a nice crunch. (Insider tip: It is best to let this pizza cool down a bit before diving in. Due to the generous cheese amount, slices can easily fall victim to the cheese slide-off. Plus, the pies taste their best lukewarm.) Plain cheese pizza is always a hit, allowing you to appreciate the overall, no-nonsense pizza quality without any distracting toppings. But if you are feeling fancy, try one of the gourmet choices like the Murray Avenue with bacon, mushrooms, and four cheeses. Aiello's is family owned and operated, so seeing a familiar face kneading dough is not uncommon—especially once the number is on your speed dial. This eat-in or take-out joint is cash only. An ATM is on-site for those who forget their dollar bills while pizza is on their brains.

Avenue B, 5501 Centre Ave., Friendship, Pittsburgh, PA 15232; (412) 683-3663; avenueb-pgh.com; New American; $$$. Chef-Owner

Chris Bonfili creates a beautifully eclectic, yet familiar, menu that elegantly displays his prowess in the kitchen. It features traditional American-style fare like Wagyu beef meat loaf with goat cheese and chive whipped potatoes, crispy onions, and tomato jam, and dishes subtly influenced by a range of other cultures. In addition to the seasonal menu, Avenue B offers daily chalkboard specials for each course. Creative beginning dishes like rosemary butternut squash soup with maple crème fraîche and main events like pan-seared halibut with parsley pesto cavatelli, cauliflower, beurre rouge, and clam relish are the norm here. Save room for dessert at Avenue B because the dessert comes architecturally plated, pretty enough to save. But we advise you to dive right in. Be sure to bring a bottle of wine with you because Avenue B is BYOB.

Bangkok Balcony, 5846 Forbes Ave., Squirrel Hill, Pittsburgh, PA 15217; (412) 521-0728; bangkokbalconypgh.com; Thai; $$. Bangkok Balcony sits on a second floor above Forbes Avenue. The small entrance can be easily missed from the sidewalk, but the discovery is worth it. Bangkok Balcony specializes in authentic Thai cuisine and does it quite well. The menu features traditional curries, noodle dishes, and house specialties. We like to start off with the Thai spring roll, but if you are a mussel appreciator, several appetizers like the Bangkok Balcony mussel fritter, featuring sautéed mussels with bean sprouts, will be a nice beginning. The pad Thai here is top-notch. Being big on noodle dishes, we also like the See-You Noodles, with your choice of meat, broccoli, and egg. Dishes can be customized on a spiciness level of 1 to 10. Depending on your mood, you could eat a mild entree or just have the fire department on standby to hose down your mouth after a level 10. Bangkok Balcony's sister restaurant, **Silk Elephant** (p. 129), is close by on Murray Avenue.

Big Jim's Restaurant & Bar, 201 Saline St., Greenfield, Pittsburgh, PA 15207; (412) 421-0532; bigjimsrestaurant.com; Neighborhood Bar; $–$$. Big Jim's in Lower Greenfield, aka "The Run," looks like a typical neighborhood bar from the outside. And on the inside, it looks like a typical neighborhood bar too, complete with wall-to-wall wood paneling, dim lighting, and tacky decor. Big Jim's attracts regulars, college students from Oakland, and folks wanting to taste the amazing food after hearing about the bar on Food Network's *Diners, Drive-ins and Dives*. Everything on the menu is recommended by the friendly staff, but when you go here, you must get a sandwich. Big Jim's Specialty Sandwiches are huge and the veal cutlet ala Parmigiana is served on half a loaf of Italian bread. Half a loaf of bread! If you don't see a Signature Sandwich you like, you can create your own half-pound sandwich. The homemade wedding soup is the perfect complement to a large sandwich—that is, if your stomach has the room. Pizza, calzones, pasta, and salads are also on the menu, but we repeat: Get a sandwich. Your stomach won't be sorry.

Bloomfield Bridge Tavern, 4412 Liberty Ave., Bloomfield, Pittsburgh, PA 15224; (412) 682-8611; bloomfieldbridgetavern.com; Neighborhood Bar; $$. Pierogies and kielbasa and potato pancakes! Oh, my! *Haluski* (cabbage and noodles), *kluski* (homemade noodles and cottage cheese), and *gotabki* (stuffed cabbage) too! If you're a die-hard fan of Polish cuisine, and we mean die-hard, don't forget to get a bowl of the *czarnina*, Polish duck soup. While it seems like someone's Polish grandmother rules the roost, don't worry; if you're craving something other than carbs, Bloomfield Bridge Tavern offers a variety of other menu items. Choose from Pittsburgh bar standards like Bridge wings, Bridge fries covered in mozzarella and American cheese, grilled chicken salad with fries and cheese, or a hot sausage sandwich. Bloomfield Bridge Tavern also has a hearty draft and bottle beer selection and live music featuring national and local talent on the weekends. Plus every Wednesday, BBT turns into "The Polish Party House" for Drum and Bass

CONFLICT KITCHEN

We don't usually mix dinner with politics, but Pittsburgh's Conflict Kitchen isn't afraid to stir the pot. This take-out restaurant doubles as a public art project headed by Carnegie Mellon University assistant professor of art Jon Rubin and artist Dawn Weleski, serving up dishes from countries that the United States is in conflict with.

Conflict Kitchen takes on a new country's identity every few months and has created Iranian, Afghan, Cuban, North Korean, and Venezuelan dishes, which have never been found in Pittsburgh until now. Some past dishes have included: *bolani kachaloo*, turnovers from Afghan stuffed with leeks and potatoes; Iranian *kabab-e kubideh*, ground beef kebab served with *mast-o khiar* (yogurt and cucumber dip), fresh herbs, and sumac on naan; and *doenjang jjigae*, a traditional vegetable and soybean paste stew from North Korea.

The purpose of the Conflict Kitchen is to engage the general public through discussion about these conflicting countries, their cultures, and the people that they may know little or nothing about outside of what is portrayed through the media. So, if you're looking to school your taste buds, we recommend you stop by for a bite to eat and an open discussion. Be sure not to throw your food wrapper away when finished eating. On it you will find interviews, ranging from popular culture to politics, from both people in the conflicting country and the diaspora in the United States.

Visit the **Conflict Kitchen**, open 7 days a week in Schenley Plaza, at 221 Schenley Dr., Oakland, Pittsburgh, PA 15213; (412) 802-8417; conflictkitchen .org.

Night, a must-go-to event to truly appreciate the uniqueness this tavern has to offer.

BRGR, 5997 Centre Ave., East Liberty, Pittsburgh, PA 15206; (412) 362-2333; brgrpgh.com; Burgers; $$. One of the most perfect meals in the world: a juicy burger and a thick milk shake. You can find this perfect meal and much more at BRGR. The burgers come gourmet, with fancy toppings and combinations of ingredients beyond the traditional mustard, ketchup, and pickles. Try the Double Yoi, a beef burger topped with pastrami, fried egg, swiss cheese, coleslaw, and Thousand Island dressing. If beef isn't your meat of choice, you can still enjoy a burger. The non-beef gourmet burgers include salmon, turkey, black bean and roasted corn falafel, lamb, and a shrimp patty. With your burger, order a side of the BRGR fries with truffle cheese whiz (who says cheese whiz isn't gourmet?) or the house-made chips with crack dip. We did not make this up. BRGR denotes its cheese dip as so good, it may become addictive like a drug, though legal in this case. To top your meal off, order a spiked milk shake or float. Additional locations: 20111 Rt. 19 and Freedom Rd., Cranberry, PA 16066; (724) 742-2333; inside PNC Park in Section 115; and the roaming BRGR Food Truck.

Brillobox, 4104 Penn Ave., Bloomfield, Pittsburgh, PA 15224; (412) 621-4900; brillobox.net; Neighborhood Bar; $$. Half watering hole, half cultural catchall, Brillobox is a creative space used for concerts, special events, and socializing. Downstairs houses a hipster bar complete with eclectic artwork, a killer jukebox, mustaches, and pants tighter than an 80s glam rocker. It also has a deliciously diverse big bottle and draft beer selection and food menu. While Brillobox has a full menu, we suggest hitting this place for appetizers. You can't go wrong with any app here, but the *pommes frites* are nicely seasoned and come piled high in a cone accompanied by awesome dipping sauces (malt vinegar aioli, red bell pepper aioli, and black pepper ketchup). The nachos are also a good choice and come piled high with red beans, nacho cheese, tomatoes, lettuce, tomatillo salsa, queso fresco, and crema. Upstairs plays home to an events venue where concerts from artists like Neon Indian, Tapes n' Tapes, and French Horn Rebellion are a regular occurrence. If you're lucky, you might be there for a dance party, community event, or some of the hardest trivia around. If you have a hipster hankering on a Sunday, stop by for the Starving Artist Vegetarian Supper, where the chef prepares a different healthy and cheap vegetarian meal each week.

Butterjoint, 214 N. Craig St., Oakland, Pittsburgh, PA 15213; (412) 621-2700; thebutterjoint.com; Gastropub; $$. Butterjoint is **Legume's** (p. 116) adjacent bar. It's cozy and always filled with patrons looking for a mighty fine cocktail. And the bartenders here know how to do just that. There is a standard drink menu, filled with beers, cocktails, and wines, but if you dare, put your trust into the bartenders and order The Mercy of the Bartender, a surprise cocktail made to the bartender's liking. To pair with your cocktail, be sure to order a few snacks from the menu. The freshly ground beef burgers are made daily and come topped with lettuce, onion, and your choice of cheese. If you are looking for something a bit fancier, ask your waiter what's on the Fancy Burger of the Day. Another standout on the menu is the white potato and homemade farmer cheese-filled pierogies. They come fried or sautéed and plated with fried onions and sour cream. They can also be ordered with sautéed greens, sauerkraut, and house-made sausage. In addition to Butterjoint's small menu, Legume's full dinner menu is available.

The Cafe at the Frick, 7227 Reynolds St., Point Breeze, Pittsburgh, PA 15208; (412) 371-0600; thefrickpittsburgh.org/start/cafe.php; Eclectic; $$–$$$. Located on the grounds of the beautiful

Frick Art and Historical Center, or quite simply, The Frick, The Cafe at the Frick soars above typical museum-quality eateries. Windows wrap around the small space, which allows diners to gaze upon the illustrious former dwellings of industrialist Henry Clay Frick. The setting makes one feel fancy, and the food served continues the trend. The Cafe prepares inspired lunch and brunch dishes that use fresh produce grown at the on-site greenhouse. Therefore, the menu changes with the growing seasons and, sometimes, the art exhibitions inside (e.g., a Faberge show produced Russian-centric meal choices). The housemade desserts are also top-notch and baked fresh daily. Afternoon tea is offered every day after 2:30 p.m., so you can feel like a coal magnate taking a leisurely break. Make sure to call ahead as tables fill up fast. Trust us, you don't want to be turned away!

Cafe Moulin, 732 Filbert St., Shadyside, Pittsburgh, PA 15232; (412) 291-8119; Breakfast & Lunch; $.

Cafe Moulin is tucked away in a basement space along Filbert Street in Shadyside. The sweet little spot takes full advantage of this underground location with a large banquette along a beautiful stone wall. Images of windmills grace the walls less rocky. You have your choice of savory and sweet crepes, omelets, or waffles. Cafe Moulin serves **La Prima** coffee products (p. 43) and has a variety of other hot and cold beverage options like Nutella hot chocolate and Turkish apple juice. If you order a crepe (which you probably should do), you can watch as the chef whips up your meal behind the counter in the back of the space. The spinach, feta, and goat cheese crepe is a great choice from the savory side of the menu. The Super Belgium, a crepe filled with cookie spread and topped with bananas, strawberries, chocolate sauce, and whipped cream, is the not-to-be-missed crepe from the sweet side of the menu. The sweet crepe options can also be transferred to a liege waffle.

Bring your laptop if you are dining solo; Cafe Moulin has Wi-Fi.

Cafe Phipps, 1 Schenley Park, Squirrel Hill, Pittsburgh, PA 15213; (412) 622-6914; phipps.conservatory.org; International; $. Phipps Conservatory and Botanical Gardens is a quiet place to escape the hustle and bustle of the city. Whether you walk through the gardens or grab a bite to eat at Cafe Phipps, nature will surround you and provide eco-friendly inspiration. Cafe Phipps is a 3 Star Green Restaurant Certified eating establishment committed to providing fresh and healthy food that is good for both its patrons and the environment. The Cafe is open for lunch Mon through Sun and for happy hour and dinner on Fri nights. Many of the food items on the menu are vegan

or vegetarian, and are made from in-season local and organic produce. Salads, paninis, sandwiches, flatbreads, and soups fill the chalkboard menu. You won't find any soda at Cafe Phipps, but you will find their own healthy substitution for it, a fruit-based beverage called Phipps Splash. In addition to the food, the Cafe makes a huge effort to be sustainable. The coffee is fairtrade and organic, the water is filtered on-site, the beer and wine are organic, and the take-out containers and serviceware are compostable. We give Phipps and Cafe Phipps two green thumbs up!

Cafe Zinho, 238 Spahr St., Shadyside, Pittsburgh, PA 15232; (412) 363-1500; International; $$$. Cafe Zinho is a small space that actually feels like you are eating in someone's living room. You are, in fact, eating in a converted garage, but the space is so warm, eclectic, and welcoming, you'll feel like an invited guest at an old friend's. Just as any good dinner guest would, bring a bottle of wine; this place is BYOB! The menu features just about every meat in the book—lamb, pork, duck—and our favorite cheeses: goat, feta, gorgonzola. Goat cheese in puff pastry appetizer, you have our hearts. Dishes like chicken stuffed with gorgonzola and portobello mushroom ravioli are generous and satisfying. The menu does get altered every so often, but the cuisine remains hearty. If you end up being hungry for dessert, the Cafe has changing, daily selections to choose from that should cap off your meal nicely. Cafe Zinho also sets up several sidewalk tables in good Pittsburgh weather.

Caliente Pizza & Draft House, 4624 Liberty Ave., Bloomfield, Pittsburgh, PA 15224; (412) 682-1414; pizzadrafthouse.com; Pizza; $$. Wedged between a laundromat and a Cricket store, Caliente Pizza & Draft House might seem like your run-of-the-mill neighborhood dive bar. But if you let the glowing red neon sign lure you inside, you'll quickly notice it's far from ordinary. Old-fashioned beer tins fill the walls. Twenty rotating craft drafts are artistically chalked on the wall the behind the bar. And three beer coolers keep exotic bottled beers cold for carryout. It's a craft beer drinker's heaven that will be hard to leave. Once you wade through the beer selections, turn your attention to the food menu. It is extensive and features starters, wings, calzones, pizza, burgers, gyros, subs, and salads. But the real star is Caliente's pizza. The crust is thick, bubbly, and hand-tossed. The sauce is homemade. The cheese is grated fresh every day. The vegetables and toppings are hand-cut and piled high. And the result is old-school pizza perfection.

Casbah, 229 S. Highland Ave., Shadyside, Pittsburgh, PA 15206; (412) 661-5656; bigburrito.com/casbah; Mediterranean; $$$–$$$$. If you want to dine in a Mediterranean-inspired outdoor patio surrounded by plants, flowers, and Greek-esque sculptures, then Casbah is the place to go. Warning: Mediterranean Sea not included. The restaurant has a large bar, lounge, and two dining rooms on the inside, but the outside front patio is where you want to be seated to enjoy your meal. The menu is inspired by the Mediterranean, with influences from North African, French, Italian, and Spanish cuisines. The menu here changes often, but one of our favorite dishes that is always on the menu is the orecchiette pasta mixed with dried cranberries and grilled chicken, and tossed in a sage cream and goat cheese sauce. Rich and heavenly enough to share with some of your dinner guests. For a meatier option, we suggest ordering the duck, lamb, or filet mignon. Casbah also serves up brunch and offers a prix-fixe option that includes a cocktail, appetizer, and entree for $24. You seriously can't beat it!

Constellation Coffee, 4059 Penn Ave., Lawrenceville, Pittsburgh, PA 15224; (814) 419-9775; constellationcoffeepgh.com; Coffee Shop; $. Coffee culture has taken a turn. No longer just gulped to aid in waking up, coffee has developed a devoted following. Similar to the current craft beer phenomenon, coffee is being appreciated and examined on a whole new level. Part of the growing coffee education in Pittsburgh comes from Constellation Coffee. The small coffee shop can be easily missed on bustling Penn Avenue. Just look for the simple handwritten logo and COFFEE sign. The minimalist vibe is carried inside, which makes it easy to focus on the task at hand: coffee. The drink menu at Constellation is a simple one: Chemex, drip coffee, and espresso. Lattes and hot chocolate are also available. Each choice is carefully crafted by an expert barista who can talk effortlessly about the specific blend of coffee from Ceremony Coffee Roasters in Maryland that you're about to enjoy. Vegan treats from **Eden** in Shadyside (p. 106) are also usually available to pair with your coffee. Constellation also has a large back room that can be booked for meetings or events.

Crepes Parisiennes, 207 S. Craig St., Oakland, Pittsburgh, PA 15213; (412) 683-1912; French; $. Crepes Parisiennes brings a little taste of Paris to Pittsburgh with its made-to-order sweet and savory crepes. The line is usually out the door on the weekends and filled with college students and families alike. Don't let that stop you from indulging; it moves fast. When you make it to the front, choose from savory or sweet crepes, or both, and enjoy a cafe au lait while you wait for your crepe to be made. The savory crepes such as egg and cheese, smoked salmon, and mixed vegetables and cheese come with your choice of one of four sauces inside (Asian-inspired soytang, béchamel, crème fraîche, and garlic olive oil) and a side salad with house-made champagne vinaigrette. The vinaigrette is so tasty you might want to order a second side salad to enjoy. For the sweet crepes, you can never go wrong with a crepe stuffed with Nutella or mandarin oranges and chocolate. You can also get Belgian waffles and panini sandwiches. Leave the plastic at home; Crepes Parisiennes only accepts cash.

Cure, 5336 Butler St., Lawrenceville, Pittsburgh, PA 15201; (412) 252-2595; curepittsburgh.com; Eclectic; $$–$$$. The scent of smoked meat will greet your nostrils the moment you enter Cure. The scent will stay with you even after leaving, which acts as a welcome reminder of a meal well done. Cure is an intimate space with wood-lined walls, a long banquette, and clear vision lines all the way back to the kitchen. The handwritten menu, which is an ever-evolving organism, is presented on a wood block. Options are limited, but the selections are sure to please your palate. Cure calls its food "extra local urban Mediterranean," but we just call it delicious. You can expect creative preparations and combinations of flavors. Pistachios and duck? Apple cider and beef cheeks? Sure, why not? You can also expect the meat (of any kind) on your plate to be perfect. A place with a heavy meat smell and a pig logo cannot disappoint in that department. Executive Chef and Butcher Justin Severino makes sure of it.

D's Six Pax and Dogz, 1118 S. Braddock Ave., Swissvale, Pittsburgh, PA 15218; (412) 241-4666; ds6pax.com; Neighborhood Bar; $. As the name suggests, at D's you can find six-packs and hot dogs. Perhaps rather unexpected is the sheer volume of brews that can fill your pack and the downright gourmet options for your dog. D's boasts a microbrew selection that is unrivaled in the area. Step into the beer cave behind the main room and prepare to have your mind blown. The menu choices may be more limited than the brewskies, but this neighborhood bar serves up truly satisfying, and most often deep-fried, snacks. The fries, which can be ordered by the handful, are a good start or nice to share. You will need to save room for a hot dog, be it all beef, turkey, or veggie. After choosing your dog, pick from a variety of preselected topping combos including the likes of the Bacon Cheddar (more, please!) or the Mason Dixon (chili and coleslaw), or make your own powerhouse compilation.

Deli on Butler Street, 4034 Butler St., Lawrenceville, Pittsburgh, PA 15201; (412) 682-6866; delionbutler.com; Deli; $. It's all about family at the Deli on Butler Street. So much so, you will feel like a member of the family after just one visit. Owner Gary Gigliotti opened the family-run deli in 2008 after the passing of his late father, Pasquale, who told him at a young age that he should own a deli. Honoring his father, a menu item is named after him, the Pasquale specialty sandwich that features ham, turkey, roast beef, red onion, two kinds of cheese (provolone and colby), and the deli's special sauce. All specialty sandwiches are served on either Italian, marble rye, or whole wheat bread, and with lettuce, tomato, and a pickle spear. We love pickle spears! Other items on the menu include salads, soups, paninis, hoagies, and wraps. Also, you can order sliced lunch meat and cheeses by the pound. There is no seating, so grab your order to go. Additional location: Deli on North Avenue, Northside, 4 E. North Ave., Pittsburgh, PA 15212; (412) 322-3354.

Dinette, 5996 Centre Ave., Shadyside, Pittsburgh, PA 15206; (412) 362-0202; dinette-pgh.com; Pizza; $$. The large windows create an open breeziness. The simple decor and table settings give it a minimalist swagger. The garden on the roof where the chef's father, Seth, grows ingredients like tomatoes, arugula, shishito peppers, figs, and herbs makes it pretty darn cool. And that's all before we've even talked about the menu. The daily rotating menu at Dinette, located on the second level of the Eastside development, is only open for dinner and focuses largely on thin-crust pizza. Yes, there are several starter course selections that will make your mouth water at the description alone, but you go to Dinette to experience gourmet pizza. Pizza with salt-cured anchovies, jalapeños, capers, fresh mozzarella, and tomato or shaved fennel, red onion, spicy sopressata, oregano, fresh mozzarella, and tomato. This is not your average pepperoni pizza here, folks. This is innovative pizza from Chef-Owner Sonja Finn, who finds inspiration for her menu through using seasonal ingredients. The pizzas are perfect for sharing and allow room to sample dessert. We suggest whatever Arborio Rice Pudding is available. Visit Dinette's website for more information about the rooftop garden.

E2, 5904 Bryant St., Highland Park, Pittsburgh, PA 15206; (412) 441-1200; e2pgh.com; Italian; $$$. Kate Romane, chef and owner of E2 in Highland Park, creates dishes you wish you could make. They're simple, rustic, and full of flavors that blend together seamlessly. E2 serves dinner, but your first experience should be brunch. The vibe is casual and cozy, and the chalkboard menu is filled with rustic, sweet, and savory Italian-influenced choices. From simple one- or two-ingredient items to the more complex, E2 completes each dish with sincerity and heart. And you can tell. Start your brunch off sweetly with a bag of doughnuts, lightly fried pieces of sourdough that are tossed with ginger and sugar; beignets, airy fried dough with a sprinkling of powdered sugar; or zeppoli rolled in Parmesan cheese and black pepper and stuffed with anchovy (the anchovy is optional). For $5 each, why not try all three? As for your main brunch entree, recommendations get a little tricky. The menu is constantly changing, but any version of the polenta, frittata, or fried egg hoagie won't steer you wrong. See Chef-Owner Kate Romane's recipe for Spaghetti Carbonara on p. 221.

Eat Unique, 305 S. Craig St., Oakland, Pittsburgh, PA 15213; (412) 683-9993; eatuniquecafe.com; Neighborhood Cafe; $. Tired of the same old chain lunch spot? Eat Unique. With a long list of created on-the-spot sandwiches and salads, Eat Unique adds some much-needed flavor to the lunchtime routine. Vegetarians and healthy food addicts can find some solace here with options packed full of veggies and freshness. The Summer Sandwich, a take on mozzarella, tomato, and pesto, is a standout choice; the classic BLT is a favorite for those who require bacon on seriously delicious farm bread; and the tomato soup sprinkled with feta is a nice introduction to some of Oakland's best homemade potage. Be sure to expect a bit of a wait for your food, especially during the lunchtime rush; crafting quality meals takes time. You can always call and order ahead if you are in a hurry. An important note: Even if you are trying to keep things healthy, don't forgo the sea salt chocolate chip cookies. Those puppies are life-changing on the delicious scale and are the size of your face—which will be smiling after your lunch.

Eden, 735 Copeland St., Shadyside, Pittsburgh, PA 15232; (412) 802-7070; edenpitt.com; Neighborhood Cafe; $$. Eden is the type of place you feel healthier just by walking inside. Dedicated to fresh ingredients and gluten-free *everything*, Eden's menu is vegetable heavy (you can order veggie fries and raw ketchup, for instance) and one of the most interesting in the city. Many of the items are also vegan friendly, like vegan waffles for Sunday brunch. Meat is on the menu too, which changes seasonally, but the stars here are absolutely the twists on the veggies. If you are feeling adventurous, take a shot . . . of kale or spinach, with hints of lemon or lime and ginger. Healthy shots not your thing? Bring your liquor; this joint is BYOB. As a fun touch, the food here isn't the only thing that is locally sourced; regional artists' work graces the white walls and pairs nicely with the otherwise minimalist interior.

Espresso A Mano, 3623 Butler St., Lawrenceville, Pittsburgh, PA 15201; (412) 918-1864; espressoamano.com; Coffee Shop; $. Espresso A Mano fits the mold for so many Pittsburghers for so many different reasons. It's the go-to meeting spot for a quick business coffee. It's the place to hang out for a couple of hours reading or working on your latest project. It's the destination for a girls' catch-up sesh. And it's great for a first date, aka can't commit to a meal just yet. It's always filled with the most interesting locals, who, regardless of the reason they came, keep coming back for another reason entirely: the coffee. This coffee shop is a welcome addition to the Lawrenceville neighborhood and is never not thumping to the pulse of the patrons. Friendly and knowledgeable folks serve up regular cups of joe, flavored espresso drinks, and seasonal beverages. It's open 7 days a week, and when the weather is warm, the best seat in the house is at one of the two tables outside of the garage door that doubles as a full-size window. There's something about sitting on Butler Street with a strong coffee watching the hustle and bustle of the reinvigorated neighborhood to get you all revved up.

Everyday Noodles, 5875 Forbes Ave., Squirrel Hill, Pittsburgh, PA 15217; (412) 421-6668; everydaynoodles.net; Chinese; $$. Pittsburgh's Squirrel Hill neighborhood is known for its variety of food offerings. Among those offerings is Everyday Noodles, an authentic Chinese restaurant. At Everyday Noodles, you can watch your noodles be made right before your very eyes. The cozy joint doesn't allow for a bad vantage point, which means that you not only get to enjoy your meal but you also get something more important: the opportunity to watch your meal be lovingly handcrafted by an experienced chef. Go hungry, as the menu is loaded with dim sum options, dry noodles, and noodle soups as well as steamed dumplings. The dumplings, served in a bamboo basket with tongs, are steamed to perfection. Choose from meat or vegetable and make sure to leave just a few minutes for them to cool before devouring them. To make your traditional meal complete, try a bubble tea. Flavors range from black and green tea to mango and coffee.

Food for Thought Deli, 194 N. Craig St. Oakland, Pittsburgh, PA 15213; (412) 682-5033; foodforthoughtdeli.com; Deli; $$. It's really hard to find a good egg salad sandwich. And at this New York-style deli, you can find a pretty darn good one along with tasty chicken and tuna salad sandwiches. In addition to these deli sandwiches, Food for Thought is serving up a plethora of specialty sandwiches, such as the Pittsburgh Reuben: grilled kielbasa, swiss cheese, sauerkraut, and Russian dressing; and the triple-decker club sandwich piled high with turkey, ham, bacon, swiss and American cheeses, lettuce, tomato, and mayonnaise. All sandwiches are served with a pickle spear and your choice of chips or pretzels. When it's chilly in the air, a hot turkey sandwich with gravy and french fries or a cup of the delicious broccoli cheese soup (served on Wednesday) or matzo ball soup (served every day) will warm you right up. In addition to serving up these comforting sandwiches, Food for Thought also sells deli meats and cheeses by the pound.

Frankie's Extra Long, 3535 Butler St., Lawrenceville, Pittsburgh, PA 15201; (412) 687-5220; Hot Dogs; $. For so long, Frankie's had been a myth to us, tucked almost unnoticeably in the early blocks of Butler Street in Lawrenceville. No idea how we missed the yellow awning or red neon FRANKIE'S sign in the window. No idea how we

missed the wafts of onion scent that lingered on the sidewalks. No idea how we missed the stories from locals who had been frequenting Frankie's for dogs and brew for years. We're here to tell you that you don't want to miss out. The dimly lit bar (hot doggery!) has two entrances for your convenience.

One door leads directly into the bar where you can take a seat, order an Iron City and a foot long with chili and kraut, and feel like a true Pittsburgher. The other door leads you right into the oft-long line where you can order up your dog(s) to go. There's not much on the menu: you can get a regular dog, a foot long, or hot sausage. Top that with kraut, onions, chili or your run of the mill condiments. You'll also get a good dose of friendly service and a mighty inexpensive meal. Bring your cash!

Fukuda, 4770 Liberty Ave., Bloomfield, Pittsburgh, PA 15224; (412) 377-0916; fukudapgh.com; Japanese; $$. Amidst the sea of meat and potatoes-esque Pittsburgh gems is Fukuda, one of the city's only Japanese-style restaurants. What began as a food cart on the streets of Bloomfield, the 'Burgh's Little Italy, transitioned into a full-fledged brick-and-mortar of the best darn sushi in town. Reservations are recommended as this teeny-tiny joint is almost always booked solid. Once inside, however, be prepared to be wowed. The chefs and servers are great about explaining what goes into each dish, as you can imagine some things on the menu are not self-explanatory. While sushi is the main course, it's not your everyday roll. Fukuda is one of those places where you pull up a seat at the counter, leave your skepticism at the door, and put your trust in the chef. After tantalizing your taste buds with fresh roe, ceviche, and maki, you'll want to take down a few cups from a teapot and dig into the famous green tea tiramisu. If you're feeling extra adventurous, tell the chef you're opting to "omakase," translated to mean "I'll leave it to you," and let them guide you and prepare a meal especially for you.

Harris Grill, 5747 Ellsworth Ave., Shadyside, Pittsburgh, PA 15232; (412) 362-5273; harrisgrill.com; Neighborhood Bar; $$. Harris Grill would easily win the "Class Clown" title in your high school's yearbook superlative contest. The owners have a sense of humor, so be sure to pay attention when you're dining, drinking, or recovering from drinking here. Harris is best in the summer. The front patio is the perfect spot to people-watch as you sip on its famous frozen pink cosmo (add a shot of Chambord for only $2). Try to not fill up on those stiff frozen treats though. Harris has quite the extensive menu. With items like *calamari mata hari* (calamari seasoned and flash-fried and tossed in a sweet and spicy chile drizzle), *macaronis et fromage de langoustine* (macaroni and cheese with Atlantic lobster and lump crab meat), and Aw, You're Pullin' My Pork (slow-cooked pork shoulder with its Big Gay Al's Strawberry Chipotle Barbecue Sauce), how could you not want to sample something? Even if you don't have room for dessert, you should try Scooter's Mom's Black Bottom . . . cupcake. It's over-sized, stuffed with chocolate cream cheese, and served with raspberry chocolate sauce. Bacon Night happens every Tuesday at Harris, where baskets of bacon are complimentary at the bar and only a dollar at the tables, so get there early if you want free bacon.

Hello Bistro, 3605 Forbes Ave., Oakland, Pittsburgh, PA, 15213; (412) 687-8787; hellobistro.com; Neighborhood Cafe; $. Everything 'Burghers love about our local **Eat'n Parks** (p. 158) can be found on the menu at the diner's sister restaurants, Hello Bistro. We're talking a massive salad bar, soups, burgers, french fries, and milk shakes. This place has thought up some creative salads for the menu, including the Caribbean Shrimp: mixed greens, roasted shrimp, black beans, avocado, corn, and tortilla strips all dressed in a citrus lime vinaigrette. But, if you're up for the challenge, you can make your own salad, choosing from over 30 fixin's. If burgers and fries are more your speed, you definitely won't be disappointed here. Order the locally famous Superburger with two beef patties, American cheese, lettuce, pickles, and a secret sauce. All beef burgers can also be substituted with a three-grain patty or turkey burger, and can be ordered on a gluten-free bun. Be sure to order up a side of french fries with your burger. Not only are

Jozsa Corner Hungarian Restaurant

Alexander Jozsa Bodnar, the restaurant's owner, opened Jozsa's in 1988 and has been single-handedly churning out authentic Hungarian food ever since. First things first: If you want to experience Jozsa Corner Hungarian, you're going to have to call and make a reservation. Groups of diners (four-person minimum) can visit during the week or weekend for a one-of-a-kind multicourse meal.

We suggest making a reservation for the "Hungarian Night" on the second Friday of each month. Don't look for a menu because there isn't one. Expect dishes like traditional *haluska*, cabbage and egg noodles; Transylvanian goulash, with sweet cabbage and meat; and chicken paprikash, chicken simmered with onions and paprika and dolloped in sour cream.

You come in as a stranger, and walk through his small, galley kitchen before you make your way into the room where Alexander serves his guests family-style. It's cozy and full of tchotchkes and memories. He'll seat your party at one of the communal tables that take up most of the room. You'll be left to absorb the unique artwork, the sounds of Hungarian tunes wafting through the air as you befriend your new dining neighbors.

What makes dining at Jozsa Corner Hungarian Restaurant one of the most unique dining experiences in the 'Burgh? "Uncle Alex's" mid-meal stories. He's known to come out between courses to talk about life outside the United States. He's not shy about sharing personal details of growing up in Hungary, including his time serving his country. If you catch him on a particularly good night, he'll treat you to a song and dance.

Don't forget to sign the guestbook, though by the time you leave you're already family.

Visit **Jozsa's Corner Hungarian Restaurant** at 4800 2nd Ave., Hazelwood, Pittsburgh, PA 15207; (412) 422-1886.

the fries delicious, they are also perfect for dipping into the famous Eat'n Park ranch dressing. It comes in its own self-serve dispenser next to the ketchup and is free of charge. So grab as many tubs of it as you want! It's that good. Wash your meal down with either an Original Birch Beer or Root Beer from Boylan Bottling Company on tap. Additional locations: See website.

Hemingway's Cafe, 3911 Forbes Ave., Oakland, Pittsburgh, PA 15213; (412) 621-4100; hemingways-cafe.com; Neighborhood Bar; $. In Oakland, the place to go for a cheap lunch is Hemingway's Cafe. To receive the half-off lunchtime special, you must have your order placed between 11 and 11:45 a.m. (Warning: Not all items are half-off during this time period, though many are.) The menu consists of your standard neighborhood bar food: appetizers, sandwiches and wraps, burgers, pastas, and pizza. Our must-eat menu item is the pita chips appetizer, though it could be a full meal on its own. These are deep-fried pieces of pita bread topped with a spicy cream cheese artichoke spread. Holy yum. Another good choice: the Philly chicken or Philly steak wraps with a side of mayo. And maybe by far the best item on the menu, the grilled cheese made with your choice of cheese (American, cheddar, pepper jack, provolone, or swiss) and thick slices of Italian bread. The half-price menu is pulled back out from 9 p.m. until midnight in case you want your second grilled cheese of the day.

Industry Public House, 4305 Butler St., Lawrenceville, Pittsburgh, PA 15201; (412) 683-1100; industrypgh.com; Gastropub; $$. Caution: Don't try this one at home. One of the most unique items on Industry's drink menu is the Smoke Stack. First, select your bourbon and then select the flavor of wood you want to infuse the bourbon with, choosing from cherry, mesquite, apple, maple, and pecan wood. The bourbon is combined with a few dashes of bitters and maple syrup in a glass. A cocktail strainer is placed on top of the glass and the wood is lit on fire and placed onto the strainer. A cocktail shaker is then placed on top of the fire, trapping the smoke into the glass, infusing the bourbon. After a few of these, you might need to send those smoke signals to your friends, letting them know where to pick you up. To ensure that doesn't happen, fill up on some of Industry's grub, including the Farmed Out Burgher, topped with wild boar bacon, aged white cheddar, a fried egg, and barbecue sauce. Be sure to order a side of the Filament Fries, which are done three different ways: loaded with chili and cheese; topped with pot roast and gravy; and tossed with truffle oil and Gorgonzola cheese.

Joe's Doghouse, Carnegie Mellon University Campus, Tech St. and Margaret Morrison St., Squirrel Hill North, Pittsburgh, PA 15213; Hot Dogs; $. Monday through Friday on the Carnegie Mellon University Campus, you can find Joe's Doghouse, a hot dog cart serving up, you guessed it, hot dogs. You can find all-beef dogs, kielbasa, soy dogs, and a few burgers, all priced under $5. Perfect for students on a budget. A variety of traditional condiments are available to complement your dog of choice, such as ketchup, mustard, relish, onions, and kraut. For an extra dollar, you can make your dog a meal with the addition of a pop (aka soda) or water and a bag of chips. On Saturday, the cart moves to Walnut Street in Shadyside and attracts the shoppers looking for a hunger fix. The lines get long, but a perfectly charred dog from Joe's is worth the wait. Daily specials are always happening, so be sure to follow Joe's Doghouse on Facebook for all the deets. Additional location: Shadyside, Walnut Street (typically outside American Apparel), Pittsburgh, PA 15232.

Kaleidoscope Cafe, 108 43rd St., Lawrenceville, Pittsburgh, PA 15201; (412) 683-4004; kaleidoscopepgh.com; Eclectic; $$$. Off the beaten Butler Street path and worth venturing to find is Kaleidoscope Cafe. Housed in one of the most colorful buildings in Lawrenceville,

Kaleidoscope serves eclectic American cuisine. The small, 36-seat restaurant is as cool as the handcrafted tables throughout the small dining room (you can take one home with you, they're for sale!). That same vibe is translated to the menu by Chef-Owner Dan Robinson. Choose from salads, sandwiches, pasta, or small plates. Our favorite meal to savor is the Gnocchi Nirvana featuring homemade deep-fried gnocchi. Just search "how to deep-fry gnocchi" on YouTube and you'll understand how crazy deep-frying gnocchi actually is. Once you pick your jaw off your desk, take a moment to check out the masterpiece placed in front of you. Fluffy gnocchi are gently placed in a bath of *kafta* (Indian spiced tomato-cashew sauce) and topped with chorizo (or Soyrizo). It's especially tasty. And lucky for you, Chef Dan is daring enough to dodge popping gnocchi to deliver it.

Kelly's Bar & Lounge, 6012 Centre Ave., Shadyside, Pittsburgh, PA 15206; (412) 363-6012; Neighborhood Bar; $$. Dive bars run rampant in Pittsburgh. Most follow a similar structure: dark nooks, lingering smoke, kitschy decor, and regulars. While that may be the norm, not all are of the same caliber, and Kelly's Bar & Lounge elevates the game. Surprisingly well lit, Kelly's smoke has long lifted, as has its kitschy decor. Regulars still rule the roost, but what makes it a standout is its classic cocktail list and "good food" menu. In the mood for a Pimm's Cup, Fire Fly, Harvey Wallbanger, or Pink Squirrel? You can get it here along with a host of other cocktails long forgotten by the masses. Plus what other dive bar has grilled haloumi and olives on its menu? Not many. You can also get Pittsburgh Bites, big chunks of either tofu or chicken in a mild or hot sauce; Cajun meat loaf with mashed sweet potatoes; or a PLT sandwich (pancetta, lettuce, and tomato). If you want to really experience Kelly's at its finest though, get the macaroni and cheese, which arrives at the table bubbling and lightly crusted with bread crumbs. And if all else fails, the jukebox is filled with punk, rock 'n roll, and soul classics that will make your night an instant hit.

Kevin's Deli, 101 N. Dithridge St., Ste. 120, Oakland, Pittsburgh, PA 15213; (412) 621-6368; kevinsdeli.com; Deli; $. Want to know a secret that only the locals know? Kevin's Deli in Webster Hall. Tucked away on the ground floor in the back of this residential building is Kevin's Deli where delicious sandwiches (served with a side of extreme kindness by the friendly staff) are whipped up in a teeny-tiny kitchen. And we're talking tiny. As needed, ingredients are passed back and forth across the small deli case from the refrigerators and freezers located near the entrance. If you become a regular, which you will, you may even be asked to hand the chef a bag of fries from the freezer. The menu is filled with sandwiches, ranging from cold deli-style tuna and turkey sandwiches to hot hoagies, grilled Reubens with homemade dressing, and cheeseburgers. Breakfast sandwiches are served all day, as well as omelets and hash browns. Seating is limited to a few tables located outside the building; so takeout is your best bet.

Khalil's II Restaurant, 4757 Baum Blvd., Bloomfield, Pittsburgh, PA 15213; (412) 683-4757; Middle Eastern; $$. You will not leave Khalil's hungry. When we go, we settle in for the long haul and begin with the mazza appetizer, a combo of its house-made hummus, baba ghanoush, medamas, tabouli, feta, and olives and accompanied by warm pita. Then we move onto a bowl of its hearty lentil soup. Next up is the main course, usually a lamb shish kabob (chicken or shrimp is also available). All main dishes are served with a salad topped with Khalil's special dressing and steamed rice with pine nuts. Okay, so sometimes we end up taking enough food home to last a week, but what's wrong with that? We never leave Khalil's without witnessing someone breaking out into song and dance, which we happily watch and secretly wish we could join in. Oh, and we never forget the baklava.

Legume, 214 N. Craig St., Oakland, Pittsburgh, PA 15213; (412) 621-2700; legumebistro.com; Eclectic; $$$–$$$$. Legume has a sleek space on North Craig Street. While the interior is vast, it still manages to feel cozy at each table. The very low light and flickering candles can take the credit for that loveliness. While the name of Legume might suggest a vegetable-heavy offering, this is not the case. Vegetarians will be pleased, but there is indeed meat to eat (part of the menu is even designated to steak house fare)! The menu here is inventive and always changing. You can find the daily menu online, or just take the chance that whatever is offered will be great (it will be). Starter salads that feature the likes of curly endive and pears will literally melt in your mouth. We didn't know it was possible for salad to actually do that, but we learn something new every day! Entrees are perfectly portioned and, again, melt in your mouth-able. Splurge on one of the desserts created in-house. Legume's truffle chocolate cake is easily one of the greatest cakes in the history of ever. Valet parking is available across the street.

Lili Cafe, 3138 Dobson St., Polish Hill, Pittsburgh, PA 15219; (412) 682-3600; Neighborhood Cafe; $. Lili Cafe has charm with a slight punk edge. It's the kind of place you stumble upon and immediately tell all your friends about. Tucked among the houses high on Polish Hill, Lili Cafe serves breakfast, lunch, and coffee. The menu is small but robust and filled with items for vegans and those with gluten sensitivity. For breakfast our go-to is the Punk Toast. Farm or rye bread comes smeared with avocado, Earth Balance spread, and nutritional yeast. It's a delicious way to start your day. If you're around on a Sunday, check out the brunch special especially if the blueberry waffle is involved. The waffle is crispy, jam-packed with blueberries, and served with butter infused with orange rind. For lunch, nothing beats a grilled cheese made on farm bread. The tempeh Reuben is also a great choice for a new twist on a classic sandwich. Just want coffee? Lili has you covered with its Americano, espresso, latte, macchiato, matcha latte, breve, and cafe au lait. If you want to sit back and enjoy your coffee, there are a few plush chairs in the back room. And one of the best parts about Lili Cafe is that it serves really great food and coffee at beyond reasonable prices. Our favorite kind of charm.

The Livermore, 124 S. Highland Ave., East Liberty, Pittsburgh, PA 15206; (412) 361-0600; Cocktail Bar; $-$$. Named for the famed American stocktrader, Jesse L. Livermore, The Livermore serves handcrafted cocktails and light fare. We suggest ending your night here. Its dark, laid-back attitude is the perfect atmosphere for sipping classic cocktails like a Manhattan, Negroni, or Aviation and discussing tomorrow's brunch options (like at **Bar Marco**, The Livermore's sister restaurant in the Strip, p. 38). A small beer menu is also available, but why get beer when you have expert bartenders shaking and stirring? Follow up your classic libation creation with a few small plates. Spicy nuts, hardboiled eggs, bacon-wrapped dates, and tomato and white anchovy toast will help cure those late-night munchies. The Livermore also has one of the best happy hour specials in the city. From 4 to 6 p.m. during the week, you can enjoy fresh oysters for $1. They make for a very happy hour in our opinion. You can also head to The Livermore to recharge after your long night. During the day the Juice UP 412 crew serves fresh juice like Aloe Zinger, Orange Sunrise, or the Green Machine.

Mercurio's, 5523 Walnut St., Shadyside, Pittsburgh, PA 15232; (412) 621-6220; mercuriosgelatopizza.com; Ice Cream; $. Sometimes strolling along the three rivers of the 'Burgh feels like strolling along the canals of Venice. Okay, it actually doesn't feel like that at all. The 'Burgh is one thousand times more romantic—lies! Anyway, just because we aren't in Italy doesn't mean we can't indulge in one of the boot-shaped country's finest treasures: gelato! This creamy, frozen treat gets us every time. With less butterfat than ice cream, you can even eat more with less guilt, or at least that is what we tell ourselves. Mercurio's in Shady-side is the perfect place to indulge, with 30 daily flavors and additional tastes on rotation. We love a cup of Birthday Cake (actual cake is mixed in, you guys!) and the Stracciatella (essentially a fancy chocolate chip). Payment per cup or cone is based on weight. Mercurio's also has several beers on tap and an assortment of Italian snacks like paninis and pizza. Nothing like pizza, beer, and a heaping cup of gelato to get the heart racing. Perhaps Pittsburgh does have Venice beat in the ways of love!

Mad Mex, 370 Atwood St., Oakland, Pittsburgh, PA 15213; (412) 681-5656; madmex.com; Mexican; $$. The original Mad Mex location opened in the collegiate neighborhood of Oakland, and locations have been popping up over the city and 'burbs ever since. You can down a Big Azz 22-ounce margarita in five fruity flavors or go traditional. You can choose from original, strawberry, mango, or one of their many seasonal flavors, such as cranberry during Thanksgiving. During their infamous happy hours, these monster margs are half off, so prepare yourself accordingly. Some of our favorite menu items include the Wing-O-Rito, boneless buffalo chicken burrito, served with waffle fries. We also recommend their loaded nachos grande, blue corn bread, and Black Beanie Quesadeenie, loaded with Kaya Yucatan black bean dip, cheese, and pineapple—a strange but delicious combination. We are suckers for their homemade bleu cheese dressing. We use the term "dressing" loosely as you'll have the best luck eating it with a fork rather than drizzling it anywhere. Seriously, it does a bang-up job of making you want to order an extra side so you can dunk the contents of your pockets in it. Additional locations: See website.

1947 Tavern, 5744½ Ellsworth Ave., Shadyside, Pittsburgh, PA 15232; (412) 363-1947; 1947tavern.com; Gastropub; $$–$$$. 1947 Tavern is not your typical neighborhood bar. Yes it's quaint, comfortable, and dimly lit, not to mention it has a killer selection of cocktails and bourbon. But this Shadyside joint is serving up basically every adult's dream: breakfast for dinner. Order up the fried chicken and biscuits drizzled in coffee red eye gravy or the Benedict Arnold, a jumbo lump crab cake and poached egg served in bacon fat potato hash and topped with spicy tomato hollandaise. If you aren't feeling breakfast for dinner, the menu features swanky starters such as crisp gnocchi tots flash fried and served with a sriracha aioli, and tavern fries topped with peppered bacon and smothered with pimento cheese. For heartier entries, order the barbecue pulled pork sandwich: pulled pork braised in Dr Pepper and topped with a sweet barbecue sauce, crisp coleslaw, and pickles, and served in a fresh baguette from **La Gourmandine** (p. 185).

Notion Restaurant, 128 S. Highland Ave., East Liberty, Pittsburgh, PA 15206; (412) 361-1188; notionrestaurant.com; New American; $$$$. Special occasions call for a special meal. What you get at Notion Restaurant in Pittsburgh's East Liberty neighborhood is something so far beyond special. The elaborately curated dishes that Chef-Owner Dave Racicot creates are equal parts elegant and appetizing. Bring a bottle of your favorite wine; Notion is BYOB. You can opt for the 4-course fixed-price meal or a 6- or 8-course Chef's Tasting menu. Your taste buds will be delighted on the daily by fresh fishes, tender cuts of beef, lean chicken, and pork all paired with fresh seasonal fruits and vegetables to the tune of beets, greens, and mushrooms. A breadbasket with salted butter and an amuse bouche gets your palate ready for the party your mouth is about to experience. Among the first-course options you'll find the Tartare, prepared with Korean flavors and peanuts on a bed of iceberg. The best part of coursed meals is that they always finish off with dessert. Among the offerings, the Milk Chocolate: Nutella cake, orange, and banana pudding.

Nu Modern Jewish Bistro, 1711 Murray Ave., Squirrel Hill, Pittsburgh, PA 15217; (412) 422-0220; Jewish; $$. Two words: latke tots. Mic drop. Oh, you need more information? Cool. Nu Modern Jewish Bistro opened in 2013. The smallish cafe nestles right up against its very famous neighbor in Squirrel Hill, **P&G's Pamela's Diner** (p. 48). The two places even share the same front door. Nu's menu is an interesting take on classic Jewish deli offerings. Let's circle back around to those latke tots, shall we? One of the delectable starters, the latke tots are shredded potatoes mixed with onions, balled up, and schmaltz fried. The tots are served in a small metal basket and accompanied by sour cream. Another excellent dish to share is the Kreplach: ground brisket stuffed into a dough. So, basically, meat pockets. Delicious meat pockets. Several prescribed sandwich combinations are available, like the Upstreet Dip with brisket, caramelized onions, and horseradish cream cheese. You can also take a stab at creating your own sandwich. House-cured meats include turkey, brisket, or smoked salmon. It should be noted that Nu is not kosher. The restaurant serves meat and cheese together. When in a rush, Nu is also a good place for takeout.

Paris 66, 6018 Centre Ave., East Liberty, Pittsburgh, PA 15206; (412) 404-8166; paris66bistro.com; French; $$. The distance between Pittsburgh and Paris is about 4,000 miles. Paris 66 just happens to have the feel of a cafe that could be a stone's throw from the Champs-Élysées, without all of the flight time. This quaint bistro, with limited seating, an all-season patio, and a "bonjour!" greeting as you enter, offers food that fits its tagline: "Everyday French cuisine." Savory crepes, traditional quiches, and classic croques headline the menu. Monday through Saturday enjoy *Plats Principaux* for dinner like beouf bourgignon or try one pound of P.E.I. mussels with white wine, shallots, and crème fraiche. Brunch on Sunday features our favorite fare, eggs Provençal: scrambled eggs, feta, tomatoes, herbs . . . *j'adore*! After your meal, try one of the many flavors of homemade French macarons with equal parts taste and prettiness. Bring your favorite travel reading, order up a *pan au chocolat* and a warm brew, and settle in under the decorative Metropolitan sign posts; you'll be in Paris in a heartbeat.

Park Bruges, 5801 Bryant St., Highland Park, Pittsburgh, PA 15206; (412) 661-3334; pointbrugge.com; International; $$. Park Bruges is the sister restaurant to the Point Breeze-located **Point Brugge Cafe** (p. 124). With a similar menu and a shared, relaxed ambiance to its relative, Park Bruges is an inviting place for a bite to eat. The cozy booths, rich color palette for the decor, and the table layout around the bar make it easy to spend hours here enjoying good conversation and a Merlot or two. The menu has a French influence with choices like the *tarte flambées,* which start with crust baked at the local **Enrico Biscotti** (p. 41), or the Montreal favorite of *poutine* (gravy and cheese curds on fries). Not all the plates are French, but they do all inspire a bit of "ooo la la." Be sure to check out the website for special event listings, like live jazz night. And if you're in the mood for brunch, stop by on Saturday.

People's Indian Restaurant, 5147 Penn Ave., Garfield, Pittsburgh, PA 15224; (412) 661-3160; Indian; $$. People's Indian Restaurant serves up some seriously sensational authentic Indian food. It may look closed from the outside, but have no fear, it's open 6 days a week (closed Sun). The quiet, dimly lit interior sets the mood for some serious naan munching. The extensive menu is filled with various kabobs, curries, peneer, and pakora dishes. Stop by for lunch and sample a bevy of dishes from the lunch buffet. Dinner is great anytime at People's, but

720 Music, Clothing, and Cafe

Not many places can combine three seemingly different features as effortlessly as 720 Music, Clothing, and Cafe in Lawrenceville. The eclectic space has soul from the front to the back. So don't worry if you're stopped in your tracks as you walk through the door. It's likely you haven't experienced a shop quite like 720 anywhere else in the 'Burgh.

Once you recover from your temporary sensory overload, you'll be greeted by a smile from the barista. 720 has a variety of coffee and loose teas (both iced and hot) to choose from.

Unlike most cafes, 720 has more than local art on its wall to gaze at as you wait for your drink. Its carefully curated vinyl collection would make any enthusiast's eyes widen. Hip-hop, funk, soul, and jazz as well as local artists can be found in the bins. No, the selection isn't exhaustive, but you'll be sure to find something worth adding to your own collection.

The clothing is also worth checking out. Pittsburgh-based t-shirts and other funky, vintage garb hang from the walls and would look really great in your closet.

Stop by on the last Sunday of each month for 720's Sunday's Best Brunch event. It's when the true essence of 720 comes alive. Exotic Brunch options from empanadas to Yakisoba noodles are lined up along the wall as a DJ spins hip-hop, soul, and funk beats. The crowd is as diverse as they come but they are all laughing and loving life in that moment.

Visit **720 Music, Clothing, and Cafe** at 4405 Butler St., Pittsburgh, PA 15201, Tues through Sat from 10 a.m. to 9 p.m. or Sun from 10 a.m. to 5 p.m.; 720records.com.

if you're there from 5 to 6 p.m. or 9 to 10 p.m., you'll receive a special offer: buy one entree, get one at 50 percent off. One of our favorite dishes is the chicken tikki masala: generous chunks of tender chicken bathed in a smoky, creamy tomato sauce. If you're looking for a vegetarian option, our go-to is the Aloo Mattar: peas and potatoes cooked to perfection in a curry sauce. You can choose your spiciness level, but be warned: People's is not afraid of spice. Be sure to take a spoonful of the colorful Mukhwas, an after-dinner breath freshener and digestive aid, at the counter on your way out.

Piccolo Forno, 3801 Butler St., Lawrenceville, Pittsburgh, PA 15201; (412) 622-0111; piccolo-forno.com; Italian; $$. While Piccolo Forno is a great spot for dinner, we suggest stopping by for lunch. The menu covers all the Italian basics: antipasti, *insalata* (salad), *zuppe del giorno* (soup), *pizze* (pizza), pasta, and panini, which means you'll probably be having a long, bountiful lunch—bring friends! Start your lunch extravaganza off with the crostini di polenta that's baked and topped with gorgonzola, mushroom spread, and marinated roasted cherry tomatoes or the *affettati*, which is an assortment of local meats from **Parma Sausage Products, Inc.** (p. 53) and imported cheeses. You may also want to try one of the *insalata*, all large enough to share. We like the *insalata di farro* made from Tuscan wheat grain with grape tomatoes, onion, radicchio, arugula, and basil. Piccolo Forno also has pasta and panini on the menu, but the pizza is too good to pass up. A classic margherita or bianca pizza is always a safe bet. If you're looking to kick it up a notch though, consider the capricciosa with crushed tomatoes, artichokes, mushrooms, olives, fresh mozzarella, mushroom, prosciutto cotto, and an egg, or the *speck e mascarpone* with crushed tomatoes, fresh mozzarella, mascarpone, and speck.

Plum Pan-Asian Kitchen, 5996 Centre Ave., Shadyside, Pittsburgh, PA 15206; (412) 363-7586; plumpanasiankitchen.com; Pan-Asian; $$. Plum is nestled at the bottom of the Eastside development. From the street you can see the large, colorful light fixtures and the sleek banquette running the length of the windows. It creates a seductive dining scene that will lure you in with its swank and promise of quality eats. Inside, the sushi bar is right in the center of the dining room. You can watch as the sushi chef masterfully crafts the special Plum rolls like the Marilyn Mon Roll (soft shell crab, cucumber, and tobika) and other divine sushi creations. On the cooked side of things, the pan-fried vegetable dumplings with savory brown sauce are pan-fried fantasticness. Entrees include curries, noodles and rice, vegetarian, and house specialties like Thai spicy duck. We personally cannot get enough of the simple dry sautéed string beans (with choice of meat, of course), again in that crazy good brown sauce.

Point Brugge Cafe, 401 Hastings St., Point Breeze, Pittsburgh, PA 15206; (412) 441-3334; pointbrugge.com; International; $$. You can't make a reservation at Point Brugge Cafe, so we suggest going before 6 p.m. If you can't, try grabbing a seat at the bar. You'll be treated to the same quality service, but you'll be a part of the ebb and flow of the restaurant. The menu is made up of Belgian-inspired cuisine and has a decent selection of wine and beer. If it is your first time visiting Point Brugge, order yourself the *moules frites* and a good Belgian beer. All the sauces are excellent, but we suggest the classic white wine sauce, which is rich and velvety. Here's a tip: Take the crusty bread that accompanies the dish and let it soak up the sauce for a good minute, then place a mussel (or two) on the soggy bread, and enjoy. When you wake up from that food coma, you can thank us.

The Porch at Schenley, 221 Schenley Dr., Oakland, Pittsburgh, PA 15213; (412) 687-6724; theporchatschenley.com; Neighborhood Cafe; $–$$. The Porch at Schenley celebrates the concept of outside-in. Located in Schenley Plaza, a bustling parklet usually full of collegiate fresh air seekers, The Porch has walls of windows that deliver plenty of outdoor scenery. A rooftop garden provides ingredients for the chef to use, in season, for the dishes on the menu with options ranging from sandwiches to rib eye. Fortunately, the waitstaff is very knowledgeable about the meals and can help you make the right choice. Atypical to most dining establishments, the starters on the menu are quite cheap and provide enough to share. The crispy taters and farm bread with apple butter are starters that will provoke a thumbs-up from everyone at the table. Colorful and flavorful pizzas arrive on a cookie sheet, right from the oven. Reservations are not accepted at The Porch, but you can put yourself on the waitlist prior to arrival by visiting the website. The Porch also has a take-out window that provides for a very nice picnic in the Plaza.

Pusadee's Garden, 5321 Butler St., Lawrenceville, Pittsburgh, PA 15201; (412) 781-8724; pusadeesgarden.com; Thai; $$. Family-owned and operated, Pusadee's Garden is a lush oasis in Upper Lawrenceville. There is an actual garden at Pusadee's Garden, in which you can sit and eat on warm days. The garden is quite lovely and the perfect tranquil spot to enjoy quality Thai cuisine. Inside the small restaurant, peace is achieved through soft lighting extended from the tin ceilings and the white table linens. The menu includes noodle dishes, rice dishes, curries, soup, salads, and a good assortment of apps. To start, we really love the tempura vegetables served with a peanut sauce for dipping. We are never ones to pass on large flat noodles, so the see yew noodle entree, with egg, broccoli, and sweet soy sauce, gets our seal of approval. The house specialties here include crispy tilapia and crab fried rice, solid choices for eating in one of the nicest urban gardens in the 412. BYOB and also bring your own dessert—for $1 per glass/person.

Razzy Fresh, 1717 Murray Ave., Squirrel Hill, Pittsburgh, PA 15217; (412) 521-3145; razzyfresh.com; Ice Cream; $. Razzy Fresh, we love you so hard. Razzy Fresh is a frozen yogurt emporium that is often equated to a desirable substitute for actual human romantic relationships. Who needs sweet nothings whispered in his or her ear when you can eat heaps of frozen yogurt that taste like dreams? Upon entering, grab a cup (only two sizes: large and bucket), fill said cup with whatever frozen yogurt suits your fancy (Razzy has 12 flavors daily, which rotate throughout the week, including original tangy yogurt and a long list of sweet options), and then pile on toppings from cookie crumbles to fresh berries. D.I.Y. magic! Pay for your creation by the ounce and then dig in! The whole process has us twitter-pated just thinking about it. Two more spots to get your Razz on in Oakland: 300 S. Craig St., Pittsburgh 15213; (412) 681-0515; and 3533 Forbes Ave., Pittsburgh 15213; (412) 586-5270.

Root 174, 1113 S. Braddock Ave., Edgewood, Pittsburgh, PA 15218; (412) 243-4348; root174.com; Eclectic; $$–$$$. Root 174 gives taste buds of the vegan, vegetarian, and meat-eating variety a reason to dance. The always-changing menu, which can be found daily online, focuses on creative preparations of fresh and local ingredients. A chalkboard on the back wall calls out the specials of the day, and your server will be happy to offer advice on selections. Flavors here toe the line between risky and comfortable. An adventurous eater could pick a dish like bone marrow crème brûlée, while one seeking a nice twist on an old favorite could choose the likes of pork with a touch of barbecue sauce. Each plate is unique and proves that Root 174's Chef Keith Fuller is a genius. Really, anyone who can make us pine for another slice of vegan chocolate cake has kitchen brilliance on lockdown. Be sure to make a reservation—the space is incredibly cozy. See Chef Keith's recipe for Falafel on p. 214.

Rose Tea Cafe, 5874½ Forbes Ave., Squirrel Hill, Pittsburgh, PA 15217; (412) 421-2238; Taiwanese; $$. Rose Tea Cafe is a popular Taiwanese restaurant known for its bubble teas; even the sign outside boasts a drawing of the famed, tapioca drop filled drinks. If bubble tea doesn't push your delight button, try a mango, mung bean, or papaya milk shake. Along with the creative drink selection, the Taiwanese cuisine also keeps diners pouring through the door. For starters, the steamed or fried dumplings here rank among the best in town. The entree side of the menu is lengthy and full of excellent choices. In fact, the menu is overwhelming in its depth. We know folks who have this spot on their regular dining rotation, and they could easily dine here weekly without meal repeats. Kimchee and hot pot options are aplenty, and unique proteins like pork intestines and squid pop up more than once. For less adventurous eaters, entrees like chicken with mixed vegetables in a savory brown sauce will appease. Anticipate quick service and plenty of food left over for tomorrow's lunch. Takeout is also available. Additional location: Oakland, 412 S. Craig St., Pittsburgh, PA 15213.

Round Corner Cantina, 3720 Butler St., Lawrenceville, Pittsburgh, PA 15201; (412) 904-2279; roundcornercantina.com; Mexican; $. Set in a building with a legit round corner (hooray architecture impacting restaurant names!), the Round Corner Cantina is a super-hip Lawrenceville haunt. An impressive amount of tequila, brews, sangria, and Micheladas for days, Round Corner Cantina could survive as a bar alone, but the food here is worth a stop-in. In the mood for some gourmet tacos? Cantina has you covered. Made with a variety of meats like pork, brisket, and house-made chorizo, the taco flavors provide a good complement to your margarita or basil julep. We give a solid score to the *carnitas* tacos: slow-roasted pork, onion, cucumber, radish, and cilantro. The chips and salsa and an order of the guacamole are a good table share. Try to get to the Cantina in the spring and summer, so you can sit in the rustic outdoor space, reminiscent of the Wild West and south of the border combined. Brunch is served on Sunday with Bloody Marys and breakfast burritos among other Latin-infused delights.

Salt of the Earth, 5523 Penn Ave., Garfield, Pittsburgh, PA 15206; (412) 441-7258; saltpgh.com; Eclectic; $$$$. No detail is overlooked at Salt of the Earth. From the floor-to-ceiling chalkboard menu to the presentation of dishes, Salt of the Earth is excellently executed. The modern design aesthetic might make you temporarily forget you're at a restaurant. That is until your sense of smell kicks in. Chef Kevin Sousa, the original mastermind behind the experience, recently relinquished his owner and chef titles to Chad Townsend, who has set out to follow Kevin's lead but with his own spin. Forego the reservations and try snagging a seat at the kitchen bar or one of the three long wood communal tables. If you wait for a bar seat, you can watch the talented staff work their magic as you dine. The menu consists of several regular items as well as rotating seasonal options. We won't make any dinner recommendations though as the menu is fluent and forever evolving each day, taking its flavor from locally sourced ingredients. The only tip we'll offer is to get to Salt of the Earth fast and sample as much from the menu as humanly possible.

Sausalido, 4621 Liberty Ave., Bloomfield, Pittsburgh, PA 15224; (412) 683-4575; sausalido.net; International; $$$. If looking for a restaurant that is open on Monday and is also BYOB, Sausalido in Bloomfield's Little Italy is the perfect fit. Upon sitting down at one of the 15-ish tables, your server will greet you with slices of crusty white bread served with a white-bean-and-olive-oil dipping sauce. For starters, try the roasted brussels sprouts with Danish bleu cheese and the sage wheat-encrusted smoked Gouda served with sautéed spinach. A few salads fill the menu, but if you plan on ordering one of the entrees, your meal will come with a small side salad filled with mixed greens, roasted beets, red onions, and toasted walnuts. As for entrees, the daily risotto is a must-try, but other entrees include ravioli, crab cakes, duck breast, and roasted chicken. We like that the waitstaff paces your meal, so you have time to finish each course before receiving the next. A relaxed dining experience rules, and so does Sausalido.

Shady Grove, 5500 Walnut St., Shadyside, Pittsburgh, PA 15232; (412) 697-0909; eatshady.com; Neighborhood Bar; $–$$. If you want consistently satisfying bar food in Shadyside, head to Shady Grove. The menu is vast and you may find yourself wanting to order one of everything. It's okay, we often feel that way too. We are here to help. For starters or even as a main meal, get the Shady Sticks. They are by far the best thing on the menu, hands down; a slightly sweet pizza dough covered in multiple cheeses and served with marinara sauce. Insiders hint: Ask for a side of ranch dressing to dip these sticks in. Simply salivating. Really, any pizza on the menu will satisfy your taste buds. For sandwiches, the California BLT is where it's at, and all of the salads are large and in charge, served in stainless steel bowls. Shady Grove always serves up great food and quality drinks, whether you go for happy hour or any hour. Be sure to stop by on Wednesday for half-price bottles of wine and Thursday for half-priced bottles of Champagne. Sit outside if you can. It's a great spot for people watching.

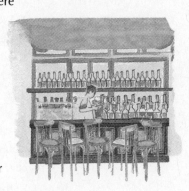

Silk Elephant, 1712 Murray Ave., Squirrel Hill, Pittsburgh, PA 15217; (412) 421-8801; silkelephant.net; Thai; $$. Norraset Nareedokmai is the chef and inspirational force behind the authentic Thai restaurant Silk Elephant. He strives to create an interplay of flavors, ingredients, and textures each time he creates a menu item. The menu at Silk Elephant is extensive. One notable feature of the menu is the variety of tapas options. Various rolls and dumplings (try the salmon!)

are available as well as several meat (marinated lamb ribs, chicken kabobs) and vegetarian selections (taro crunch and corn fritters). If you haven't filled up on small plates, we suggest trying the pumpkin curry with grilled chicken. The chicken spends some time marinating in a blend of Thai herbs and spices then takes a swim in the rich pumpkin curry and is finally finished with sweet basil and bell peppers. While you may want to be more adventurous, the pad Thai at Silk Elephant won't let you down. And if the food doesn't blow you away, maybe the entertainment will. Every Thursday and Sunday two young ladies perform traditional Thai dances throughout the restaurant complete with commentary explaining what each dance means.

Silky's Pub, 5135 Liberty Ave., Bloomfield, Pittsburgh, PA 15224; (412) 683-6141; Neighborhood Bar; $$. Located on the corner of Liberty Avenue and South Evaline Street is Silky's Pub. It's your classic neighborhood bar and a great place to watch Pittsburgh sport events, especially if you're a Penguins' fan. The bar is typically filled with people in Malkin, Crosby, and Letang jerseys swigging beers and cheering on the black and gold. It's only slightly less crowded if there isn't a game on, which is an ideal time to get in a game of shuffleboard. The long, well-worn board is a welcome change from the typical pool tables and dartboards found in most bars. In between the cheering and fierce shuffleboard competition, sample something from Silky's standard or special menu. Both are sprinkled with typical bar favorites and unexpected dishes like lobster ravioli. The zucchini planks are always a great choice to start things off. The thinly sliced planks are lightly breaded and especially delicious dipped in Pittsburgh's favorite condiment, second to ketchup: ranch dressing. Burgers are also a great choice at Silky's Pub. Our standard go-to is the bleu burger. It's topped with creamy bleu cheese dressing, bacon, lettuce, and tomato and comes served with your choice of a side like waffle fries, coleslaw, or potato salad.

Additional locations: Silky's, Squirrel Hill, 1731 Murray Ave., Pittsburgh, PA 15217; (412) 421-9222; and Silky's Crow's Nest, 19th and River Rd., Sharpsburg, PA 15215; (412) 782-3707.

Smiling Banana Leaf, **5901 Bryant St., Highland Park, Pittsburgh, PA 15206; (412) 362-3200; smilingbananaleaf.com; Thai; $$.** Great for lunch or dinner, Smiling Banana Leaf offers classic Thai favorites. Choose from curries, fried rice, noodles, noodle curries, and noodle soups. The interior of the restaurant is cheerful yet relatively small so if you can't get a table, try takeout and head to Highland Park for an impromptu picnic. One great dish to consider, which constantly delivers flavor and a bounty of veggies, is the green curry. The sauce is not as thick as some other green curries around town but still packs a rich, spicy flavor punch. It comes with your choice of meat (choose from chicken, pork, or tofu and vegetables), eggplant, basil leaves, broccoli, green beans, and bell peppers. The spicy green bean entree is also a favorite among diners. Green beans, carrots, and your choice of meat come served in a spicy and tangy chili sauce. Most dishes at Smiling Banana Leaf come served with perfectly cooked white jasmine rice that is delicate and only slightly sticky, which makes it an excellent accompaniment for your meal. Don't forget—Smiling Banana Leaf is BYOB!

Soba Lounge, **5847 Ellsworth Ave., Shadyside, Pittsburgh, PA 15232; (412) 362-5656; sobapa.com; Pan-Asian; $$$.** Sleek, swanky, and sexy are all words that describe Soba Lounge in Shadyside. The dark, intimate setting is a perfect spot to take a date and indulge in late-night cocktails and dinner. Reservations are recommended for any night, but don't worry if you find yourself with a short wait at the bar. The cocktail and wine list is extensive (over 10 pages at the moment), the drinks are strong, and the bartenders are very attentive. Toted as "Pittsburgh's premiere example of Pan-Asian cuisine," Soba is known for dishes that exemplify creativity. Start your meal off with the Burmese tea leaf salad. Napa cabbage, peanuts, tomato, cucumber, yellow split peas, sesame seed, cilantro, and crispy shallot seamlessly blend to create a uniquely fresh flavor unmatched elsewhere. For entrees we recommend the seared rare tuna, encrusted with white and black sesame seeds gently placed in a sweet and tangy Korean barbecue sauce and served with house-made kimchee and ginger-fried rice. Watch its website for upcoming tasting menus that usually feature four courses and the option to add wine pairings. See Soba's recipe for Bangkok Tea on p. 207.

Social at Bakery Square, 6425 Penn Ave., Larimer, Pittsburgh, PA 15206; (412) 362-1234; bakerysocial.com; American; $$. During the warmer months in Pittsburgh, we are all looking for places to dine outside. And, Social is a fun place to do just that. Grab a few of your friends and pull up a table on the large outside patio and kick it with an array of cocktails and solid, good food. Drink specials run daily, including $6 martini Mondays, half-priced pitchers of beer on Thursday, and half-priced bottles of wine on Friday. Share a few of the ahi tuna tartare nachos and the thai shrimp taco appetizers and one or two large pizzas. Beyond the classic margarita and pepperoni pizzas, Social has some unique variations, including the pierogi pizza and the green eggs and ham pizza. A variety of sandwiches also make up the menu, and one standout is the turkey burger served with melted smoked Gouda cheese, lettuce, tomato, and a spicy mango ketchup. What you will not want to share with your friends is the build your own ice cream cookie sandwich. Chocolate or vanilla ice cream is slathered in between two freshly baked chocolate chip or peanut butter chunk cookies. It's the perfect sweet treat on a warm summer evening.

Spak Bros., 5107 Penn Ave., Garfield, Pittsburgh, PA 15224; (412) 362-7725; spakbrothers.com; Pizza; $. Vegans and vegetarians rejoice! Plenty of tasty options await you at neighborhood pizza shop Spak Bros. The menu features over 10 vegan options like the ever-popular seitan wings covered in your choice of wing sauce (the barbecue sauce is vegan) or the seitan "steak" hoagie filled with shaved seitan, fries, mushrooms, hot peppers, green peppers, grilled onions, egg, provolone, and mayo. If you're not into meat substitutes, Spak Bros. can still feed a hungry belly. Hoagie options are available and come packed with local ingredients. The Philly steak or hot sausage, made with local sausage, is always a good place to start. Spak Bros. also makes a mean pizza. The topping selections are enough to keep your pie interesting without getting too zany. We suggest going with spinach, mushrooms, and feta cheese. The salty cheese slightly melted tangles perfectly with the spinach and mushroom. It makes a near perfect pizza every time. Spak Bros. only has a short counter so order your food to go and play a round of pinball while you wait.

Spoon, 134 S. Highland Ave., East Liberty, Pittsburgh, PA 15206; (412) 362-6001; spoonpgh.com; New American; $$$. Sister restaurant to the adjacent BRGR (p. 97), Spoon offers beautifully presented American cuisine. It's the perfect place for a fancy date if you ask us. Start off with a glass of wine carefully selected by the wine director or cocktail. Then order a few of the hot and cold plates for sharing. We recommend the dim sum and the Gorgonzola bleu cheese soufflé. A breadbasket will also arrive to your table, including house-made chive and cream cheese biscuits and slices of French baguette, all served with whipped butter. Heartier entrees are also offered, including duck two ways, duo of beef, and ancho chile crusted pork tenderloin. The menu changes often, but one item that remains constant is the Spoon burger topped with white cheddar cheese and served on a brioche bun with a side of Parmesan and herb fries. Whatever you order, you will be impressed and so will your date.

Square Cafe, 1137 S. Braddock Ave., Edgewood, Pittsburgh, PA 15218; (412) 244-8002; square-cafe.com; Breakfast & Lunch; $–$$.

Square Cafe is a happy morning or afternoon eatery. Bright blue and orange walls, vinyl retro-ish seating, and artwork by local creatives create sunny surroundings. On days when the sun is shining for real, lucky patrons can grab seats on the sidewalk. The staff here also add to the friendly, welcoming atmosphere. Get a milk shake, even at 8 a.m., and then choose from a solid variety of breakfast and lunch options. We tend to order breakfast when we visit here. The omelet ranchero (ham, Amish cheddar, and locally made salsa) and the brussels sprouts and bacon hash can start the day off right. Might as well get a pancake (perhaps a pumpkin walnut or gluten-free pancake?) or french toast on the side while you're at it! Lunch here is tasty too, with crepes, wraps, and burgers rounding out the menu. While its logo may be a circle, entrees are served on square plates and bottomless coffee is served in square mugs. We sure do love a theme and think it really is hip to be square.

Station Street Hot Dogs, 6290 Broad St., East Liberty, Pittsburgh, PA 15206; (412) 365-2121; stationstreetpgh.com; Hot Dogs; $. Station Street Hot Dogs isn't located on Station Street, but back in 1915, it was. Today, this hot dog shop is located on Broad Street in East Liberty and features gourmet dogs. In February 2012, locally celebrated Chef Kevin Sousa and his brother, Tom Sousa, gave the menu a face-lift with flavorful, 100 percent beef, natural casing dogs. The Devil Dog comes topped with egg salad, Tabasco sauce, potato chips, and scallions. The Chili Cheese Dog has smoked brisket chili, cheese, and onions stacked high. The buns are substantial; think more of a roll, preventing sogginess. Vegetarian dogs are also available, and most of the hot dog menu items can be made meat free as well. Just one hot dog will fill you right up, but you'd best save room for a side of poutine or chili cheese fries. Besides dogs, Station Street is also serving up a variety of $5 tacos filled with chicken livers, fried squid, tofu, braised chicken, and beef brisket, and the traditional

Hawaiian salad poké made with Copper River salmon. Definitely not your average hot dog joint.

Szmidt's Old World Deli, 509 Greenfield Ave., Greenfield, Pittsburgh, PA 15207; (412) 904-3558; szmidts.com; Deli; $. Homemade. That's what you'll find at Szmidt's Old World Deli (pronounced Szchmeeds) in Greenfield. From the meat to the bread, everything you'll taste is made the old-fashioned way . . . by hand. Corned beef, pastrami, roast beef, turkey—all of it is brined, cured, and roasted in-house. The bread, it's mixed, proofed, and baked in-house. Sauces are developed from family recipes. The pierogies? Yep, homemade. And every Pittsburgher can appreciate the time it takes to make a homemade pierogies. When you pair that old-fashioned work ethic that courses through the veins of Szmidt's, with quality ingredients, you have a recipe for success. The menu at Szmidt's includes sides, salads, pierogies, and most importantly sandwiches. You really can't go wrong with anything off the menu but here's our suggestion: The Hoya (grilled corned beef oozing with swiss cheese, kraut, and Thousand Island dressing on grilled rye) with a side of cucumbers sliced razor thin and marinated in a candied white vinaigrette. Be sure to save room for the sweet potato and pumpkin pierogies for dessert.

Tamari, 3519 Butler St., Lawrenceville, Pittsburgh, PA 15201; (412) 325-3435; tamaripgh.com; Asian-Fusion; $$$. Did someone say outdoor dining? Tamari has some of the best! Tamari also happens to have much more than just a killer spot to eat in the sight-line of the Steel City; cocktails, tapas, and sushi should bring you through the door over and over again. If the weather isn't up for outdoor dining, inside Tamari is classy times. The long bar and open kitchen extend from the front to the back. After you settle in, choose from a variety of beautifully presented, Asian-Latin fused dishes to get the sampling going. The lobster macaroni and cheese with truffle aioli is pretty bomb, as are any maki choices. Tamari also features a robata grill, which is a Japanese technique of charcoal grilling, for items like hanger steak and quail egg. Tamari is a fun place to bring a group, because sharing is caring, guys. Order up a bunch of tapas and get the party started. Tamari shares the love with a second location, 701 Warrendale Village Dr., Warrendale, PA 15086; (724) 933-3155.

Tazza D'Oro Cafe & Espresso Bar, 1125 N. Highland Ave., Highland Park, Pittsburgh, PA 15206; (412) 362-3676; tazza doro.net; Coffee Shop; $. Tazza D'Oro is by far one of our favorite places to grab a coffee and do some writing in Pittsburgh. Located on the busy North Highland Avenue in Highland Park, the cafe is surrounded by large trees, which almost makes it unnoticeable from the road. But once you visit the cafe, you will never miss it again. The coffee drinks at Tazza D'Oro are crafted by expert baristas who have gone through extensive training, including professional certification. If you enjoy a shot of espresso, this is just the place to go. And be sure to swing by on Monday for "Free Espresso Monday," when dine-in customers are treated to a free double shot of espresso. Coffee here comes exclusively from Counter Culture Coffee in Durham, North Carolina, and the offerings change weekly. To educate the public about the coffees offered, Tazza D'Oro holds cupping classes. Be sure to follow Tazza D'Oro on Facebook for announcements on these classes. Additional location: Carnegie Mellon University, Gates Center, 3rd Floor, Computer Science Building, Forbes Ave., Pittsburgh, PA 15213.

Tender Bar + Kitchen, 4300 Butler St., Lawrenceville, Pittsburgh, PA 15201; (412) 402-9522; tenderpgh.com; Cocktail Bar; $$$.

Pittsburgh has a habit of repurposing buildings. Churches become breweries, schools become apartments, and banks become bars. While we may have a few bank-to-bar converts, Tender Bar + Kitchen is by far the most grandiose. Once home to the Arsenal Bank, Tender now showcases classic American fare and an extensive cocktail list with a Prohibition-era flare. Head to Tender on a Monday for the special Burger Menu and get yourself a 1/3 pound burger for just $7. If you're a first-timer, try the Tender Burger with cheddar cheese and stacked with arugula, white onion, and pub sauce. Pair that juicy burger with a house-created cocktail, punch, or vintage-inspired cocktail for one heck of a meal. The tenders of the bar at Tender are experts at their craft if you're feeling overwhelmed by the cocktail list so feel free to ask for a recommendation. After all, it's free—the menu says so! Tender also often hosts special 20s-themed events and live music. So dust off your bowties and sequin party dresses and prepare for a rip-roaring good time.

Teppanyaki Kyoto, 5808 Bryant St., Highland Park, Pittsburgh, PA 15206; (412) 441-1610; teppanyakikyoto.com; Japanese; $$. Teppanyaki Kyoto is a unique place to dine. Step inside the tranquil space and try to sit along the bar. You will be able to watch the chefs craft the traditional Japanese dishes on the menu. A few tables of seating are available along the wall. Teppanyaki also offers the opportunity to sit in spaces designed after traditional Japanese guest rooms, called "Zashiki." You and the rest of your dinner party will need to remove your shoes and sit on a mat to dine. A truly immersive experience! Regardless of where you are seated, you can be sure your meal will be remarkable. Teppanyaki is known for the Japanese pancake dishes called *Okonomiyaki* and *Hiroshimayaki*. Both *Okonomiyaki* and *Hiroshimayaki* start with a pancake batter of wheat flour, egg, and cabbage and your choice of meat layered on top. The *Hiroshimayaki* includes a layering of yaki saba noodles and a fried egg. The distinction is derived from the native areas of each pancake style. The *Hiroshimayaki* is the style used in Hiroshima. The *Okonomiyaki* is from the Kyoto region of Japan. Expect a hearty helping of fish flakes on each dish. Make sure to sip some sake while you are here. Teppanyaki has a sake list that includes helpful explanations of flavor interpretations.

Thai Cuisine, 4627 Liberty Ave., Bloomfield, Pittsburgh, PA, 15224; (412) 688-9661; Thai; $$. Restaurants are a'plenty along Penn Avenue in Pittsburgh's Little Italy neighborhood. One restaurant that doesn't fit Bloomfield's Italian niche is Thai Cuisine. It is tucked in a corner space, doors down from an Italian market in one direction and doors down from a gourmet bistro in the other. Always full of hungry patrons, Thai Cuisine serves up traditional style fare with flair. Talk your party into ordering appetizers of every variety. Steamed dumplings, satae chicken, and spring rolls will pave the way for a spicy, spectacular meal. When it's time to order your entrees, we recommend the Hawaiian fried rice, chock-full of your choice of meat, pineapples, cashews, raisins, onions, and egg. Crispy duck is another fan favorite, complete with peas and carrots, drenched in a pepper and garlic sauce. Curries and noodles abound, available in all spice levels and with seafood, beef, or chicken (or for you vegetarians, veggies and tofu are also available). To polish off your meal, go for the unique banana spring roll and a jasmine hot tea.

The Thunderbird Cafe, 4023 Butler St., Lawrenceville, Pittsburgh, PA 15201; (412) 682-0177; thunderbirdcafe.net; Neighborhood Bar; $$. The Thunderbird Cafe is one of the premier venues to see rockin' live music in the city. Local acts are at The Thunderbird daily, and the joint is almost always packed to capacity. It may just be a neighborhood bar, but do your neighborhood bars have indoor balconies that are perfect for band watching? Whether you're there fist bumping to a local band on a Thursday evening or toe-tapping along to blues on a Saturday night, you are going to get hungry. We recommend you grab a few friends who aren't afraid to have a good time, order up a few local craft beers, and head to the second floor of The Thunderbird Cafe. The menu items are inexpensive so we don't feel guilty when we can't make up our minds. A few of our favorite choices include the chicken and waffle sandwich, the shoestring fries, and the Garlic parm wings. We do our fair share of eating out, but eating out is especially fun when you can also be rocking out!

Toast! Kitchen & Wine Bar, 5102 Baum Blvd., Shadyside, Pittsburgh, PA 15224; (412) 224-2579; toastkitchen-winebar.com; Eclectic; $$$. Contrary to what its name might suggest, Toast! Kitchen & Wine Bar has more than varieties of toast on its menu. The daily rotating menu features locally sourced items that influence the features of the day. Along with the food menu, the wine menu rotates based on availability. The portion sizes at Toast! are ideal for sampling something for each course. Try the sweet onion bisque if it's available for a warm start to your meal. Onions are cooked down and pureed, releasing a sweet, mild flavor that even non-onion lovers will enjoy. Plus it's topped with a few pieces 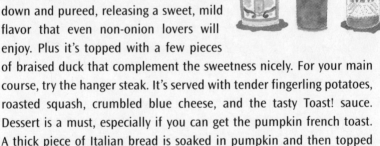 of braised duck that complement the sweetness nicely. For your main course, try the hanger steak. It's served with tender fingerling potatoes, roasted squash, crumbled blue cheese, and the tasty Toast! sauce. Dessert is a must, especially if you can get the pumpkin french toast. A thick piece of Italian bread is soaked in pumpkin and then topped with a rich scoop of pumpkin ice cream. Breakfast for dessert never felt so right.

Umi, 5849 Ellsworth Ave., Shadyside, Pittsburgh, PA 15232; (412) 362-6198; bigburrito.com/umi; Japanese; $$$. Follow the sea dragon up the stairs to the Japanese restaurant Umi. Here you can savor menu items hard to find elsewhere in Pittsburgh. While the space above **Soba**

(p. 131) is half the size, it serves equally inventive and delicate dishes. Sit at the sushi bar and watch the chef prepare maki handrolls, sushi, and sashimi with seasoned ease. Tables and tatami tables (traditional Japanese-style low tables) are also available for your dining pleasure. The knowledgeable waitstaff welcomes you with a warm hand towel as you peruse the menu. Once your menu is open, your eyes should go directly to the multicourse *omakase* meal. It's recommended as the best way to thoroughly experience Umi. Choose from 7 or 11 courses plus dessert options. If you're celebrating a special occasion or feeling adventurous, go with the "Trust Mr. Shu" option. Whichever option you choose, you'll receive masterpieces presented like pieces of minimalistic art made from the freshest ingredients available. A two-person minimum is required, so be sure to bring a friend for the food adventure.

Union Grill, 413 S. Craig St., Oakland, Pittsburgh, PA 15213; (412) 681-8620; American; $$. Union Grill is an ideal collegiate lunch, dinner, and after-exam hangout spot. It is rare to find the place not hopping. Thankfully, there are plenty of seating options either at the bar or in the larger-than-it-appears-from-the-street dining area. During the warmer months, the front opens up onto the always bustlin' Craig Street, and a handful of diners can bask in the urban outdoors. The portions at this joint are incredibly hardy. If you order the fish taco, you will wind up with what looks to be more like a whale taco. Not that we are complaining—the more good food the merrier! Choose a burger or a sandwich from the menu (and choose the waffle fries—always the waffle fries), and you can't miss. The turkey burger in particular gets a serious "heck yes!" in our book, as its deliciousness sometimes haunts our dreams. Perhaps the most important feature of the Union Grill is on the drink side of the menu: Union Grill has a $10 wine list. We repeat: $10. Bottles. Of. Wine. Enough said.

Union Pig & Chicken/Harvard & Highland, 220 N. Highland Ave., East Liberty, Pittsburgh, PA 15206; (412) 363-7675;

unionpgh.com; Barbecue; $$. One of a few Kevin Sousa establishments in the city of Pittsburgh, Union Pig & Chicken sits nestled in East Liberty. Catering to palates that are fine-tuned to southern barbecue and all the beverages that pair so perfectly, Union Pig & Chicken has become a fan favorite. Of course, the rustic restaurant serves more than pig and chicken, with menu items ranging from brisket to tofu and either slathered in sauce or fried up to your liking. The meats are hearty portions so we recommend sharing in order to save room for the equally hearty sides. Some of our favorites: the meaty mac and cheese made with bleu cheese and wasabi and loaded with brisket and ribs, and the the underrated accouterment, corn bread. Save room for something sweet: You'll want a whoopee pie from local bakery, **Vanilla Pastry Studio** (p. 191). After you fill your belly, peel yourself from the communal, picnic-style tables (red and white tablecloths, check!) and make your way upstairs to Harvard & Highland, Union's cocktail bar, for a glass of American whiskey or a mixed drink (try the Hot Pink Gin!), and if you're lucky enough to be out on a night when there is a live band, you'll be in hog heaven. Catering and private events available.

Verde Mexican Kitchen & Cantina, 5491 Penn Ave., Garfield, Pittsburgh, PA 15206; (412) 404-8487; verdepgh.com; Mexican; $$.

If you like tequila, then Verde Mexican Kitchen & Cantina is the place for you. With over 160 varieties made of 100 percent blue agave, Verde Mexican Kitchen & Cantina has one of the largest selections around. Try one of 160-plus varieties in a seasonal or flavored margarita or a tequila flight. If you choose one of those flights, it will be accompanied by a shot of traditional sangrita. A great complement to smooth out the flavor. The menu features traditional Mexican flavors and authentic ingredients with a modern flair. Try the guacamole made fresh with your choice of ingredients and spice level. And if you're in the mood for a show, you can have the guacamole made tableside. If you're with a group (or just have a hungry appetite), try the Family Style Taco deal. Choose from either the small or large option; it comes with six or nine tacos and allows you to try either two or three different taco styles like beer-braised chicken, wild mushroom, or chile-rubbed pulled beef. Rice and beans are also included.

Landmarks

Coca Cafe, 3811 Butler St., Lawrenceville, Pittsburgh, PA 15201; (412) 621-3171; cocacafe.net; Neighborhood Cafe; $$. Coca Cafe, in Pittsburgh's Lawrenceville neighborhood, is a tiny place on Butler Street with large windows, red walls, and an impressive menu of coffees and teas, Italian sodas, and fresh fruit smoothies. During its Sunday brunch, you can order a made-to-order omelet and carb it up with your choice of cinnamon, seven-grain, herbed focaccia, pumpernickel, or country white toast. If you like your toast french, like we do, you're going to want to go for the french toast, served with fresh berries. You'll be licking the plate afterward. For lunch, there are salads and sandwiches aplenty. And for dinner you can indulge in a mushroom tart, mussels, and more. Something that we love about Coca Cafe is the local artwork you can find when you look around. It's all for sale so you can get a cappuccino, a biscotti, and a painting to go! Coca Cafe also caters the cafe at the Mattress Factory so you know you'll be eating well if you decide to snack after peeping the art exhibits.

Dave and Andy's Homemade Ice Cream, 207 Atwood St., Oakland, Pittsburgh, PA 15213; (412) 681-9906; Ice Cream; $. You will know you are near Dave and Andy's when the sweet smell of freshly made waffle cones fills the air. Just follow this scent for some of the best ice cream around town. Since 1983, Dave and Andy's has been satisfying the sweet teeth of University of Pittsburgh students and anyone who comes in close contact with that sweet smell of waffle cones. There is a list of the flavors of the day on the chalkboard behind the freezers full of ice cream tubs. If you have a hard time choosing one of the 200-plus flavors that are on constant rotation, try our two faves: birthday cake and chocolate chip cookie dough. The ice cream is rich and smooth, and you will want to get at least two scoops of your favorite flavor. Once you are done licking away your scoops, a surprise awaits you at the bottom of the waffle cone—a piece of chocolate candy, which is placed in the cone to prevent ice cream drippage. Sorbet, yogurt, and fat-free/sugar-free ice cream are also available.

Girasole, 733 Copeland St., Shadyside, Pittsburgh, PA 15232; (412) 682-2130; 733copeland.com; Italian; $$. Girasole is a cozy, basement-level restaurant with stone walls that give the appearance of dining in a Tuscan wine cellar. This association is appropriate as the fare here references Italy as well. With seasonal menus for winter, spring, summer, and fall, you can anticipate slightly different variations of Italian classics depending on the time of year. Unchanging throughout the calendar is the excellent marinara sauce and the surprising house salad—no sad iceberg lettuce here! The salad, coined as the "Girasole," is prepared with mixed greens, garbanzo beans, gorgonzola cheese, and a flavorful sunflower vinaigrette. Girasole has a solid wine list spanning all regions of Italy and a bar that can serve you up a delicious bellini. If the weather is cooperating, a welcoming, substreet-level patio is the perfect spot for outdoor eating. Less than 1 block off of Shadyside's busy Walnut Street, you'll still be in range to shout "ciao!" to friendly passersby.

Le Mardi Gras, 731 Copeland St., Shadyside, Pittsburgh, PA 15232; (412) 683-0912; lemardigras.com; Neighborhood Bar; $. Are you in the mood to be transported to a time when drinks were stiff and indoor smoking was prevalent? Then Le Mardi Gras is your new stomping ground. This small neighborhood bar has been around since 1954 and features a regular cast of locals just waiting for you to pull up a stool. Its cramped, dark quarters help it pull off that cool-without-trying vibe. Squeeze your way up to the bar and ask for a Greyhound. It's vodka and half of a freshly squeezed grapefruit. Be warned: It's heavy on the vodka, and light on the juice. The booze is the star in every drink the bartenders pour at Le Mardi Gras so find yourself a designated driver if you plan on staying for the long haul. If one of the four red retro booths open up, be sure to slide in and make yourself comfortable. The jukebox is filled with blues, jazz, and countless classics, and don't forget to play a round of Ms. Pac-Man. Oh, and watch those stairs when you're leaving. They'll make for a painful reminder of just how much fun you had.

The Original Hot Dog Shop, 3901 Forbes Ave., Oakland, Pittsburgh, PA 15213; (412) 621-7388; theoriginalhotdogshop.com; Hot Dogs; $. Open until the wee hours of the morning, The Original Hot Dog Shop, commonly known to Pittsburghers as "The O," is the perfect place to grab greasy food after a long evening of drinking. Be prepared to meet and mingle with all of the party-hardy University of Pittsburgh students. To prevent any kind of stampede for fries, there is a security guard stationed in the middle of the shop. Casing hot dogs and overloaded, twice-fried french fries are this landmark's specialty. Up front, you order your hot dogs and then in the back is where all the french fry magic happens. The fries are piled high like skyscrapers, and condiments here don't come in those little packets. You get tubs of condiments large enough to jam all of those fries in. There are more than just fries and hot dogs at this place—you can get pizza, booze, and burgers, too!

Tessaro's, 4601 Liberty Ave., Bloomfield, Pittsburgh, PA 15224; (412) 682-6809; American; $–$$. Tessaro's has been crafting impossibly good burgers before gourmet burgers became the hottest menu item around. The meat is butchered on-site, and that freshness translates to a good meal. The menu has a lot more than burgers, but really, you should get a burger. You can order it plain, with cheese (American, bleu, swiss, provolone, or cheddar), with bacon and cheese, with bacon, mushrooms, and cheese, or with coleslaw. On the side, decide from potato salad, coleslaw, chips, broccoli, or home fries. Always the home fries. Wood walls, paper placemats, and tablecloths create the perfect no-nonsense 'Burgh ambiance. There is a long bar and sports on the televisions. No better place to kick back and eat a burger the size of a small vehicle. Being a Pittsburgh tradition, sometimes a wait is inevitable. With all your time spent in anticipation, think of all the locals who have stood in your spot—waiting for a classic bite of the 'Burgh.

Tram's Kitchen, 4050 Penn Ave., Bloomfield, Pittsburgh, PA 15224; (412) 682-2688; Vietnamese; $$. You probably wouldn't notice Tram's Kitchen if you walked by. There's nothing fancy about it. Quite frankly, some might avoid it altogether. Tram's Kitchen serves inexpensive Vietnamese dishes to a typically packed dining room of patrons Tues through Sun. Start things off with an order of fresh spring rolls. This appetizer regularly wins "best of" categories from the local media, and you'll know why after the first bite. Each roll is tightly wrapped in translucent rice paper and pops with an explosive fresh flavor. As far as main dishes go, pho is king at Tram's. It arrives piping hot with thick noodles, choice of meat, and an array of mix-ins like bean sprouts and basil swimming in a perfectly seasoned broth. The vermicelli is also an excellent choice with thinly sliced meat, delicate rice noodles, broccoli, and peanuts sitting in a shallow pool of broth.

Add a bit of complexity or spice to any dish you choose with one of the bottles of sauce found on the table. Don't forget your booze and cash. Tram's Kitchen is BYOB and cash only!

Uncle Sam's Sandwich Bar, 210 Oakland Ave., Oakland, Pittsburgh, PA 15213; (412) 621-1885; unclesamssubs.com; Sandwiches; $. Uncle Sam's Sandwich Bar has some pretty tasty cheesesteaks for both meat and veggie lovers. Order the classic Uncle Sam's Special Steak, a cheesesteak loaded with provolone cheese, peppers, and mushrooms. Fun fact: For a little up-charge, you can substitute chicken instead of steak on any sandwich. Vegetarian? Uncle Sam's has you covered with five sandwiches on the menu, including the grilled portobello sub and the Mediterranean sub: fresh zucchini, tomatoes, black olives, cucumbers, grilled onions, lettuce, and provolone cheese topped with a house-made vinaigrette. We suggest you dine in at Uncle Sam's because you can take advantage of the free shoestring-cut fries that come along with sandwiches. If ordering a sandwich to go, the fries will cost you a few dollars, but trust us, they are worth every penny. If you can't finish your sub, be sure to get it wrapped in butcher paper on the way out. Locations outside of Oakland also offer a variety of salads, cheese fries, and sweet potato fries (see website).

Specialty Stores, Markets & Producers

East End Food Co-op, 7516 Meade St., Point Breeze, Pittsburgh, PA 15208; (412) 242-3598; eastendfood.coop. If you're in search of a healthy but hearty meal in Pittsburgh, the East End Food Co-op could be just what you're looking for. Open daily, the East End Food Co-op cafe and market caters to the diverse East End crowd. House-made soups, smoothies, and juices, and sandwiches are available for dining in or taking with you on the go. Local and organic ingredients help you feel good about what you're eating. Visit during the weekend for their brunch and then fill your recyclable cotton bag with fresh fruit, vegetables, and all-natural snacks for you and the family and friends you're looking out for. The staff is friendly and knowledgeable so don't be afraid to ask questions, even if they look way cooler than you.

Groceria Italiana, 237 Cedarville St., Bloomfield, Pittsburgh, PA 15224; (412) 681-1227; groceriaitaliana.com. Long before chain grocery stores moved into town, communities shopped at their neighborhood market. Groceria Italiana in Bloomfield takes you back to a simpler time when life was home-made. The first thing you might notice is the counter where nimble fingers with years of practice are busy making fresh pasta and ravioli. Pasta includes fettuccine, linguine, vermicelli, spaghetti, angel hair, and about a dozen types of ravioli like artichoke and gorgonzola, mushroom, prosciutto, roasted red  pepper, and spinach. Take a box home with you along with some home-made meat or marinara sauce and you have a quick, authentic Italian dinner. Next to the pasta is the deli counter where you can find cold cuts, dry cured meats, olives, and cold salads. If you need a hot quick lunch, check out the hot food section. Features change but expect to find dishes like meatball sandwiches, eggplant Parmesan, stuffed peppers, lasagna, and pepperoni rolls. Groceria Italiana also has shelves stocked with tomato sauces, olive oil, balsamic, and spices.

Shadyside Market, 5414 Walnut St., Shadyside, Pittsburgh, PA 15232; (412) 682-5420. Shadyside Market has been a staple on Walnut Street for 50 years. This specialty grocer keeps stock in fresh produce, fresh meat, and interesting boxes, cans, and jars. No cheap alternatives here; this is higher echelon food product. We once went in for just regular old pasta sauce; when we realized this was not an option, we found ourselves with some of the best sauce ever. Thank you, Shadyside Market, for your off-the-beaten path finds! The market also has an on-site deli where you can indulge in a sandwich, salad, or daily entrees. Lunch and dinner can be picked up or delivered. Cookies and the like are often at the front register, which makes it hard to resist the charm. Pay for your groceries and snag some baked goods.

Waffallonia, 1707 Murray Ave., Squirrel Hill, Pittsburgh, PA 15217; (412) 521-4902; waffallonia.com. A mystical land dedicated to waffles? Welcome to Waffallonia! This tiny, tiny, blink-and-you-miss-it waffle shop specializes in Belgian liege waffles. The secret to the liege-y-ness is the specific, Belgian sugar that provides a different texture and outer crunch than other waffles. It's science. It's delicious. You can take your plain waffle and run, or you can kick back in the hip, minimalist space and get your waffle piled high with a variety of extras. Strawberries, whipped cream, Nutella, ice cream—take your pick. Perhaps you should be running toward Waffallonia right now. You can also order from a predetermined menu, which looks like a train schedule, on the wall with combos like the Antwerp, which includes chocolate sauce and whipped cream, or the Bruges, which includes strawberries and whipped cream. Additional location: Oakland, 4212 Forbes Ave., Pittsburgh, PA 15260; (412) 685-4081.

Suburban Gems & Places Worth the Drive

The suburbs are as varied as the collection of neighborhoods that make up the 'Burgh. Proud, tiny towns to posh, stately villages. We've outlined the best bets for tasty visits to these nearby hamlets. Your taste buds will delight in each area, and you'll continue to be a recipient of the Pittsburgh charm.

Sure, leaving Pittsburgh may be a struggle. Our roads are wacky, disjointed, and in no way parallel. Our drivers think they can turn left before you go straight through an intersection. And everyone—*everyone*—stops before going through tunnels. The reward for emerging on the other side is great for you and your stomach, as plenty of quality dining options abound beyond the city limits.

Yinz guys better get moving—the 'Burbs are anticipating your arrival.

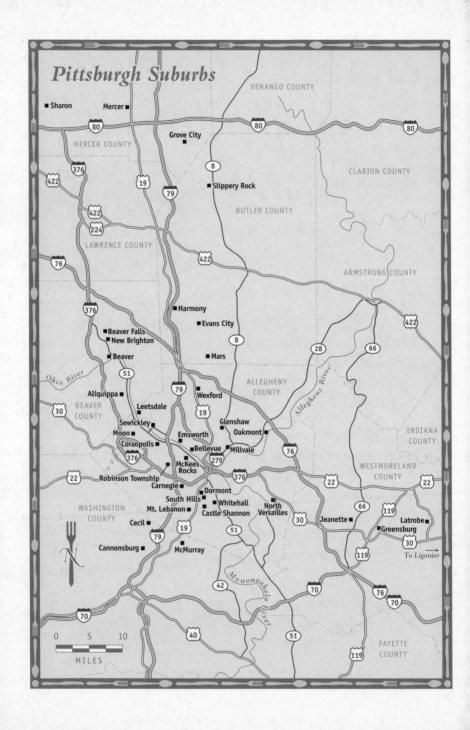

Pittsburgh Suburbs

■ Sharon   Mercer ■

VENANGO COUNTY

MERCER COUNTY

Grove City ■

CLARION COUNTY

Slippery Rock ■

BUTLER COUNTY

LAWRENCE COUNTY

ARMSTRONG COUNTY

Harmony ■

Evans City ■

Beaver Falls ■
New Brighton ■

Beaver ■

Mars ■

ALLEGHENY COUNTY

Aliquippa ■

Wexford ■

Leetsdale ■

INDIANA COUNTY

Sewickley ■
Moon ■

Glenshaw ■
Oakmont ■

Emsworth ■

Coraopolis ■

Bellevue ■   Millvale ■

WESTMORELAND COUNTY

McKees Rocks ■

Robinson Township ■

BEAVER COUNTY

Carnegie ■

Dormont ■

South Hills ■
Whitehall ■

North Versailles ■

WASHINGTON COUNTY

Mt. Lebanon ■   Castle Shannon ■

Cecil ■

Jeanette ■

Latrobe ■
Greensburg ■

Cannonsburg ■   McMurray ■

To Ligonier

FAYETTE COUNTY

Ohio River

Allegheny River

Monongahela River

N

0   5   10
MILES

Amel's Restaurant, 435 McNeilly Rd., Baldwin Twp., Pittsburgh, PA 15226; (412) 563-3466; amelsrestaurantpgh.com; Mediterranean; $$. Amel's Middle Eastern restaurant in the South Hills is one of those rare gems that can take on whatever form of restaurant you're looking for. If you want a romantic dinner for two, Amel's is your place. Family fun night? Amel's. Drinks and appetizers with the girls (or guys)? Amel's. Its bar has a special almost every night of the week. If you get there on a Monday, you're definitely going to want to take advantage of the 33-cent wings (the wings are to die for). Amel's menu ranges from soups and sandwiches to pasta, seafood, and kabobs out the wazoo. It has traditional Mediterranean fare like hummus and grape leaves, and we hope you're no stranger to feta cheese because it's found on the majority of the menu items. If you are hungry for something a little more American, order a juicy filet cooked to perfection. Warm pita bread is complimentary so be cautious not to fill up before your entree arrives; trust us, we've made that mistake before!

B Gourmet, 428 Beaver St., Sewickley, PA 15143; (412) 741-6100; bgourmet-pgh.com; Neighborhood Cafe; $$. Sister eatery to Avenue B (p. 93) in Friendship is B Gourmet, a neighborhood cafe and gourmet marketplace on busy Beaver Street in Sewickley. Different from the more upscale Avenue B, B Gourmet offers tasty lunches and meals-to-go. There are a handful of tables located at the front of the space where you can dine in during lunch hours and enjoy sandwiches, wraps, salads, and daily soups that are ordered off the wall menus behind the deli cases. In addition, B Gourmet has freshly prepared foods to go that fill the deli-style counter. The offerings change frequently and can include meat loaf, roasted chicken, crab cakes, stuffed peppers, and a variety of sides and salads. During the dinner rush, B Gourmet turns into a takeout-only restaurant. "Dinners to go" can be ordered in

PIEROGIES PLUS

Need gas? Then don't head to Pierogies Plus. Because at this renovated gas station, you are not going to find fuel for your car. Instead, there's fuel for your stomach.

Pierogies Plus was started by Helen Mannarino, a Polish immigrant, in 1991. And ever since, it has been a Pittsburgh institution. If you ask a 'Burgher where to get pierogies, he or she will tell you one of two places: the nearest church basement or Pierogies Plus. The pierogies here are jam-packed with so much filling, we wonder how they don't explode when cooked. The daily offerings include the traditional fillings of potato and onion, potato and cheese, sauerkraut and potatoe, and cottage cheese and chives. Meatier fillings, such as hot sausage and ground meat, are also available daily. All pierogies can be ordered hot and drenched in an oh-so-delicious butter and onion sauce, or can be taken home cold and prepared to your liking. In addition to these traditional offerings, specialty flavors such as lekvar, spinach and ricotta, potato and jalapeño peppers, and even a breakfast pierogi stuffed with scrambled eggs, bacon, cheddar cheese, and chives, can be ordered with at least 2 days' advance notice. Besides the delicious pierogies, Pierogies Plus serves up other Eastern European delicacies, such as halushki, stuffed cabbage, borscht, and potato pancakes. Are you salivating yet? A quick tip: If you can't quite pick out what you want to eat at this take-out joint, order one (or two) of the sampler platters.

Pierogies Plus pierogies are also found on the menus at several local restaurants, including the **Bloomfield Bridge Tavern** (p. 95) and **Diamond Market Bar and Grill** (p. 23), and sold at **Soergel Orchards Family Farm** (p. 176) and the **Pennsylvania Macaroni Company** (p. 53). You can also order them up online and have them shipped to you!

Visit **Pierogies Plus** at 342 Island Ave., McKees Rocks, PA 15136; (412) 331-2224; pierogiesplus.com.

advance or you can swing by and pick up a meal-to-go. Whether here for lunch or picking up dinner, be sure to grab a few locally sourced items from the gourmet grocery section.

Bartram House Bakery, 2000 Village Run Rd., Wexford, PA 15090; (724) 719-2442; bartramhousebakery.com; Neighborhood Cafe; $. Part bakery, part cafe, part deli, Bartram House Bakery is a little bit of everything. At Bartram, breakfast is served all day. You can treat your palate to a made-to-order quiche or warm crepes with your choice of filling. Pair your first meal of the day with a fruit smoothie, seasonal flavored cappuccino, or large Bartram House Blend coffee. When lunchtime rolls around, you can dive into a bowl of homemade mac and cheese or cabbage and noodles before indulging in a signature sandwich. Choices include the Bartram House Burger, Cuban, and Egg Salad. Lighter fare is also offered in the way of salads with toppings galore. Always opt for the house-made vinaigrette. Last but not least, you'll want to pick a pastry or slice of cake to polish off or take home to enjoy later. Bartram has standard doughnuts, croissants, and cookies but outdoes it on the dessert bars: layer upon layer of all things magical. And the cakes! Additional location: 4120 Washington Rd., McMurray, PA 15317; (724) 260-0702.

Biba, 406 3rd St., Beaver, PA 15009; (724) 728-7700; bibabeaver .com; Latin American; $$. Taco Tuesdays are not just the day your mom announces she is making tacos with a store-bought taco kit. They are an event at Biba during dinner service. Tacos are priced two for $5, and include a small variety of options, such as braised pork, roasted chicken, and short rib, and change from week to week. The tacos are made with char-grilled taco shells and topped with flavorful slaws, guacamole, salsas, sour cream, and queso. Two tacos are plenty to feed your appetite, because you are going to want to order a few other small plates to try, such as the sharable skillet fries: french fries topped with goat cheese, bacon, chili, mayo, and sour cream. And, of course, be sure not to skip out on the chips, salsa, and guacamole. After your tacos and apps have settled in your belly, a must-order dessert, even if you don't like desserts, is the churros served with a chocolate habanero ganache dipping sauce. A truly sweet (and spicy) ending to a meal. Biba is BYOB and a reservation is highly recommended.

Bistro 19, 711 Washington Rd., Mt. Lebanon, Pittsburgh, PA 15228; (412) 306-1919; bistro19.com; New American; $$$. Bistro 19 is open for lunch and dinner, and brunch on Sunday. It's sophisticated and is the perfect place for a first date, a business dinner, or to impress the in-laws. The dinner menu is wide ranged and has items that include sea bass and duck. Whether you order the Hawaiian Tuna or the boursin-encrusted filet, you'll be enamored with Bistro 19, tenfold. Start with their French Onion soup and Pan-Seared Sea Scallops before making your way to the entrees. The dishes are served with unique sides like risotto, roasted vegetables, and polenta. The restaurant's sauces are all housemade, as are the pickles that adorn the bacon cheddar bistro burger. If you find yourself there on Sunday morning, our favorite menu items are the Bananas Foster Pancakes, complete with fresh bananas and caramelized whiskey sauce, and the eggs benedict with prosciutto.

Brighton Hot Dog Shoppe, 1128 3rd Ave., New Brighton, PA 15066; (724) 843-4012; brightonhotdogshoppes.com; Hot Dogs; $. Hot dogs, burgers, fries, chili, cheese, milk shakes, and fountain pop served in take-home plastic cups with hot dog characters on them. You can get all of these tasty treats and more at the Brighton Hot Dog Shoppe. Started in 1959 in New Brighton, the Brighton Hot Dog Shoppe is a staple of Beaver County, which has since crossed county lines, opening up locations in Allegheny, Butler, and Lawrence Counties, and state lines with a location in Salem, Ohio. When you visit you must order a chili sauce and onion hot dog, a side of cheddar and chili fries, and a milk shake. There are no fancy hot dog names here, no wacky toppings, and nothing gourmet. Just simple, good food that will stick to your ribs. Though the place is known for their wieners, their burgers are outstanding. Just plain, simple burgers with traditional toppings. You really don't go wrong with either a burger or a hot dog here. Several locations also serve breakfast of omelets, pancakes, french toast, and home fries, which are simple and delicious. Additional locations: See website.

Burgatory, Waterworks Mall, 932 Freeport Rd., Fox Chapel, Pittsburgh, PA 15238; (412) 781-1456; burgatorybar.com; Burgers; $$. Burgatory is all kinds of clever. Playing off the dichotomy of heaven and hell, Burgatory describes its offerings as "Helluva Burger" and "Heavenly Shakes." You know, just stuck between the two in Burgatory! There is no better place to be in limbo, folks. The burgers here really are sinfully delicious. You can build your own burger, starting with the specialty rub or seasoning (we really like the Angel Dust, a salt-and-pepper blend) and every condiment you can dream of. Each burger comes with house chips—a mix of regular and sweet potato. The shakes, good heavens the shakes, are absolutely fantastic. Using handcrafted ice cream, the team at Burgatory are miracle workers with both the nonalcoholic and alcoholic variety of frosty delights. We would go as far as saying the campfire s'mores milk shake, in particular, is the best milk shake we've ever had (and we have had a lot). A giant roasted marshmallow and expertly mixed graham cracker crumbs contribute to this magnificence. Word is out that this place is awesome, so the wait can sometimes be intimidating. You can check the wait time on the website before you go. Don't be deterred! Burgatory has additional locations: See website.

Carnegie Coffee Company, 132 E. Main St., Carnegie, PA, 15106; (412) 275-3951; Coffee Shop; $. Mail used to be delivered here, but now coffee is served. The Carnegie Coffee Company is located in the former Carnegie Post Office. And though the coffee shop has a modern style, old fixtures of the post office remain, like the bank of P.O. boxes that make up the coffee counter. The space is bright, and the wall of books will make you want to cozy up on a plush chair and spend an afternoon reading while sipping a cappuccino. The Carnegie Coffee Company serves Illy coffee and a variety of pastries and cafe selections. If looking for a little snack to go with your coffee, you can't go wrong with one of the doughnuts made by **Big Daddy's Donuts** (p. 179), or grab a Savory Plate (artisan cheese selection served with olives and nuts) from the grab-and-go cooler. If you're looking for a little more substance, the Carnegie Coffee Company has salads, soups, and made-to-order sandwiches, such as a grilled peanut butter and jelly and a gourmet BLT. This coffee shop is one of the best in the 'Burbs, so when you find yourself out near Carnegie, be sure to stop by for a latte, mocha, or fruit smoothie.

Central Diner & Grille, 6408 Steubenville Pike, Robinson Twp., Pittsburgh, PA 15205; (412) 275-3243; Diner; $$. So hungry you want to eat breakfast, lunch, dinner, and dessert in one sitting? Central Diner & Grille is the place you want to go. The menu is huge, filled with omelets, pancakes, salads, soups, burgers, pasta, wraps, paninis, triple-decker sandwiches, and a variety of ice cream parlor treats, cakes, and pies. If confused on where to even start in the menu, the friendly staff will surely guide you in the right direction. We suggest ordering one of the Greek specialty entrees, such as the spanakopita, (which also comes as an appetizer), or moussaka, a Greek-style lasagna with layers of sliced eggplant, potatoes, meat sauce, and béchamel sauce. If breakfast is calling your name, the challah french toast, eggs

Benedict, or one of the 10 plus omelet combinations will surely please your cravings. Just like the menu, the portions here are huge, but you definitely need to order one of the homemade desserts. Choose from a piece of baklava, scoop of rice pudding, slice of pie or cake, or the incredible giant brownie ice cream sundae.

Clifford's Restaurant, 514 Upper Harmony Rd., Evans City, PA 16033; (724) 789-9115; cliffordsrestaurant.com; American; $$$. Located literally in the middle of nowhere in Butler County, Clifford's is a destination restaurant worth every bit of the drive and gas money. The restaurant is located on farmland in an old stone house, which makes you feel as though you are going to your Great-Aunt Jennie's for dinner. It is only open for dinner Wed through Sun and is BYOB with no additional cork charge. There is a standard menu of whole boneless trout, veal osso bucco, and grilled pork chops, to name a few, but Clifford's is known for their large daily menu, which is developed according to what is in season the day you go. Talk about freshness. With your meal, you receive homemade rolls so good you better take an extra-large purse to shove a few in for the drive back to civilization. Though you may be in the middle of nowhere farmland Pennsylvania, the meal you get will be as five star as any major restaurant in a metropolitan city. Reservations are a must, so call ahead before you go.

Dive Bar & Grille, 12017 Perry Hwy., Wexford, PA 15090; (724) 719-2060; divebarandgrille.com; Neighborhood Bar; $$. Though the name suggests this place is a dive, it is far from it. From the modern interior to the classed-up bar food, this place is worth the drive for a few drinks and many plates of snacks. It's hard not to want to try everything listed on the small bites menu, but if you only pick a few items, choose the buffalo chicken eggrolls. These house-made rolls are filled with a creamy mixture of grilled chicken, buffalo sauce, and bleu cheese, deep-fried to a golden perfection, and served with a side of ranch dressing. And the loaded croquettes: panko-crusted potato pancakes topped with the daily pulled barbecue pork, shredded cheese, and sour cream will kick sad potato skins to the curb. Loaded fries are a dive bar staple, but at this Dive Bar, you can build your own loaded fry bowl, choosing from a variety of toppings including mac n' cheese, chimichurri, and a fried egg. If you are nursing a weekend hangover, Dive Bar has you covered with brunch on Saturday and Sunday. A peanut butter chocolate chip funnel pancake, breakfast burrito, or sandwich will have you feeling better in no time. Additional location: Lawrenceville, 5147 Butler St., Pittsburgh, PA, 15201; (412) 408-2015.

Dor-Stop Restaurant, 1430 Potomac Ave., Dormont, Pittsburgh, PA 15216; (412) 561-9320; dorstoprestaurant.com; Breakfast & Lunch; $. The Dor-Stop has been serving up no-nonsense diner eats on the corner of Potomac and Glenmore Avenues in Dormont for over 25 years. The hotcakes here are legendary, as are the restaurant's German potato pancakes—both worth a taste. Its reputation as one of the Pittsburgh area's must-eats was bolstered by a visit from Guy Fieri on Food Network's *Diners, Drive-ins, and Dives*. If you visit on a weekend, you are almost guaranteed a long wait on the sidewalk. Be patient and remember your reward: those giant, sweet Dor-Stop hotcakes. The menu includes lunch options as well, like a hot meat loaf sandwich, classic burgers, and homemade soups. There is a solid chance that you will see the owners, Bob and Vicki Lawhorne, making their way around the small, retro space. Look up the Food Network's *Diners, Drive-ins, and Dives* episode before you go so you can be aware when you have your brush with celebrity.

Eat'n Park, 245 E. Waterfront Dr., Homestead, PA 15120; (412) 464-7275; eatnpark.com; Diner; $. Pittsburgh's first carhop? Eat'n Park. In 1949 Eat'n Park opened up as a carhop and 13-seat restaurant in the South Hills. The day it opened, a traffic jam was caused. That tells you how much Pittsburghers dig this place. The original carhop location is gone, but this local chain restaurant now has over 70 restaurants in the tri-state area (Ohio, Pennsylvania, and West Virginia). Many locations are open 24 hours a day to satisfy your hunger at any hour of the day. Possibly the most noteworthy item on the menu is actually a cookie, a Smiley Cookie to be exact. The second most popular item, at least in our eyes, is the Grilled Stickies, served a la mode or as a breakfast meal. Grilled Stickies are Eat'n Park's signature sticky-bun type creation that coats your soul in sweet goodness. Besides these sweet treats, the menu includes a wide variety of sandwiches, burgers, dinners, and a soup and salad buffet. A great spot if you are looking to please your family and kids. Additional locations: See website.

Fede Pasta/Cenacolo Restaurant, 1061 Main St., North Huntingdon, PA 15642; (724) 515-5764; cenacolorestaurant.com; Italian; $$$. Located in an industrial park deep in North Huntingdon is Fede Pasta. The small artisanal pasta company started in 2005 and has since grown to include a national clientele list and a restaurant called Cenacolo Restaurant. Using recipes and techniques he grew up making, Owner Steve Salvi offers 20 or so varieties of fresh, handmade pasta. Traditional shapes like tortellini, rigatoni, and linguine are a staple, but Fede also offers lesser-known varieties like ricciolina, tagliolini, and garganelli. Stop by Fede and pick up your favorite varieties fresh at the retail store or visit Cenacolo for lunch or dinner. Cenacolo offers several varieties of the handmade pasta on a quarterly basis. Try the delicate ricotta gnocchi with short rib ragu, porcini mushrooms, and roma tomatoes; or the orecchiette with corn, red peppers, zucchini, basil, and pistachio pesto. Don't forget to start the meal with a hearty variety of *affettato* (sliced meat) and *formaggi* (cheese). Or go with our favorite, Fior di Late. Three fresh mozzarella balls are sprinkled with coarse sea salt and pepper and accompanied by crusty bread smeared with pesto and topped with sweet red peppers.

The Flame BBQ, 1805 Babcock Blvd., Shaler, Pittsburgh, PA 15209; (412) 821-0202; theflamebbq.com; Barbecue; $. It's hard to find good barbecue north of the Mason Dixon Line, and it's even harder to find good barbecue in a region primarily known for its doughy dumplings. The Flame BBQ brings some southern flair to us Yankees by way of pulled pork, racks of ribs, brisket, coleslaw, and collards. They serve up traditional-style barbecue, add spice and heat if asked, and even modernize the meals by stacking the meat of your choice with homemade mac and cheese into sandwiches. They also stir meat with rice to create a casserole and bundle into burritos for a hot hand-held lunch, thereby offering something for everyone. Because barbecue is a food that lends itself well as a party food, Flame BBQ has a catering menu with pans of their best dishes including barbecue meat loaf and sweet potato bake. Additional location: 20300 Rt. 19, Cranberry Township, PA 16066; (724) 772-2270.

Freedom Farms Sandwich Shop, 4323 Shearsburg Rd., New Kensington, PA 15068; (724) 212-3844; freedomfarmspa.com; Sandwiches; $. More famously known as the Farm Kings, the fine folks at Freedom Farms are turning their locally grown foods into spectacular dishes for all to enjoy. Freedom Farms Sandwich Shop is open Wed through Sun and shelves and serves an array of locally sourced, locally grown, and locally raised food. Your meal can be made to order, or you can opt for the special of the day, which never disappoints. Farm-fresh sandwiches range from the farmer's cheesesteak, piled high with seasoned steak, sautéed onions, and mushrooms and then topped with melted provolone and lettuce, tomato, and mayo all shoved into a warm Italian hoagie roll. Or you can order the schnitzel: pan-fried pork with melty swiss on Italian with veggies and Dijon dressing. After deciding on a sandwich, you'll need to decide on what side will accompany said sandwich. Choices are fresh cut fries, seasonal veggie, cup of soup, chopped salad, or mac and cheese! What makes this shop special is the variety of carryout items. A cafe and market in one, you can dine in and take out! Farm-fresh eggs, milk, and cheeses line the coolers and the shelves are stocked with salsas and soups you can enjoy at home.

Golden Pig Authentic Korean Cuisine, 3201 Millers Run Rd., Cecil, PA 15321; (412) 220-7170; Korean; $. The Internet and GPS were created to find places like Golden Pig Authentic Korean Cuisine. Without either, word may have never reached the masses that a place like it exists. Golden Pig is in the middle of nowhere, about 30 minutes outside of Pittsburgh in a town called Cecil. The menu at Golden Pig is small. Really small. That's because it's a one-woman show in the kitchen. Actually it's a one-woman show entirely. The owner, Yong Kwon, does all the cooking and adds a little bit of her heart to each dish. She decided to open the 10-seat restaurant in 2008 during the Year of the Pig in honor of her grandson being born. So we'd like to take this opportunity to officially thank her grandson! All of Yong's dishes are made with the freshest ingredients, which make the simple yet complex flavor shine. Authentic dishes like *man-du*, beef and vegetable-stuffed dumplings; *bibimbap*, white rice, seasoned vegetables, chili pepper paste, and sliced meat; *bulgogi*, beef marinated in a mixture of soy sauce, sesame oil, black pepper, garlic, onions, ginger, wine, and sugar; and spicy squid are as close to South Korea as you can get in Pittsburgh.

Hank's Frozen Custard, 2210 3rd Ave., New Brighton, PA 15066; (724) 847-4265; go2hanks.com; Mexican; $. At Hank's, you're going to find a unique combination of cuisine: frozen custard and Mexican food. Sounds strange, but it's oh so delicious. Hank's has been a Beaver County staple for over 60 years, though the Mexican food didn't show up until the 1960s. Ordering here can be quite a challenge, so let us give you a heads up. At the left window, frozen custard creations are ordered, like shakes, floats, malts, and cones. The cookie dough flurry (layers of custard and cookie dough pieces) is out-of-this-world crazy good. Custard flavors include vanilla, chocolate, and the flavor of the day. Black raspberry is on Sunday and peanut butter on Wednesday. Be sure to check Hank's website for the flavor of the day before you go. At the right window, Mexican food is served up. The menu is filled with tacos, enchiladas, burritos, taco salads, nachos, and quesadillas. And it is okay in our book if you feel the urge to dunk a nacho cheese-covered chip into your vanilla custard. Be sure to get your fill of custard and Mexican food during the spring, summer, and fall months, because Hank's closes up shop each year in November, reopening again in March.

Il Pizzaiolo, 703 Washington Rd., Mt. Lebanon, Pittsburgh, PA 15228; (412) 344-4123; ilpizzaiolo.com; Italian; $$. Far from its European roots lies a magical place where one can feast on wood-fired pizza and sip wine while enjoying the sights and sounds of a garden patio reflective of any movie scene that takes place in Italy. That place is Il Pizzaiolo. It features something few restaurants in Pittsburgh do—a wine bar. If that doesn't sell you right there, there is also a brick oven where hand-tossed pizzas are cooked to perfection before being served to anxious patrons. The toughest choice you're going to make is what to put on top of your pizza. The toppings are made in house and include sausage, meatballs, and mozzarella. If you're not the pizza-going type, don't worry; you can still have a Neapolitan experience at Il Pizzaiolo. Order up any of their veal menu items or lasagna made with Pasta Faella, San Marzano tomatoes, and fresh ricotta and mozzarella. You might forget you're in western Pennsylvania so don't be surprised if you're saying *grazie* as you leave. Additional location: Downtown, 8 Market Square, Pittsburgh, PA 15122; (412) 575-5858

Jerry's Curb Service, 1521 Riverside Dr., Beaver, PA 15009; (724) 774-4727; jerryscurbservice.com; Car Hop; $. If you want to experience a real-working car hop that isn't a part of any chain restaurant, head up the Ohio River to Beaver. Jerry's Curb Service has been hoppin' since 1947, dishing out burgers, fries, and sandwiches from the kitchen to your car. Burgers and cheeseburgers are stacked by the single, double, and triple patties, and there is even a burger for your dog, the Mutt Burger, that comes plain so your mutt can have some Jerry's lovin' too. If you are watching your caloric intake, then don't get the Burnt Herbie, a deep-fried ham and cheese sandwich. But honestly, you probably should just try it at least once. The fries here are delicious, so definitely get them no matter what. You can also get grilled chicken and fries or chopped steak and fries, which come with cheese and dressing of your choice. We will caution that the ketchup is bound to spill in your car as you dunk your fries into the saucy goodness, so be sure to go prepared with extra napkins.

Jioio's Restaurant, 939 Carbon Rd., Greensburg, PA, 15601; (724) 836-6676; jioios.com; Italian; $. Pizza is always just pizza, right? Wrong. Jioio's Restaurant has created something truly unique with its Original Thin Crust Pizza. This crispy, squared pie is unapologetically sweet and gosh darn amazing. It is any good Greensburger's responsibility as a human to introduce outsiders to its goodness and sit gleefully by as the visitors take their first bites. Sweet sauce. Sweet crust. Savory cheese. The pizza comes in 4, 8, 12, and 30 cuts (if you must share). Jioio's serves other Italian favorites, like pasta and homemade ravioli, with that same sweet sauce. You can dine in at Jioio's in the no-frills space or call in for take out. Jioio's also takes pickup orders online. We know folks who will drive the 35 miles from the 'Burgh for so much as a slice. If you make the trip, order more than necessary. This is one of the best reheated or cold pizzas you will ever encounter.

Kelly O's Diner, 1130 Perry Hwy., Ross Township. Pittsburgh, PA 15237; (412) 364-0473; kellyos.com; Diner; $. Kelly O's Diner shot to fame after its appearance on *Diners, Drive-ins, and Dives* in 2009. Since then it's expanded and opened a second location in the Strip District that welcomes hungry new customers with open arms. Both locations serve equally delicious home-cooked breakfast and lunch fare with a classic diner flair. The breakfast menu at Kelly O's is egg heavy with an abundance of omelets and egg sandwiches. But our favorite items include the pancakes, which are fluffy, slightly sweet, and oozing with butter, and the biscuits and Southern-style sausage gravy. Be sure to add the crispy shredded potatoes with green peppers and onions to your order and thank us later. If you'd rather have lunch, try the turkey potpie soup or the homemade hot meatloaf with mashed potatoes and gravy. Both will warm you up on cold Pittsburgh days. Additional location: Strip District, 100 24th St., Pittsburgh, PA 15222; (412) 232-3447.

The Kitchen on Main, 136 E. Main St., Ligonier, PA 15658; (724) 238-4199; thekitchenonmain.com; New American; $–$$$. The small town of Ligonier, east of Pittsburgh, can be described many ways: adorable, quaint, old-timey. It is time to add another superlative: delicious. The Kitchen on Main, both delicious and adorable, fits in quite nicely to the town's surroundings. This tiny spot boasts a small seating area and a large, open kitchen. Hearty breakfasts are served on Saturday and Sunday, lunch is served Wednesday through Sunday, and dinner is served Wednesday through Saturday. The breakfast menu features a nice selection of benedicts along with classic morning fare. And since the establishment is BYOB, diners are encouraged to build their own Bloody Mary for breakfast. Bring your choice of booze, and The Kitchen on Main will provide you with housemade Bloody Mary mix and fixings. Lunch includes excellently crafted sandwiches and salads, and dinner proves a bit fancier with filets and sea bass and the like. The Kitchen on Main also provides cooking

classes for those of us who are eager to learn about preparing amazing meals.

Kous Kous Cafe, 665 Washington Rd., Mt. Lebanon, Pittsburgh, PA 15228; (412) 563-5687; kouskouscafe.com; Moroccan; $$$. It seems so unfair that the South Hills of Pittsburgh should be home to some of the city's tastiest Mediterranean restaurants, but here we are, folks. Kous Kous Cafe is a tiny place; seriously, it's very small—intimate is perhaps a more apropos term but we digress. It's a family-run Moroccan restaurant that serves food with flair and allows you to BYOB (with a small corkage fee). We love the beet salad, which is mixed with Moroccan spices and gorgonzola cheese; it's a great way to begin your meal. A variety of meats and fish are available, including lamb, duck, beef, chicken, salmon, and sausage. These are combined with fresh vegetables and Moroccan spices like saffron, cilantro, and ginger. Try the beef in plums tanine with almonds for a dish that is a little sweet with a little crunch.

Mineo's Pizza House, 713A Washington Rd., Mt. Lebanon, Pittsburgh, PA 15228; (412) 344-9467; mineospizza.com; Pizza; $. Mineo's is a family-owned pizzeria with two great locations and is a Pittsburgh staple. The Mount Lebanon and Squirrel Hill spots both serve pizza the way pizza should be served—slice by gigantic, cheesy slice. The best way to enjoy Mineo's is by ordering with your face pressed up against the glass counter, watching as your pizza is heated up (or if you're us—two slices) so it's warm and ready to eat. Be sure to work out before heading out to eat at Mineo's, though; they load enough cheese onto their pies that you'll swear you're holding onto an infant or a stack of three *Encyclopedia Britannicas*. They've also got your classic Italian dinners like manicotti, rigatoni, and ziti, and if you want to make it a complete meal, you can top it off with some of Pittsburgh's own Reinhold Ice Cream. Additional location: Squirrel Hill, 2128 Murray Ave., Pittsburgh, PA 15217; (412) 521-9864.

The Original Gab and Eat Restaurant, 1073 Washington Ave., Carnegie, PA 15106; (412) 276-8808; gabneat.com; Breakfast & Lunch; $. Under the Gab and Eat sign, complete with rooster, is a paper on the window that proclaims: "No whining." Eating at this authentic, Pittsburgh gem certainly won't provoke it. The long space has several booths that line a wall full of autographs from Pittsburgh news anchors, local sports heroes (high school included), and other hard-to-determine flourishes. If a booth isn't your style, saddle on up to the counter and watch the line cooks in action. Diner food rules the menu complete with absurdly low prices. It is possible to eat a week's worth of calories here for under $4. The breakfast options are all solid; the pancakes are the size of Allegheny County, and the bacon has the perfect ratio of grease to crispness. The classic burgers will make your heart sing or, at the very least, bleed black and gold along with all of the locals eating beside you.

Police Station Pizza, 1007 Merchant St., Ambridge, PA 15003; (724) 266-3904; Pizza; $. Driving through Merchant Street in Ambridge, you will probably miss this take-out pizza joint. Why? Because the sign outside reads "Original Pizza House." For us locals, we call it Police Station Pizza, due to its proximity to the former police station. Anytime you visit, you will surely encounter a crowd inside and even may have to park a few blocks away. But it's so worth it. A piece of advice before entering this Beaver County landmark is to know the proper way to order. As soon as you step foot through the door, a man from behind the counter will ask you how many slices you want. He won't write it down, but he'll memorize your order, and everyone else's order, with precision. After a few minutes, he'll ask you what you want on them, as he assigns another worker to quickly assemble your order. The pizza here comes cut square and is baked with tomato sauce and a sprinkling of mozzarella cheese. And the toppings, such as pepperoni, crumbled Italian sausage, sweet peppers, and anchovies, are applied cold to the piping hot slices. Be sure to bring cash, because this place kicks it old school. But if you're craving pizza and you only have plastic, its sister location in Oakdale can hook you up: 7235 Steubenville Pike, Oakdale, PA 15071; (412) 788-2227.

Rachel's Roadhouse, 1553 Perry Hwy., Mercer, PA 16137; (724) 748-3193; springfields.com; American; $$$. Rachel's Roadhouse, in the heart of Amish Country, gives patrons a taste of down-home cooking with a few frills and a few surprises. The standout menu item is the New York–style pretzels that come with your choice of dippers. We recommend ordering all three—mustard, nacho cheese, and hot fudge! What?! Trust us. Rachel's is best known for their filet slices sandwich. Order that and you'll be served filet medallions on a garlic croissant topped with mozzarella. There are many accompaniments to the sandwiches, but we recommend the homemade chips, deep-fried and served with a homemade dip. For dinner, you can't go wrong with one of the many varieties of Reubens or carefully crafted sandwiches. We're partial to the Bourbon Street burger because it's on a toasted onion roll, slathered in barbecue sauce, topped with grilled onions and bacon, and finished off with provolone cheese. . Speaking of barbecue, they rub their ribs with a special blend of seasoning, so if you're in the mood for a rack, we say go full and pair it with a pumpkin. Oh, excuse us, we mean sweet potato (but they're HUGE!). Additional location: 100 Fairfield Ln., Butler, PA 16001; (724) 841-0333.

The Sewickley Cafe, 409 Beaver St., Sewickley, PA 15143; (412) 749-0300; sewickley-cafe.com; Neighborhood Cafe; $$$. The Sewickley Cafe is a place where you can take just about anyone to break bread. Take your family for lunch, have a client meeting over a cocktail, and even court a date with dinner in the back garden patio. The Cafe has the feel of an old bar, but the food reflects a much fancier cuisine. Lunch service offers a variety of sandwiches from the gourmet lobster club to the classic grilled cheese.

Complement your order with the truffle french fries because saying "I'll have the truffle french fries as my side" sounds really fancy. During dinner service, the menu completely transforms to include mostly entrees: seafood, pastas, chicken, beef, veal, lamb, and pork. No matter who you go with or when you dine at The Sewickley Cafe, save room for cake. A variety of cakes are on display in the pie case at the entrance. These cakes are stacked so tall, we don't know how they stand up straight.

Sidelines Bar & Grill, 621 Evergreen Ave., Millvale, Pittsburgh, PA 15209; (412) 821-4492; sidelinesbarandgrill.com; Wings; $. Wings. Wings. More wings. They come by the basketful and they are divine. Whether you choose to coat them in garlic parmesan, classic buffalo, or dry seasoning, you'll make the right choice. That's because there isn't a wrong choice on the menu at Sidelines. You'll want to order a side of fries to accompany your wings (because duh, you have to get the wings), and we suggest the dusting of dry ranch sprinkled on top. Dunkers are available in the way of bleu cheese, restaurant ranch (yinz know what we're talking about), and who can forget the celery! We highly recommend you wash all that down with one of the 12 beers on tap. Careful, you may begin to feel at home. And that's okay; just ask to join the beer club if you want to become a regular. Your Monday nights will never be the same. Additional location: 518 Locust Place, Sewickley, PA, 15143; (412) 741-0300.

Sir Pizza, 320 Sewickley Oakmont Rd., Ross Twp., Pittsburgh, PA 15237; (412) 367-1333; sirpizza-pittsburgh.com; Pizza; $. This pizza is one pie you'll want to tip your hat to. Sir Pizza, around since the mid-70s, has been tossing dough that literally has no crust. Not in the traditional crusty pizza sense anyway. Their slogan "Good to the Very Edge" rings true, as the pies are virtually flat with cheese, sauce, and toppings loaded all the way to the very edge. Something else that differentiates Sir Pizza is the way they slice. You won't get square slices or pie slices, but more party-style pieces that are great for nibbling and dipping. Sir Pizza makes a mean sandwich, and for those non-pizza-loving folks (if such folks exist), pasta options also adorn the menu. Though who could turn down the Royal Feast, a pizza loaded with pepperoni, mushrooms, red and green peppers, onions, and sausage? Additional locations: See website.

Smoke Barbeque Taqueria, 225 E. 8th Ave., Homestead, PA 15120; (412) 205-3039; Barbecue; $. Smoke Barbeque Taqueria feels familiar as soon as you walk through the door. Weathered hardwood floor and mismatched tables and chairs; it feels like you stopped by a friend's apartment for dinner. Only we bet your friend can't make a taco like this place can. Smoke combines perfectly smoked meats with hand-made tortillas and a hint of sauce and toppings. The pork taco comes with chunks of pork that easily shred and is lightly sauced with apricot habanero and caramelized onions. The brisket in the brisket taco is thinly sliced and falls apart in your mouth. A fiery spice is added with sautéed onions, hot peppers, and barbecue mustard sauce. Smoke's latest taco combinations are also worth a look. The chicken apple taco comes with bacon, cheddar, and a smoky jalapeño mayo. Breakfast tacos are also available all day long. While tacos are the main attraction at Smoke, we could die happy just eating items from the Snacks and Sides section. Macaroni and cheese is cooked to a creamy, cheesy perfection with roasted garlic, shallots, mascarpone cheese, and sharp white cheddar, and filling up on crispy chips with pico de gallo queso is a perfectly acceptable dinner.

The Supper Club, 101 Ehalt St., Greensburg, PA, 15601; (724) 691-0536; supperclubgreensburg.com; American; $$. The Supper Club is housed in the historic Greensburg train station and is adjacent to where the Amtrak train stops now. It is a beautiful space with soaring ceilings and old-timey transportation charm. The only thing more interesting than the location here is the farm-to-table menus, as the list of local purveyors the restaurant entrusts is truly impressive in length. The Supper Club serves from two menus: Gastropub and Farm-to-Table. From the more casual gastropub fare, do yourself a favor and order the house-made tater tots. These tots are not your normal tots—these beauts harbor mashed potato insides! The result is a surprising twist on a dish found on cafeteria trays across the nation. The pizza here is also quite delicious with topping combos that will elicit a "yes, please!" We like the brie/pear/arugula/balsamic reduction mash-up. The Farm-to-Table menu is more refined than the Gastropub, with offerings like the Jamison Farm lamb, served with **Fede Pasta**'s (p. 159) ricotta gnocchi. The Supper Club also plays host to live music multiple times per week. Call The Supper Club for more details.

Vivo Kitchen, **432 Beaver St., Sewickley, PA 15143; (412) 259-8945; vivokitchen.com; New American; $$$.** Vivo Kitchen, a minimalist space on the main drag in Sewickley, offers modern American fare in a sleek setting, both indoor and outdoor. (It should be noted that the restrooms here are all kinds of lovely. Do yourself a favor and freshen up at least once while you dine—you'll want to check them out!) Like a good number of its contemporaries, Vivo Kitchen has a changing menu due to its affinity for locally sourced ingredients prepared in its flavorful dishes. Try a starter plate like the cheese board with bacon jam or octopus. Meat lovers will rejoice over the variety presented as entrees on the menu, from duck to lamb to elk to lamb. And can we get a "mm hmm" from the bread lovers? Vivo Kitchen serves crusty bread with spiced-up olive oil. Nothing like a little kick-start to the meal!

White Rabbit Cafe and Patisserie, **113 N. Main St., Greensburg, PA 15601; (724) 216-5229; Coffee Shop; $.** Close your eyes and imagine the most perfect coffee shop. Okay, open your eyes and start driving to Greensburg. No need to imagine, because the perfect coffee shop exists, and it is the White Rabbit Cafe and Patisserie. This gem on the main road of town has it all: atmosphere, late hours (for the suburbs), friendly patrons, excellent beverages including locally roasted coffee and a variety of specialty teas, and fresh-baked snacks and desserts. The large space, complete with chandeliers and quirky vintage-inspired prints, has plenty of table and gathering space. This is the place to get lost in a good book, battle a group of friends in checkers, or catch up on your hometown gossip. The hot beverages are beautifully presented with foam designs ALMOST too pretty to sip down. The well-stocked baked goods, crafted from scratch and on-site behind the whimsical "In" and "Out" double doors behind the counter, are presented elegantly and taste divine. Daily bakery specials are highlighted on the Rabbit's social media. The eclectic and inventive treats will wow you online, which will get you offline to indulge. Grab a guy or gal, order up a pastry and some lattes, and settle in for an evening of conversation. Losing track of time will be easy. Leaving this truly perfect neighborhood gathering spot will be hard.

Wild Rosemary Bistro, 1469 Bower Hill Rd., Upper St. Clair, Pittsburgh, PA 15241; (412) 221-1232; wildrosemary.com; Mediterranean; $$$$. It's tough to get a reservation at Wild Rosemary. Like really tough. But trust us, it's worth the sometimes months-long wait. Located at the bottom of windy Bower Hill Road sits the tiny 28-seat restaurant. The inside may seem cramped but as you settle in, it quickly becomes intimate, inviting, and casual. Especially after a glance at the menu, most of which is made in house. And if it isn't, it's made close by. The menu changes every week, but order the signature scallops dish if it's available. It's served with fresh bucatini from **Fede Pasta** (p. 159), crème fraîche, white wine, roasted tomatoes, wilted arugula, and batons of reggiano. It's heaven in a bowl. While waiting for the main course, the kitchen sends out your complimentary starter—ranging from housemade focaccia bread with red pepper jelly to grilled veggies. The kitchen also so kindly sends out a salad to complement your main course. Arugula is lightly dressed with white balsamic vinaigrette, salt, pepper, and a sprinkle of sugar. Be sure to get dessert even if you have to share it. It's not something you want to miss. Don't forget your favorite bottle of wine. Wild Rosemary is BYOB.

Willow, 634 Camp Horne Rd., Ohio Twp., Pittsburgh, PA 15237; (412) 847-1007; willowpgh.com; American, $$. A special occasion calls for a night out on the town, right? Ditch the city and head to the suburbs to Willow. It boasts 9 different dining rooms including a patio, private dining room for parties, and a communal dining room for large celebrations. When we celebrate at Willow, we go all out and order the filet mignon and a glass of Shiraz, and we always stick around for an espresso and a slice of the decadent cheesecake. Though the menu often changes seasonally, some menu staples don't change with the weather. Some of our favorites include the signature crab cakes and the cranberry chicken, slow-roasted chicken breasts coated in an almond and corn flake mixture and served with a maple-cranberry reduction. We think we'll be celebrating at Willow the moment we see this book for sale. Whether your visit will be for a celebratory meal, like ours, or a casual lunch, we know you won't be disappointed.

Wings, Suds & Spuds, 8806 University Blvd., Coraopolis, PA 15108; (412) 264-1866; wingssudsandspuds.com; Wings; $–$$. So you flew into Pittsburgh International Airport and are dying for something to eat? Wings, perhaps? Before you make your way into the city, swing by Wings, Suds & Spuds in Moon Township for just that: wings, suds (beer), and spuds (curly fries or chips). All three of these items are delicious in our book. The wings come in a variety of wet sauces and dry seasonings and can be ordered either small or large. If you are really hungry and think you can put away a large order, hold off because you must order the half pound curly fries here. We typically top our fries with cheese and ranch dressing. And to wash both of these down, beer of course. Besides wings, suds, and spuds, this neighborhood (dive-ish) bar has salads, sandwiches, chicken fingers, burgers, and other bar-food favorites that will please both wing lovers and non-wing lovers alike.

Specialty Stores, Markets & Producers

DeLallo Italian Marketplace, 6390 Rt. 30, Jeannette, PA 15644; (724) 523-6577; delallo.com. Started in 1954 by George and Madeline DeLallo, DeLallo Italian Marketplace specializes in authentic Italian food and products. Your journey through an Italian heaven starts as soon as you walk through the door. Peppers, greens, onions, tomatoes, plums, apples, and more line the walls as you weave your way into the heart of the store. Once you make your way through the vibrant rainbow of produce, head to the 40-foot olive and antipasti bar. There you can find olives in all shapes, colors, and sizes, and antipasti favorites like hot Italian garden mix, artichokes, and roasted red peppers. The next showstopper is the extensive cheese and deli selections, but don't be intimidated by the sheer volume of choices. The friendly staff will answer questions and offer up samples for testing. Not feeling inspired by your surroundings? Check out the prepared food section. Choose from cold salads and food that needs to be warmed like lasagna and stuffed peppers. Finish your DeLallo's trip with a decadent pastry or loaf of bread at the bakery.

Fresh From the Farm Juices, 11883 Perry Hwy., Wexford, PA, 15090; (412) 224-2650; freshfarmjuices.com. Feeling gross after binge-eating cheeseburgers? Need some veggies in your diet? Look no further than Fresh From the Farm Juices. Just by walking in this place, you feel healthier. Owner Ankit Goyal grew up juicing. From a young age, his mother would cold press juice for the family from local, organic fruits and vegetables, oftentimes coming from the garden his father planted. He is carrying on the family tradition by sourcing produce from local farms and producing a variety of cold-pressed juices for daily consumption, as well as juice cleanses for 2, 4, or 6 days. Some signature juices include the "Black and Yellow," a blend of pineapples, blackberries, oranges, and lavender, and the "Limey Green," a combination of kale, spinach, carrots, apples, lime, and cilantro. Each 12-ounce bottle of "Limey Green" contains 3 pounds of fresh produce and will put all those ill-tasting green juices to shame. Besides juice, Ankit is also serving up freshly made salads with all those local organic greens. Be sure to swing by when you are in the neighborhood. You never know what juice concoction Ankit is pressing up.

Giant Eagle Market District, 100 Settlers Ridge Center Dr., Robinson Twp., Pittsburgh, PA 15205; (412) 788-5392; market district.com. Literally anything you need to make a meal, from the produce to the plates, you can buy at the Giant Eagle Market District store in Robinson Township. This store is a beefed-up version of the regular grocery store and an adult food enthusiast's Disneyland. It has a cafe, complete with hot and cold food bars, coffee and juice bar, sushi station, crepe station, and other freshly prepared foods. You can get these foods to go or eat in the second-floor restaurant area. In addition to the regular grocery items, this Market District has a housewares store, charcuterie, sweets shop with house-made chocolates and gelato, and olive oil bar. In the fresh produce marketplace, the Market District grows its own herbs and lettuce in a hydroponic garden. If you don't know how to cook, you can learn here in the Cooking School. You can also buy beer here to dine in or take out. Remember: No drinking and buggy driving. Additional locations: See website.

Jamison Farm, 171 Jamison Ln., Latrobe, PA 15650; (800) 237-5262; jamisonfarm.com. All of the little lambs are primed for the eating at Jamison Farm in Latrobe. Yes, Pittsburgh's neighbors to the southeast, in the rolling hills of the Laurel Highlands, produce some of the world's best lamb. The Jamison family farm truly resembles a postcard, with sheep roaming the fields of the Westmoreland County countryside and lovely barns nestled into the landscape. Watching the sheep get corralled by the resident sheep dogs transports you miles away from the big city, both in body and mind. The farm prides itself on keeping the animals antibiotic- and hormone-free. The attention to care and detail is evident in the meat. Lamb can be ordered online, or you can place an order and pick it up at the farm. This meat is not inexpensive, but you get what you pay for. And quality is number one at Jamison.

McGinnis Sisters Special Food Stores, 700 Adams Shoppes, Rte. 228 and Adams Ridge Blvd., Mars, PA 16046; (724) 779-1212; mcginnis-sisters.com. Back in the day, people went to their local grocery stores almost daily and stocked up on fresh bread, fresh meat, and fresh produce for the day's meals. A place reminiscent of the grocery stories of years past is McGinnis Sisters Special Food Stores, a local chain of three family-owned grocery stores. The Mars location is located in a tiny strip mall off a busy highway. If you can make it through the traffic and red lights, it is worth the hassle. The meats are all sold fresh to order, as is the seafood. The produce is bright and colorful, and the bakery is filled with muffins, breads, and other baked goods. The aisles are tiny and small, so try not to bump your cart into a stranger. If you are on the go, you can pick up a meal from the prepackaged meal section or dine in at the in-store cafe. The cafe menu consists of pizzas, burgers, paninis, and fish sandwiches, dinners, and tacos. Additional locations: See website.

Sarris Candies, 511 Adams Ave., Canonsburg, PA 15317; (724) 745-4042; sarriscandies.com. Pittsburgh icon Frank Sarris opened a small candy shop in 1963 in the heart of Canonsburg. Twenty years later, he opened a larger shop complete with an ice cream parlor that drew in crowds from all over the city. You seem to step through a time portal when you walk in the door. If you didn't know any better, you'd swear you walked into a soda fountain wearing Hush Puppies and humming "Mr. Sandman." Alas, it's present day, but the ambiance of Sarris Candies hasn't changed a bit. You can take in the bright colors of the ice cream toppings and almost taste the chocolate in the air as you ponder which delicate candies will grace your lips. Once you've created your own box of chocolates (lift the lid on ours and you'll find the famous chocolate-covered pretzels, coconut clusters, and dark chocolate pecanettes), you can enjoy a scoop of homemade ice cream topped with a milk chocolate hardcap. We dare you not to smile while you're there—and be warned, you'll be jitterbugging right out the door.

Soergel Orchards, 2573 Brandt School Rd., Wexford, PA 15090; (724) 935-1743; soergels.com. Just 20 minutes north of Downtown lies Soergel Orchards. Soergel's was started in the 1850s as an apple orchard by German-immigrant John Conrad Soergel and has expanded since to include much more than apples, though these are still the farm's namesake and a must-purchase along with the apple cider. When you visit Soergel's, the first place you will want to stop by is the Market, which is home to a bakery turning out delicious pies and pastries; a small deli providing take-home meats and cheeses as well as made-to-order sandwiches; a fresh produce section filled with colorful fruits and vegetables; gourmet grocery items; and a wine shop, which sells wines from Arrowhead Wines of North East, Pennsylvania (near Erie). If food allergies or healthy eating is of concern, visit Naturally

Soergel's, which specializes in allergen-free and gluten-free products. In addition to the Market and Naturally Soergel's, Soergel's has a home and garden center, a Gift Barn carrying a variety of unique gift items from body scrubs to stationery, and an Amish Furniture shop. If you are looking for a quick getaway from the urban city, head north to Soergel's to enjoy the fresh air.

Yetter's Candies, 504 Grant Ave., Millvale, Pittsburgh, PA 15209; (412) 821-1387; yetterscandies.com. A trip back in time: that's where you're going when you step into Yetter's Candies in Millvalle. The tiny shop on Grant Avenue boasts homemade candies and chocolates with sweet offerings for every major holiday including solid milk, dark, and white chocolate bunnies at Easter. Among the other treats include dipped potato chips, marshmallows, and cookies. There are some throwback items in stock as well. Flying Saucers anyone? Stock up on your goodies and then head to the counter and take a seat on one of the retro stools. Round, chrome, and wrapped in red sparkly vinyl. Order up a milk shake (pro tip: Order a strawberry shake with their strawberry ice cream, it has real berries!) to sip on, just like you're in a soda fountain. Or go with a single scoop in a glass dish and spoon it out until you hear the wonderful sound of finished! If savory is more your style, there is a menu loaded with sandwiches to satisfy you.

Bakeries

Let's talk about fresh-baked confections!

Pittsburgh holds the world record for most bridges (we have 446 in the city proper; take that Venice, Italy!). Pittsburgh also has a ridiculous number of bakeries. As our gift to you, we ate hundreds of doughnuts, cookies, cakes, brownies, breads, and croissants to narrow down your bakery decisions to a select few. You're welcome. The bakeries highlighted on the next few pages are the cream of the crop, the icons, the sweetest, and the most savory.

Prepare yourself for awesome. If you work through the list, you will need to run all 446 'Burgh bridges to cancel out the calories. Worth it.

Arcade Bakery & Cafe, 400 5th Ave., Downtown, Pittsburgh, PA 15222; (412) 232-2384. Arcade Bakery & Cafe: bar none the best bakery Downtown. A bold assertion backed by excellent pastries. The cakes? Delightful. The cookies? Superb. The ANYTHING? Outstanding. This nondescript bakery inside of a department store is an absolute surprise. So joy of joys, you can visit Macy's for a pair of pants AND an on-point pastry. A one-stop shop! Expert tip: Eat the pastry after you try on those pants. When you walk inside Arcade, which is on the arcade level of the store, your eyes will land on cases of decadent choices. The prices here are very fair, borderline low, giving you the ability to fill up a box of goodness with less guilt (at least in regard to your wallet). First things first, buy a cake gem. A cake gem is chocolate cake filled with a light and airy buttercream frosting and coated with a chocolate layer.

Try to resist the whimsical character cookies and cakes; it will be impossible. Finally, take an outsize cookie for the road. The thumbprints are monsters of the most delicious variety. Arcade also serves lunch options including pasta salads and chicken salad sandwiches. But we encourage cookie salads and cakewiches.

Big Daddy's Donuts, 90 Noble Ave., Crafton, Pittsburgh, PA 15205; (412) 921-4441. Across the street from the Crafton Volunteer Fire Department is Big Daddy's Donuts, open overnight from 10 p.m. to 3 p.m. 7 days a week. The doughnuts are fresh, large, and definitely don't hold back with the toppings. One of the standouts on the menu is the Crafton Angel, a yeast doughnut filled to capacity with white cream and dusted heavily in powdered sugar. Be sure to grab napkins because wherever you eat this sweet treat, powdered sugar is going to be everywhere . . . for days. A unique cream-filled doughnut is the Elvis, stuffed with a sweet banana cream and iced in a sinfully sugary peanut butter icing. The King would be proud of this one. Other standout favorites include a toasted coconut doughnut and a chocolate cake doughnut iced with white cream and topped with crushed Oreo crumbles. Besides all of these sugary sweet doughnuts, Big Daddy's Donuts can satisfy your savory craving with one of its breakfast sandwiches. Order one and sit at the diner counter or take it to go. Whichever you prefer, just remember this place only accepts cash.

Boldy's Homemade Goodies/Freedom Farms Donut Shop, 663 Pittsburgh Rd., Butler, PA 16002; (724) 586-5567; freedomfarmspa.com. Call it Boldy's, call it Freedom Farms Donut Shop, call it breakfast. Either way, it's darn good. For years, the tiny shop in Butler County ran under the name Boldy's Homemade Goodies before being bought and transformed into Freedom Farms Donut Shop.

Nancy B's Bakery

Nancy B's has the best chocolate chip cookies in Pittsburgh. This isn't an opinion. This is fact. Gooey, enormous, and addicting, these bad boys are on an entirely different level than any other cookie in town. The crunchy exterior of the cookie is balanced perfectly with a baked-JUST-enough center that is chewy and soft. There is a hint of something—maybe peanut butter?—that sets the whole confection off.

Nancy B's, the unassuming bakery tucked away in Homestead that has churned out these chocolate chip delights for over 30 years, is a no-frills spot. Once you navigate to the location, you may ask yourself, "Is this it?" A sign outside heralds your arrival, but the bakery has no street presence. No windows. Just a door. Open that door! You will be smacked in the face with the heavenly aroma of freshly baked goodies. If you happen to be lucky enough to arrive when the chocolate chip variety is fresh out of the oven, you better have some milk waiting at home! You are going to want to down those babies!

Nancy B's is one of those rare places that doesn't lean on design-flare, or cutesy packaging. This bakery survives purely on the quality of its products. Honest to goodness, delicious baked goods are all Nancy B's needs, and this place delivers. Along with the aforementioned amazingness that is the chocolate chip, Nancy B's also bakes up a variety of other stellar cookies. The snickerdoodles will rock your world. The peanut butters will charm your pants off. There is no wrong choice here. Actually, the wrong choice would be to say, "No thank you. I don't need any cookies." You definitely need Nancy B's cookies.

When you exit Nancy B's, make sure to look toward the river. The old smokestacks from the Homestead steel mill pop up from behind the buildings across the street. It is fitting that this is the cityscape in which Nancy B's resides. Steel will always be in the fabric of Pittsburgh's people. Places like Nancy B's, a spot that has produced quality food for decades, will always play a part in defining the city's palate.

Nancy B's is cash only and located at 415 W. 7th Ave., West Homestead, PA 15120; (412) 462-6222; nancybsbakery.com.

The folks who run Freedom Farms have not only maintained its delicious integrity, they've actually enhanced it. You have to arrive early to see the racks packed full of carby, circular treats in all their glory. They open at 5 a.m., so fill up the travel mug and settle in for a scenic drive. The thought of freshly baked pastries will give you the fuel to keep going. Once there, dive into the Apple Fritter or go old-fashioned and get a plain cake to dunk in your coffee. The locals will be lining up, so don't be shy, scoot right up to the counter and make friends.

BreadWorks Bakery, 2110 Brighton Rd., Perry South, Pittsburgh, PA 15212; (412) 231-7555; breadworkspgh.com. If you are dining out in one of the city's restaurants and fall in love with the bread that is included in the bread basket, it is likely that it came from BreadWorks Bakery if it wasn't made in house. This well-known Pittsburgh bread company supplies many local restaurants and specialty stores with its products, and Pittsburghers buy them like hotcakes. If you can't find these products in one of the specialty markets like at the **Pennsylvania Macaroni Company** in the Strip (p. 53)—they sell out fast—you can still carb up by heading to the retail location housed within the bakery. You can purchase rolls, loaves, and buns straight from the oven 7 days a week. Be sure to pick up a loaf of the delicious focaccia bread that serves as a perfect base for homemade pizza. Hopefully the bread you purchase makes it back to your house or other intended location, because once your car starts to smell like a bakery, you may find yourself tearing off pieces of goodness until just an empty white bag is left.

Eadie's Market & Catering, BNY Mellon, 500 Grant St., Downtown, Pittsburgh, PA 15219; (412) 391-3993; restaurantcatering systems.com/eadiesmarket. This breakfast and lunch take-out spot has some appetizing soups, salads, and sandwiches, but here it's all about the cakes. Coconut cream cake, chocolate chip cheesecake, funfetti cake, orange creamsicle cake, German chocolate cake, carrot cake, and the list goes on, and on, and on. Sheet cakes, cupcakes, cookie cakes, and tiered round cakes can all be ordered for special occasions, or you can swing by and pick up a slice from the back cooler. In addition to cakes, Eadie's is baking up monstrous chocolate chip, peanut butter, and gingersnap cookies; strawberry tarts; pies; brownies; and other pastries. If you swing by Eadie's on your way into the office, be sure to pick up one of the breakfast sandwiches, such as the bacon, egg, and cheese on a croissant roll, or the egg, capicola, and cheese served on grilled Texas toast. And don't forget a piece of cake. Whether you stop by for breakfast or lunch, be sure to get the cake.

Food Glorious Food, 5906 Bryant St., Highland Park, Pittsburgh, PA 15206; (412) 363-5330. Baked goods, glorious baked goods! The bakery that used to be a secret is a secret no more: Food Glorious Food is good stuff. This small shop in Highland Park, which operated as a cooking school and still offers classes and culinary trips, at one point in time had very limited bakery hours. The doors would open, the store would sell out, the doors would close. If you were in the know, you were in for a treat. Word has spread that this place is no joke, and thankfully, more bakery hours were added. The tempting selection of decadent delicacies available at the shop, including cakes, pies, biscuits, and savory quiches, is totally beyond. Try the White Lily Cake, which is the most coveted of the Food Glorious Food specialties. This delicate confection is layers of vanilla cake, mousse, and fresh raspberries. If you can't wait to eat the heavenly purchases you made, you can enjoy your selections inside at several small tables at the front of the store. This bakery would also be the perfect place for a wedding cake or other special occasion cakes, like an "It is Wednesday, I want a special cake day." Whatever you're reason, get to Food Glorious Food soon!

Gaby et Jules, 5837 Forbes Ave., Squirrel Hill, Pittsburgh, PA 15217; (412) 682-1966; gabyetjules.com. The product of **Paris 66** (p. 120), Gaby et Jules became a staple in Squirrel Hill and is a must-stop pastry shop. Simply and beautifully decorated, with striking red lacquer accents, the French patisserie offers a touch of the Parisian gourmet to Pittsburghers. Known for the seemingly endless flavors of perfectly crafted macrons, from pistachio to earl grey, sea salt caramel to passionfruit and fan favorite almond, Gaby et Jules also serves almost-too-good-to-eat cakes and mousses, decadent chocolates, and fresh fruit tarts. As you walk along the jewelry-like glass cases housing and showing off the sugary gems, the French-speaking servers help you decide which delicacies to take home. And just as you see the end of the cases, baskets of fresh baked baguettes and croissants come into view, adding just a little more weight to your shopping bag.

Gluuteny, 1923 Murray Ave., Squirrel Hill, Pittsburgh, PA 15217; (412) 521-4890; gluuteny.com. Gluuteny looks a lot like other bakeries you may have visited. It has a classic black-and-white-checkered floor, it smells like Grandma's kitchen and has a display case full of mouthwatering sweet and savory treats. The difference: Everything inside is gluten- and dairy-free. The menu at Gluuteny features cupcakes, cookies, brownies, tarts, whoopee pies, and breads. A must-purchase is the pumpkin pound cake. It's moist, delicately soft, and smells like a perfect fall day with hints of pumpkin and allspice. If you're more of a chocolate fan, we suggest a brownie or chocolate chip cookie. It's so rich we bet you won't even know it's gluten- and dairy-free. Gluuteny also offers special event and holiday cakes and cookies so you can offer your someone special something special they can enjoy. Want to know one of the best parts about Gluuteny (besides everything it bakes, of course)? It ships its dry baking mixes anywhere in the world. So even when you're far away, you can have a little bit of gluten- and dairy-free Pittsburgh with you.

Jean-Marc Chatellier's French Bakery, 213 North Ave., Millvale, Pittsburgh, PA 15209; (412) 821-8533; jeanmarcchatellier .com. Get out your passport, because Jean-Marc Chatellier's French Bakery will send you on a trip to France through the sheer power of tastiness. The baker, Jean-Marc, opened the space in 1992. Since that time, the Bakery has become renowned in the 'Burgh for its pastries and for its incomparable French macarons. If you haven't had a French macaron in your lifetime, get to Jean-Marc's immediately. If you have had a French macaron in your lifetime, get to Jean-Marc's immediately. These light, almond-based treasures are phenomenal. We are always partial to chocolate, but other creative flavors like salted caramel and peanut butter and jelly are refreshing twists. Brightly colored, these stunning macarons would be perfect presents for the sweet tooth in your life. Other tempting treats include croissants (again, we like ours filled with chocolate), cakes, cookies, and pies. The short trip to Millvale for a visit will be worth it no matter what fills your bakery boxes. Traveling never tasted so good.

Kretchmar's Bakery, 664 3rd St., Beaver, PA 15009; (724) 774-2324; kbakery.com. Anything you receive in a brown- and yellow-striped bag from Kretchmar's Bakery is going to be delectable. But the decorative cakes are really where it's at. The yellow cake batter has a hint of vanilla and lemon flavoring and makes the perfect base for the rich and fudgy chocolate icing. If you're looking for something a little lighter, order a cake made with the white almond cake batter, raspberry filling, and fluffy whipped cream icing. Besides cakes, cookies, breads, doughnuts, pies, tortes, an array of other pastries fill the display cases. You can't ever go wrong with the iced cut-out star cookies or the peanut butter bars. Though most of their bread comes from **BreadWorks Bakery** (p. 181), a few breads are made in-house. Slices of the cobblestone bread make a pretty fine toast in the mornings and the butterflake rolls, once warmed up in the oven for a few minutes, make the perfect accompaniment to any holiday meal. Kretchmar's accepts debit and credit card purchases, but if you pay with cash, you will receive a 3 percent discount. A definite treat for purchasing some sweet treats.

La Gourmandine Bakery and Pastry Shop, 4605 Butler St., Lawrenceville, Pittsburgh, PA 15201; (412) 682-2210; lagourmandine bakery.com.
La Gourmandine's husband-and-wife owner team of Fabien and Lisanne Moreau both hail from France; we are sure glad they moved to Pittsburgh and brought the baked goods with them! La Gourmandine offers French pastries that are visually stunning and absurdly delicious. You will want to order one of everything just to stare at each delicate confection for longer-than-appropriate amounts of time. And your schedule has been cleared to do so, as there is no longer a need to wander the streets searching for the perfect croissant—it is right here. While it is hard to pick favorites at this petit bakery, the *eclairs au chocolat* and *tarte aux frambroises* border on the divine. Stop by for lunch and order up a sandwich on a baguette or a helping of quiche. The handwritten chalkboards on the exposed-brick wall and baskets of bread behind the bakery glass all make for a charming scene. In warm weather, small tables appear out front on the sidewalk, adding to this Lawrenceville spot's certain *je ne sais quoi.*

Lincoln Bakery, 543 Lincoln Ave., Bellevue, PA 15202; (412) 766-0954.
Lincoln Bakery of Bellevue has been treating residents to deliciousness since 1945. This tasty spot is known for its holiday and theme cakes. The over-the-top cake decorations lure people in, and the airy frosting hooks 'em for life. The cake masters here could surely create whatever your heart desires. Maybe this Thanksgiving, try a cake turkey instead of a real one. You know, just giving the family something to be truly thankful for. Lincoln Bakery is well stocked in other amazing sweets as well. Try one of the many flavors of cheesecake (you

BETTER-MAID DONUT CO.

Once you find the Better-Maid Donut Co., you know you have found a legend. In perhaps the most random location for a successful doughnut shop, or a store of any kind, Better-Maid's pink building sits on a curve of a hilly road that leads to residential neighborhoods. A small, beat-up sign announces "fresh donuts." If you didn't know that Better-Maid crafted excellent doughnuts, you might turn around. Keep on course. You know better. You know that Better-Maid has the best doughnuts in town. Maybe the state. Maybe the country. Perhaps the WORLD.

The doughnuts are crispy on the outside, fluffy on the inside. Science.

Better-Maid can sell out of doughnuts fast, so we suggest calling ahead to make sure you won't be making the journey in vain. Once the doughnuts are gone, the locks are clicked. Don't be that person on the side of Steuben Street crying into the wind, locked out of treats. No one wants to see a grown person sob over doughnuts, even though we would all be feeling your pain.

Better-Maid is cash only. Located in Crafton at 1178 Steuben St., Pittsburgh, PA 15220; (412) 921-9526.

can score individual servings here, so try them all), or pick up a loaf of bread from the bread racks near the counter. If you are a fan of the simple things in life, you, like us, will be enthralled by the crazy devices that hang from the ceiling and dispense string to wrap up your baked good boxes. You will be taken by the simple goodness of your Lincoln treats, too!

Mac's Donut Shop, **2698 Brodhead Rd., Aliquippa, PA, 15001; (724) 375-6776.** The smell of fried doughnuts has been filling the

Aliquippa air since 1959. This old-timey doughnut shop opens early—we're talking 4 a.m. early every day of the week. But the days you want to go are Friday, Saturday, and Sunday. On these days, hot doughnuts fresh from the fryer are served, along with other Mac's specialties. Walking through the front door and viewing the cases and cases of doughnuts can be overwhelming, so we recommend getting at least a dozen. You can never go wrong with a cake doughnut topped with chocolate icing, a sugary-dusted jelly-filled doughnut, or any doughnut topped with sprinkles. Honestly. Besides these standard doughnuts, Mac's also offers up a specialty doughnut of the day, such as a s'mores doughnut: a vanilla cake doughnut, topped with chocolate frosting, white cream, and sprinkled with crushed-up graham cracker pieces. Be sure to follow Mac's on Facebook to be in the know. And there's more than just doughnuts here: Mac's is baking up variety of pastries, cupcakes, and cookies, and nutrolls during the Christmas holiday.

Mancini's Bread Company, 1717 Penn Ave., Strip District, Pittsburgh, PA 15222; (412) 765-3545; mancinisbakery.com. It's all about the fresh, crusty bread at Mancini's Bread Company. We're talkin' Tuscan, Italian, multigrain, baguettes, rolls, buns, loaves, and more! Upon entering the door, you can smell the aromatics of the fresh bread baking. But if that doesn't draw you in, then the employees hand-making pepperoni rolls in the front of the store definitely will. Jam-packed with pepperoni and cheese, these rolls are served hot with or without sauce and are a definite must on your Strip shopping list. Buy them to take home or buy one to eat as you explore the other specialty shops in the Strip. Other gourmet goods sold at Mancini's include homemade pizza sauce, olive oil, bread crumbs, and bruschetta spread, which all make the perfect companion to its breads. If you head out of the city, be sure to check out the Bakery's home in McKees Rocks, which is open 24 hours a day, 7 days a week. Additional locations:

Downtown, 440 Market St., Pittsburgh, PA 15222; (412) 281-8116; and 601 Mancini Way, McKees Rocks, PA 15136; (412) 331-2291.

Mediterra Bakehouse, 801 Parkway View Dr., Robinson Township, Pittsburgh, PA 15205; (412) 490-9130; mediterrabakehouse .com. Finding this place can be difficult, but once you do you will be grateful: grateful for discovering some of the best-baked bread around town. Mediterra Bakehouse is located in the Parkway West Business Park in building 8. Inside the bread baking warehouse, there's a small room dedicated to retails sales and filled with shelves of freshly baked loaves, baskets filled to the rims with rolls, and a handful of pastries such as scones, cookies, and muffins. One of the signature breads you should definitely try is the Mt. Athos Fire Bread. The round loaf has an almost burnt, dark brown exterior, with a dense, sourdough interior. You may wonder why we are telling you to buy almost burnt bread. But, the bread is baked this way on purpose. A darker crust allows for a sweeter, nuttier taste that balances out the taste of the sourdough. It is the perfect accompaniment to a rich and hearty tomato soup or simply dunked in olive oil. In addition to selling out of the warehouse, Mediterra Bakehouse breads can be found at **Giant Eagle Market District** (p. 174), **Shadyside Market** (p. 147), and in a variety of other stores.

Oakmont Bakery, 531 Allegheny Ave., Oakmont, PA 15139; (412) 826-1606; oakmontbakery.com. The Oakmont Bakery is, not surprisingly, located in the town of Oakmont. About a 20-minute drive from Pittsburgh, by way of Allegheny River Boulevard, Oakmont Bakery should lay claim to the title "most likely to inspire joy-induced tears through cookie eating." Sweet, sweet sugar-filled tears. We think Oakmont Bakery is the producer of the best sugar cookies in the region (if the region includes all of North America and parts of Latin America, as well). Other gold-standard treats include the butter stars (soft butter cookies with chocolate frosting) and the variety of rich cakes. Breads, pepperoni rolls, and doughnuts also make a strong showing. Oakmont Bakery has been serving folks since 1988. It is an impressively large space with an overwhelming selection of baked goods under a long, L-shaped glass case. There is a second building across the parking lot where one can assume all the baking magic happens, making the Oakmont Bakery more like a compound of deliciousness. Tables are provided inside the bakery and outside, in nice weather, for eager snackers.

Oram's Donut Shop, 1406 7th Ave., Beaver Falls, PA 15010; (724) 846-1504; orams.com. Old-fashioned glazed doughnuts are the name of Oram's game up in Beaver Falls. It's been the name of the bakery game since 1938, when William and Lillian Oram moved to the Falls and started baking up their delicious fried treats. The most famous and most delightful doughnut on the menu is the signature cinnamon roll. This breakfast must-have is easily twice the size of any cinnamon roll we've ever encountered. They are a favorite of locals and out-of-towners alike, so much that they often sell out early morning. It's best to get a head start on your day if you'd like to try one of Oram's cinnamon rolls. We may be partial to the cinnamon rolls, but we will not turn away a black raspberry-filled doughnut sprinkled with powdered sugar, nor will we blink an eye before devouring a coconut-coated specialty doughnut. Get there early, folks, and if you run into the four of us, we'll happily wave as we stand hungrily over our box of dozen.

Potomac Bakery, 1419 Potomac Ave., Dormont, Pittsburgh, PA 15216; (412) 531-5066; potomacbakery.weebly.com. Looking for a soft cinnamon roll the size of a county? Potomac Bakery has you covered. This spot for sweetness has been cranking out the goods in the center of Dormont since 1927. Along with these cinnamon delights, Potomac has plenty to offer from breakfast pastries, breads, pies, and a long list of specialty cakes. You can't go wrong here, but the doughnuts are a standout as are the delicate petit fours, along with the aforementioned cinnamon rolls. The cake doughnuts are fresh and don't leave you with that "ugh, I just ate a doughnut" feeling. The petit fours are bite-size, moist cakes that come in chocolate or vanilla, dotted with a tiny flower. Like all of the treats at Potomac, they almost look too good to eat. Almost. Additional location: Mount Lebanon, 689 Washington Rd., Pittsburgh, PA 15228; (412) 531-5067.

Prantl's Bakery, 5525 Walnut St., Shadyside, Pittsburgh, PA 15232; (412) 621-2092; prantlsbakery.com. If Pittsburgh had an official dessert, it would be Prantl's burnt almond torte. Just like a luxury purse, there are knockoffs out there. But don't give in to them. In Pittsburgh you must get a burnt almond torte from Prantl's. Plain and simple. You may ask, "What is a burnt almond torte?" Well, it is two layers of yellow sponge cake filled with custard, iced with buttercream, and covered in toasted almonds. The torte is so popular that it can be ordered online and shipped all over the country. Prantl's has been a Pittsburgh institution for over 100 years and bakes a wide variety of goods, ranging from breads, rolls, and doughnuts to cupcakes, cookies, and brownies. You can also special order cakes and have a Prantl's cake made for your wedding. Honestly, everything sold at Prantl's is excellent and enjoyable with your morning cup of coffee. Trust us. Additional location: Downtown, 438 Market St., Pittsburgh, PA 15222; (412) 471-6861.

Priory Fine Pastries, 528 E. Ohio St., East Allegheny, Pittsburgh, PA 15212; (412) 321-7270; prioryfinepastries.com. Priory Fine Pastries is announced on East Ohio Street with a colorful wooden sign jutting out into the Northside air. The cheerful shop is owned and operated by the Graf family, who run the nearby Priory Hotel and Pittsburgh's Grand Hall. The bakery occupies the site of the first D.L.

Clark Candy Company (think Clark bars and the like). The history here is fascinating, but it takes a backseat to the current confection magic. You may enter the bakery to buy cookies or cupcakes, but you should probably eat a doughnut while you are here too. Doughnuts that are as fresh as the Priory's are uncommon, and it is always breakfast somewhere, right? Fill up the rest of your bakery box with any combination of treats—they are really all delicious. Some suggestions if you get overwhelmed while pondering your sugar high: the burnt almond torte cupcake (truly moist yellow cake with an airy cream frosting), the chocolate crackle cookie, and the lady locks (as close to a grandma-made cookie as you can get).

Vanilla Pastry Studio, 1130 S. Braddock Ave., Swissvale, PA 15218; (412) 242-9820; vanillapastry.com. CUPCAKES! You'll feel like shouting with joy too after trying a cupcake from Vanilla. Filled with bright, cheerful colors and cute nooks to enjoy your sweets, Vanilla Pastry Studio is more chic boutique than traditional bakery inside. The display case is filled with treats just like Mom made, only a little less lopsided. Once you get past the intoxicating smells, it's time to get down to business and choose your cupcake. The cake is moist, and the buttercream or chocolate fudge icing they're topped with won't send you into a sugar coma. They're also just the right size to keep you craving more. The cupcake list varies depending on the day, but if the chocolate/peanut butter, vanilla/dulce de leche, or mango-passionfruit is available, try one, or two. Vanilla Pastry does specialize in other sugary confections like lollys (dessert on a stick), whimsical custom cakes, and wedding cakes as well as decadent goodies like brownies, cookies, and whoopee pies. You can even use the space upstairs to host your next party complete with cupcake decorating lessons.

Local Drink Scene

Pittsburghers love to eat, but Pittsburghers also love to drink. Maybe we are always thirsty because we are surrounded by water? Or we get inspired to wet our whistles by the lovely Pittsburgh rain?

Regardless, 'Burghers enjoy beverages with some kick. Luckily, craft breweries, wineries, and distilleries have been moving into town, and we are happy to have them as neighbors. We won't ask to borrow a cup of sugar, but we will ask for a growler fill-up.

Arsenal Cider House & Wine Cellar, Inc., 300 39th St., Lawrenceville, Pittsburgh, PA 15201; (412) 260-6968; arsenalcider house.com. Arsenal Cider House in Lawrenceville is dedicated to producing hard cider, mead, and wine coolers. If Arsenal feels like a home, well, it is; Owners Michelle and Bill Larkin live upstairs in this repurposed house. What was once the Larkins' living room, dining room, and kitchen is now the Civil War–themed taproom. Bill brews in the basement. Using the local Soergel Orchards apple cider as a base, each brew has a distinct twist. Offerings rotate, with notes of blueberry to cinnamon to sour cherry, among others, popping up throughout the year. The names assigned to the drinks are as unique as their taste. The ciders categorized as "Bone Dry" are named after Civil War military terms (think picket and pioneer). All the other thirst quenchers are named after local Civil War servicemen. Always on tap, the Fighting Elleck

Hard Apple Cider is a dry, crisp, and refreshing cider, which shares the nickname of Civil War General Alexander Hays. Purchase a 1-liter growler to fill with your pick of "Daily Rations" and included is a Civil War title of your very own.

Boyd & Blair Potato Vodka, 1101 William Flynn Hwy., Glenshaw, PA 15116; (412) 486-8666; boydandblair.com. Vodka made from locally grown potatoes? Sounds crazy but it's happening in Pittsburgh, and the world has taken notice. Boyd & Blair Potato Vodka was ranked #22 best liquor in the world (out of 120 spirits) according to F. Paul Pacult's Spirit Journal in June 2013. And it was the highest-ranking vodka on the list! Boyd & Blair Potato Vodka was started by Prentiss Orr and Barry Young of Pennsylvania Pure Distilleries in August 2008 and named after inspirational figures in each of their lives. The name Boyd comes from Young's father-in-law, James Boyd Rafferty, and Blair is the surname of Orr's great-grandfather, Dr. William Blair. The potato vodka is currently sold in Pennsylvania state liquor stores, as well as in other states in the United States and internationally in Canada and Singapore. If you don't want to purchase an entire bottle while you are here (though you may be persuaded after a few Boyd & Blair cocktails), many local restaurants craft cocktails centered around this smooth product. In addition to the Boyd & Blair Potato Vodka, Pennsylvania Pure Distilleries produces Boyd & Blair Professional Proof, a 151 proof version of the potato vodka, and Stonewall Rum.

The Church Brew Works, 3525 Liberty Ave., Lawrenceville, Pittsburgh, PA 15201; (412) 688-8200; churchbrew.com. You might feel a bit strange drinking in a church, but it's totally okay and actually encouraged at The Church Brew Works. Since 1996, The Church Brew Works has been brewing one-of-a-kind beers for the Pittsburgh beer-drinking community. The brews are crafted right on the altar in beautiful, shiny copper pots. The best-selling beer is the Pious Monk Dunkel, a dark lager, but The Church Brew Works also offers several ales and stouts, as well as seasonal beers. If you're looking for a nonalcoholic beverage, try the homemade ginger ale and root beer. Feel free to ask questions about the brewing process, and the history of the building itself, a restored Catholic church, which achieved Historic Landmark status in 2001. Visitors are known to say it's somewhat of a religious experience.

Copper Kettle Brewing Company, 557 Greenfield Ave., Greenfield, Pittsburgh, PA 15207; (412) 906-9400; copperkettlepgh .com. Copper Kettle is the first of its kind in Pittsburgh—you can brew and bottle your own beer. It has over 50 recipes that range from ales to stouts. Once you choose your recipe, you get started on the process. Take a few of your closest beer-loving friends and prepare to get your brewin' on. You'll be making the equivalent of two or five cases of beer so there will be plenty to go around. Once the beer has fermented for 2 to 3 weeks, head back to collect your prize! Extend the fun a little further and think of a great name for the custom label for your newly brewed bottles. After you brew your beer at Copper Kettle, be sure to stop by and celebrate your achievement at Hough's Taproom & Brew-pub, with over 200 bottled craft brews and over 70 craft taps.

Duquesne Brewing Company, 2581 Washington Rd., Suite 221, Upper St. Clair, Pittsburgh, PA 15241; duquesnebeer.com. Once the leading brand of beer in Pennsylvania, Duquesne Brewing Company was resurrected in 2010 by local entrepreneur and attorney Mark Dudash. Brewed in the South Side from 1887 to 1972, its new home is in Latrobe, Pennsylvania, alongside another Pittsburgh beverage legend, Iron City. The recipe is as close to the original as possible with a few ingredient upgrades. The Pilsner has a familiar golden color, bright white foaming head when poured, and tastes less hoppy than other similar-style beers. For light beer drinkers try Duquesne LT, the low-calorie version of the Pilsener. It can be found in various locations around Pennsylvania and comes in bottles, cans, and draft. Not only has the beer been resurrected but also its mascot, "The Prince of Pilsner." So be sure to salute the Prince as he raises his glass to you!

East End Brewing Company, 147 Julius St., Larimer, Pittsburgh, PA 15206; (412) 537-2337; eastendbrewing.com. East End Brewing Company calls itself Pittsburgh's "micro-est microbrewery." While it may be a small outfit, word is out that these brews are super fine and 'Burghers can't get enough. East End has year-round beers and, like any quality microbrewery, a rotation of seasonal beers and some occasional one-off beers for the hops aficionado in us all. Our favorite year-rounder is the Black Strap Stout, a rich, dark beer made with blackstrap molasses and brown sugar. One of the seasonal ales, the Pedal Pale Ale, is kicked off with the brewery's annual Keg Ride bike ride. The ride starts at the brewery and is led by the owner and volunteers who pull kegs of Pedal Pale Ale behind them on trailers. Hundreds of fans are led by the owner to a mystery bar location that receives the first kegs of PPA. Fun bonus: In late fall, the brewery leads a Reverse Keg Ride to pick up the kicked kegs from the lucky bar that got the first batch of PPA! Check out the website for event details and to get the Brewery's growler hours. You can also fill up your growler at the **Pittsburgh Public Market** (p. 54).

Engine House 25, 3339 Penn Ave., Lawrenceville, Pittsburgh, PA 15201; (412) 621-1268; enginehouse25.com. In this former Lawrenceville firehouse, you will find a mixture of spaces—part rental space, part photography studio, part winery, and part Roberto Clemente Museum. The man running these unique businesses is celebrated advertising photographer Duane Rieder. After years of making wine as gifts for his photography clients, Duane decided to start producing and selling Cabernet, Zinfandel, and Malbec to a more public consumer.

PGH Taco Truck

If you see the red and yellow PGH Taco Truck zooming around town, you should follow it to its intended destination. The tacos are crazy delicious. Owner James Rich started hitting the streets around Pittsburgh in the PGH Taco Truck in January 2013. And ever since, he has created a cultlike following for his tasty street food creations.

His inspiration for the taco-centric truck came from his love affair with tacos at an early age. At age 15, James traveled to Mexico City with his grandmother. One night, he snuck out of his hotel room and into an open air market, purchasing as many tacos as he could with his $20 weekly allowance. He immediately fell in love.

We're glad he fell in love with tacos, because James is creating some of the best tacos around. For about $4–$5, you can sink your teeth into some of his mouthwatering creations like the zesty Thai peanut chicken taco topped with a sweet chili slaw, and the pork taco braised in **East End Brewing** (p. 195) beer and sprinkled with queso blanco cheese. All taco lovers can rejoice with James's creations, as he always has a few vegan and vegetarian options, such as the curried organic potato taco topped with chipotle crema or the zucchini and mushroom taco topped with queso chihuahua cheese and guacamole, on his ever-changing menu.

In addition to tacos, which are all gluten-free, James is grilling up quesadillas, serving up hearty beef and bean chili, and even offering some secret "off the menu specials." Several of these specials have included honey sesame chicken wings, Korean steak tacos with kimchee, and lobster rolls served on crusty **La Gourmandine** (p. 185) baguettes

Though you can find the truck mostly posted up in the front parking lot of Coffee Buddha Coffee Shop in the suburban North Hills or outside of the custom screen-printing company, Ink Division, in Braddock, you just never know where the truck will be next. To find out where the truck will be and what the daily menu offerings are, follow **PGH Taco Truck** on Twitter (@PGHTacoTruck), Facebook, and online at pghtacotruck.com.

The Engine House No. 25 Wine is produced in the engine house's cellar with Californian grapes, and the wine bottle labels all don photographs shot by Duane over the years, including portraits of Pittsburgh Penguins and Steelers and, of course, Roberto Clemente. The basement provides a dark and cool climate for aging wine, especially due to the 21-inch-thick walls (coincidentally, 21 was Roberto Clemente's Pirates jersey number). You can schedule a tour of the winery by contacting Engine House 25 via email or phone. And while you're at it, plan a trip to the Clemente Museum, too. Because a trip to Pittsburgh isn't really complete without learning a little something you didn't know about Clemente.

Full Pint Brewing, **1963 Lincoln Hwy., North Versailles, PA 15137; fullpintbrewing.com.** What happens when beer-loving gents put their heads together over a few pints and start dreaming? They start a brewery! Full Pint Brewing combines the tasty talents of several local brewmasters and provides Pittsburgh with some of the best beers around. Most famous of those brews is the White Lightning. It's a light beer with citrus flavor, and it can be found in bars all over the city. While White Lightning is one of the favorites among 'Burghers, we recommend the Perc E Bust, their full-bodied porter brewed with coffee. Who doesn't love a two-fer? Full Pint is well-known for their sample tastings, which take place at local bars and restaurants around town. They also offer growler fill-ups.

Maggie's Farm Rum, **3212A Smallman St., Strip District, Pittsburgh, PA 15201; (412) 709-6480; maggiesfarmrum.com.** Pittsburgh's history is rich with spirit. Or should we say spirits? Prohibition shut down the scene in the 'Burg for years and years and lately, the libations have begun to creep back into town. Local whiskey, gin, vodka, and cider can be found at distilleries and watering holes in and around the city these days. One liquid was missing from the pack until Maggie's Farm Rum came along to round out the alcoholic offering: rum. At Maggie's guests can peek behind the bar and watch the magic happen. Said magic can't be missed since it happens inside a humongous copper pot. The perfectly crafted booze is bottled up and sold to 'Burghers by the fifth at the unsuspecting shop on Smallman Street in the historic Strip District. While most might miss the Rum for Sale sign on the sidewalk, others know just where to look and come in to enjoy a cleverly named cocktail during happy hour while they load up on some take-home treats.

North Country Brewing, 141 S. Main St., Slippery Rock, PA 16057; (724) 794-2337; northcountrybrewing.com. North Country Brewing is worth the 50-mile drive upstate. The brewery is a rustic building on the main street in Slippery Rock, Pennsylvania. Log cabin-esque, North Country is riddled with wood inside and out, from the sturdy deck out front to the long bar downstairs and the ceiling beams up above. It's definitely a place you can feel cozy in, especially when you're cuddled up in a corner booth with a frosty pint glass of their Liquid Love Double Stout. We think the brewery is one of the best places within a 60-mile radius that serves seriously slammin' barbecue. Slap that smoked pork barbecue on a kaiser roll, slather it with North Country's dark and decadent barbecue sauce and famous slaw, and you have yourself one heck of a dinner date. It brews everything on location and beers can change daily, so if you find something you like, be sure to fill up a growler on the way out. We recommend the Vanilla Porter, always a fan favorite for its desserty aftertaste; the brewmaster's Fruit Bowl, which is the North Country Ale with whatever fruit the brewmaster is fancying that day; and the Double Vision I.P.A. that is so strong there is actually a 2-pint maximum.

Penn Brewery, 800 Vinial St., Troy Hill, Pittsburgh, PA 15212; (412) 237-9400; pennbrew.com. Penn Brewery has an interesting claim to fame. The modern-day Penn Brewery opened back in 1989, under the name of Allegheny Brewery & Pub, and was the first "tied house" (restaurant tied to a brewery) in the entire state of Pennsylvania since Prohibition. The brewery cranks out numerous craft beers that can be found in many local bars. The flagship, Penn Pilsner, is by far the most popular, but Penn Dark and Penn Summer Berry Weisse are some of our favorites. Depending on the season, the Brewery crafts select beers, so be sure to ask your server or bartender what the current flavor is. One of our favorite seasonal brews is the St. Nikolaus Bock, available during the Christmas holiday season. The St. Nikolaus has subtle notes of chocolate and is the perfect adult beverage to enjoy on a cold winter night. The Brewery also offers unique menu items to complement the brews. We dig its buffalo chicken pierogies because there's nothing quite like a Pittsburgh twist on traditional fare to make our hearts skip a beat. We also recommend the Polish Hill Plate, which is a heaping helping of smoked kielbasa, potato cheese pierogies, grilled onions, and sauerkraut.

Pittsburgh Brewing Company, 3340 Liberty Ave., Lawrenceville, Pittsburgh, PA 15201; (412) 682-7400; pittsburghbrewing.com. If you ask any Pittsburgher what the most famous local beer is, chances are, he or she will tell you it's "Arn City," aka Iron City. If you are watching your calories, then it's I.C. Light. Why? Because Pittsburgh Brewing Company has been brewing Iron City Beer for over 150 years. In addition to Iron City Beer and I.C. Light, the Pittsburgh Brewing Company brews up I.C. Light Mango, American, American Light, and Old German. Over 150 years ago, Iron City was brewed in Lawrenceville but has since moved brewing operations to Latrobe, Pennsylvania. (Don't fret. The company's headquarters are still located in Lawrenceville.) Though the beers are brewed on the city's outskirts, Iron City bleeds black and gold. Besides boosting Pittsburgh pride in every can, Iron City has achieved some firsts in the beer industry. In 1962 Iron City was the first beer to be sold in a snap top can, and in 2004 Iron City and I.C. Light were the first beers in the nation to be sold in aluminum bottles. So, when you are in Pittsburgh, you have to order at least one "Arn City" or I.C. Light on draft, because, well, that's just how it's done around here.

Pittsburgh Seltzer Works, 1671 Monongahela Ave., Swiss-vale, Pittsburgh, PA 15218; (412) 431-1898; pittsburghseltzerworks .com. Vintage charm and bubble-filled water await you at Pittsburgh Seltzer Works, just east of the Squirrel Hill tunnels. Pittsburgh Seltzer Works crafts crisp, carbonated water, bottles it up in gorgeous, antique glass bottles, and delivers right to your front door. Seltzer is sold in cases of 10 at just $1.50 per bottle, after a one-time, refundable deposit of $35. The absolutely lovely bottles steal the show, each one a happy hue and boasting a different town of origin. All the glass bottles predate the 1940s as the factory that manufactured the bottles was destroyed during World War II. You'll be sipping your seltzer from a bit of history! So how do you fulfill your carbonation craving? The best way to order is by visiting the company's Facebook page and posting on the wall any form of "hey, I need some seltzer." Pittsburgh Seltzer Works delivers to the East End neighborhoods only, but you can always arrange a seltzer pickup and see the amazing bottle inventory firsthand. The Seltzer crew is usually around on Monday and Friday, but call ahead just in case. After a sample, your love for this specialty water will never fizzle.

Rebellion Ciderworks, 499 Grove City Rd., Slippery Rock, PA 16057; (724) 967-1609; rebellionciderworks.com. Western Penn-sylvania is lucky enough to be home to many an apple orchard, and lucky for Pittsburghers, some of those apples make their way into deli-cious hard cider. North of the city, in Slippery Rock, sits a renovated barn, and in that renovated barn sits a cider press. From that press comes drop after drop of some of the region's best booze. At Rebellion Ciderworks, you're invited to watch, learn, taste, and enjoy. The family operation is dedicated to preserving the process of creating cider from a press that is over 90 years old and producing a quality product not rivaled in this area. Bottled up in beautiful blue growlers emblazoned with Rebellion's mark, the cider is sold in local eateries, farmers' markets, and at the orchard. If you're new to this type of alcoholic drink, they'll help you choose which of their ciders will please your palate. From the still, dry Wagon Wheel, which they say "pairs well with bluegrass music" to the lighter, semi-sweet Mackenna's Premiere, which is named after the owners' daughter (awww!), you will be sure to find something that you'll enjoy sipping on as you count your lucky stars you live in (or are visiting) Western Pennsylvania.

Red Star Kombucha, 5001 Penn Ave., Garfield, Pittsburgh, PA 15224; (412) 897-6943; inglobwetrust.com. Located in Garfield, Red Star Kombucha is Pennsylvania's first licensed kombucha brewery. It started brewing this ancient Chinese health elixir made by fermenting tea back in 2012. Today, the brewery has three "adult" kombuchas: Original Green made with green tea; 1877 made with black tea and lemon; and Zingerbuch made with fresh ginger and hibiscus flowers. You can find Red Star Kombuchas on tap at **Franktuary** (p. 24) and Belevederes Ultra-Dive in Lawrenceville, and in 4-pack bottles to go at the **Beehive Coffeehouse** in South Side (p. 68), **Mineo's Pizza House** in Squirrel Hill (p. 165), and many other local markets. Check Red Star's website for more information.

Rivertowne Brewing, 5578 Old William Penn Hwy., Export, PA 15632; (724) 519-2145; myrivertowne.com. You know you're drinking a Rivertowne beer when you see the brewery's mascot, Wylie the fish, on the can. His image graces each can of lager and ale that the brewery produces. He appears very Warhol-esque on the can of his namesake beer, Old Wylie's IPA, an India pale ale that took the brewmaster one and a half decades to perfect. And on a can of the sweet and fruity Hala Kahiki Pineapple Ale, he's donning a grass skirt and lei. In addition to crafting a line of beers offered year-round, seasonal beers also pop up, like Patrick's Poison Imperial Red Ale around St. Patrick's Day. At Rivertowne Brewery you can take a tour of the facilities on Saturday or stop by the tasting room to pick up a keg, six-pack, or case of beer. In addition to finding the beers at local restaurants and bars, you can visit one of Rivetowne's four restaurants in Monroeville, the North Shore, North Huntington, and Verona to taste the locally brewed beers and scarf down some sandwiches, pizzas, pastas, and more.

Roundabout Brewery, 4901 Butler St., Lawrenceville, Pittsburgh, PA 15201; roundaboutbeer.com. The brewmaster at Roundabout Brewery is well-traveled. He's acted as brewmaster in cities around the world including one stint in Pittsburgh. So when the chance to start brewing his own beer came about, he jumped at the chance. Steve and his wife Dyana Sloan opened their small brewery in what used to be a granite and marble countertop factory in late 2013. Inspired by Steve's past brewing experience and Dyana's New Zealand heritage, Roundabout offers a unique craft portfolio including stouts, wheats, ales, and IPA's. Beers rotate frequently, but if the delicious and light Ginga Wheat is on tap, it's one we recommend. It's an American-style wheat beer made with fresh pressed ginger, McCormack honey from an Aliquippa farm, and lemon. Roundabout currently only sells 32- or 64-ounce growlers, priced at $8 to $9 and $13 to $18 respectively. Head to the tasting room to sample what's on tap before buying.

Wigle Whiskey, 2401 Smallman St., Strip District, Pittsburgh, PA 15222; wiglewhiskey.com. Wigle Whiskey is the first distillery of its kind in Pittsburgh since Prohibition. It's named after Phillip Wigle a rebellious whiskey-lover and igniter of the Whiskey Rebellion. Paying close attention to tradition while implementing modern innovation,

Wigle Whiskey produces a variety of spirits: organic white (wheat and rye) and aged Pennsylvania-style whiskies (both are made with local resources and by following a similar process Phillip Wigle once used); organic Ginever, a Dutch-style whiskey-based gin; and spiced and Landlocked Rum (made with Penn-  sylvania buckwheat honey and unlike any rum you've ever had). Wigle also makes small-batch bitters to help kick your cocktails up a notch. Group and private tours of the distillery are available, during which you'll get a complete history lesson of the distillery's namesake. But let's not forget about the best part of a distillery tour—tasting the product! You can sample and purchase the various spirits in the tast- ing room. Be sure to look up while you're slowly savoring the flavor: a lighting fixture made from its glass whiskey bottles brightens the room.

Recipes

So, you've read about where to dine out in Pittsburgh, now try your hand at some of these restaurants' recipes. From cocktails and milkshakes, to pasta and pot pie, these recipes are sure to please any food lover of Pittsburgh. And, if you aren't daring enough, just remember: You can always make a reservation.

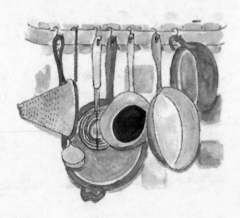

Bangkok Tea

Soba's fundamental cocktail characteristics make up this signature drink. Made with house-made green tea vodka, fresh squeezed sours blend, and house-made ginger-honey syrup, Soba's recipe makes a refreshingly unique cocktail.

1½ ounces green tea-infused vodka (recipe follows)

1 ounce ginger-honey simple syrup (recipe follows)

½ ounce sours mix

1 ounce club soda

In a shaker half-filled with ice, combine the infused vodka, ginger-honey syrup, and fresh sours. Shake well. Strain into a collins glass almost filled with ice cubes. Add club soda. Stir and garnish with a lemon slice.

Green Tea Vodka

750 ml bottle vodka

6 teaspoons sencha green tea leaves

Place tea leaves into the bottle of vodka and let sit for 2 days. Strain and re-bottle.

Ginger-Honey Simple Syrup

1 cup roughly chopped fresh ginger (skin on)

2 cups honey

½ cup white sugar

3 cups water

In a medium saucepan add all ingredients and bring to a boil. Reduce to simmer; let simmer for 30 minutes. Turn off heat and let cool for 1 hour. Remove ginger and strain.

Courtesy of Ryan Burke, General Manager of Soba Lounge (p. 131)

Candied Yams

Carmi Family Restaurant is home to fantastic Southern cooking and hospitality to match. Carleen King, along with husband and chef, Michael King, never actually lived in the South, but she got schooled on soul food from her aunts and grandparents starting at a very young age. Soul food preparation was always treated as a special occasion, with all the women of the family gathering to cook . . . and gossip! "This is where I developed my poker face. The trick was not to react to anything you heard," says Carleen.

After years of absorbing juicy stories and delicious culinary tips, while quietly shelling peas and peeling potatoes, Carleen is full of good secrets. She shares one with all of you in the form of a sweet side dish. Assemble your relatives; start cooking and start talking.

5 pounds fresh yams, peeled and sliced 1 inch thick

3 cups sugar

1 cup brown sugar

⅛ teaspoon nutmeg

½ teaspoon cinnamon

1 tablespoon lemon juice or ¼ teaspoon lemon zest

1 teaspoon vanilla extract

1 cup butter

½ cup water

Preheat oven to 350°F.

Mix all ingredients together in a large bowl.

Bake loosely covered for approximately 2 hours.

Courtesy of Carleen Kenney, Owner of Carmi Family Restaurant (p. 61)

The Captain Spaulding

The Smiling Moose has character, and so does its cocktail menu. Each cocktail is named after legendary movies, movie characters, and props. One of those drinks that best represents The Smiling Moose is The Captain Spaulding because, like the menu says, it's "Tutti F-ing Frutti!"

1½ ounces vodka
1 ounce peach schnapps
1 ounce Malibu rum

½ ounce Triple Sec
½ ounce Grenadine

Fill shaker with above ingredients and add 1 part orange juice and 1 part cream. Shake and serve with ice in a pint glass.

Courtesy of Mike P. Scarlatelli, Owner of The Smiling Moose (p. 84)

Carrot Cake with Cream Cheese Icing & Caramel Sauce

Pineapple in a carrot cake? Crazy, but delicious. Pastry Chef James Wroblewski at Habitat has taken his mother's original carrot cake recipe and classed it up with pineapple and caramel sauce. This recipe was one of the first dishes his mother taught him to make, and throughout the years since, he has found a way to make the original his own. This more sophisticated carrot cake reflects the cooking style of both him and Habitat: using quality ingredients, bringing out their natural flavors, and creating a killer presentation. Chef James says not to be intimidated by this recipe. The preparation is easy, and the few extra steps definitely make a world of difference.

Makes 10 individual servings

Roasted Pineapple

1 fresh pineapple
10 ounces brown sugar
¼ teaspoon cinnamon

¼ teaspoon vanilla bean seeds
   (beans split and scraped)
2 ounces honey
¼ cup Myers's Rum

Peel, quarter, and core pineapple. Spread brown sugar evenly on the bottom of a roasting pan and place pineapple on brown sugar. Sprinkle with cinnamon and vanilla bean seeds. Pour honey and rum over pineapple and roast at 350°F for 30 minutes. Flip each piece and roast for an additional 30 minutes or until tender. Cool and dice, then store in an airtight container in refrigerator.

Carrot Cake

10 ounces peeled and shredded carrots
6 ounces granulated sugar
4 ounces brown sugar
6 tablespoons vegetable oil
5 ounces whole eggs
2 teaspoons whole milk

¼ ounce cinnamon
¼ ounce salt
10 ounces all-purpose flour
½ ounce baking soda
9 ounces diced roasted
   pineapple
1 ounce raisins

Grease an 8-inch x 8-inch pan and line bottom with parchment paper. Mix carrots, sugars, and oil. Whisk eggs and milk together, add to carrots, and mix well, scraping occasionally. Add dry ingredients and blend until well mixed. Add diced pineapple and raisins and mix until just incorporated. Pour mixture into pan. Bake at 350°F for about 40 to 50 minutes. Allow to cool.

Cream Cheese Icing

4 ounces unsalted butter	18 ounces cream cheese
8 ounces powdered sugar	1 teaspoon vanilla extract

Beat butter and powdered sugar in mixer until light and fluffy. Scrape bowl to prevent lumps. Add cream cheese and continue to mix until smooth, scraping frequently. Add vanilla extract and blend well. Store in an airtight container.

Caramel Sauce

4 ounces unsalted butter	1 ounce heavy cream
8 ounces granulated sugar	

Cook butter and sugar over medium-high heat until dark amber color; do not stir. Remove from heat and add cream slowly, whisking to incorporate. Strain and cool. Store in an airtight container in refrigerator.

To assemble the cake, trim top of the cake so that it is even. Flip the cake over so the cut side is down. Spread cream cheese icing over top, ¼ inch thick. Refrigerate for at least 20 minutes. Cut into bars 4 inches x 1¼ inch. Drizzle with caramel sauce.

Courtesy of James D. Wroblewski II, Pastry Chef of Habitat Restaurant (p. 25)

Chicken Potpie

At Meat & Potatoes, the menu is filled with much more than these two food staples. Chef Richard DeShantz's menu at this Downtown gastropub is filled with items he would eat himself after a busy day in the kitchen. Bone marrow, wings, burgers, tacos, and of course, steaks fill the menu, as well as his take on a traditional chicken potpie. In his recipe, chicken skin is deep-fried golden brown and added to the pie's flaky crust. Though the recipe has a few extra steps in the preparation, you will never want to have another frozen potpie again after making this one.

Chicken Stock

1 whole chicken
2 cups chopped onion
1 cup chopped carrots
1 cup chopped celery
1 cup chopped leeks

2 bay leaves
1 bunch thyme
1 bunch parsley, with stems
1 tablespoon peppercorns

Pull skin off chicken and reserve. Add all ingredients to a stockpot and simmer on low for 2 hours. Pull chicken out, dice into medium-size pieces, and set aside. Drain stock and return stock liquid to a pot and reduce by half.

Crust

Skin from chicken, cut into
medium pieces
2½ cups all-purpose flour

1¼ teaspoons salt
2½ sticks butter, cold
5–6 tablespoons ice water

Cut chicken skin into medium-size pieces and deep-fry. In a bowl mix flour and salt together. Add butter and mix until butter is no larger than the size of a pea. Add in water and chicken skin. Knead dough into a ball and set aside.

Potpie Base

1 cup pearl onions	1 cup quartered red-skinned potatoes
1 cup medium-diced carrots	Roux (recipe follows)

Place all ingredients into reduced chicken stock and simmer on low for 45 minutes. After 45 minutes, add in roux.

Roux

1 tablespoon butter	6 tablespoons flour

Cook on stovetop until light golden color for about 4 to 6 minutes. Add cooked roux to potpie base 1 tablespoon at a time until the base becomes thick.

Assembling the Chicken Potpie

To thickened chicken stock, add in reserved chopped chicken, 1 teaspoon thyme, 2 tablespoons parsley, 1 teaspoon chives, 1 teaspoon tarragon, and season with salt and pepper. Place mixture into a pie pan. Roll out dough and place on top. Crimp pie edge and slice a center vent into the crust top. Brush with egg wash (1 egg mixed with 3 teaspoons water) and bake at 375°F 30 to 40 minutes until top is golden brown. Cool for 10 minutes before slicing.

Courtesy of Tolga Sevdik of Meat & Potatoes (p. 27)

Falafel

Root 174 Chef Keith Fuller has a playful approach to food preparation, with creative food ideas peppered into every dish that leaves the kitchen. Keith was inspired to cook up this recipe because of a childhood trip to a Middle Eastern restaurant that left a lasting impression and love for falafel. This love had a catch, though, as falafel texture was always dry and gritty. So Keith resolved to make his own dish creamier and less gritty, while still staying true to its falafel roots. Enjoy the product of Keith's experimenting—a creamy falafel packed full of fresh herb flavoring—and don't forget to have a little fun!

2 (15-ounce) cans chickpeas, drained and rinsed
½ teaspoon cayenne pepper
3 cloves garlic, chopped
3 cloves roasted garlic
½ teaspoon paprika
½ teaspoon ground coriander
½ teaspoon granulated garlic

2 teaspoons lemon juice
3 tablespoons olive oil
Salt and pepper to taste
¼ cup each chopped parsley and chopped cilantro
2 eggs, beaten, for dredge
1 cup panko bread crumbs, for dredge

Add all ingredients except for herbs, eggs, and panko bread crumbs to the work bowl of a large food processor. Process on high until uniform and creamy. Remove to a large mixing bowl. Fold in herbs. Portion into 1-ounce balls and dredge in egg wash followed by panko bread crumbs. Fry in 350°F oil until crispy. Yields approximately 30 1-ounce portions. Serve with tzatziki (recipe follows).

Tzatziki

½ cucumber, seeded and diced
½ red onion, finely diced
Zest and juice 1 lime
1 tablespoon chopped mint
1 tablespoon chopped cilantro

2 tablespoons red wine vinegar
1 cup plain yogurt
¼ cup sour cream
Salt and pepper to taste

Mix all ingredients thoroughly and let stand in refrigerator for at least 20 minutes or up to 1 hour.

Courtesy of Keith Fuller, Chef and Owner of Root 174 (p. 126)

PB & J Milk Shake

Beyond dessert, milk shakes are the perfect way to end a meal or even to have as a meal on their own! In Pittsburgh, we have The Milk Shake Factory by Edward Marc Chocolatier, which can shake up over 50 flavors. In the summer of 2010, The Milk Shake Factory held a contest for customers to pick their favorite out of five flavors. The PB & J Milk Shake won as the most popular and was placed on the menu. It is still one of the most popular milk shakes on the menu, and we can see why. Both a milk shake and a PB & J sandwich are reminiscent of our childhoods, and having them blended together is the perfect combination.

Strawberry Syrup

1 pint fresh strawberries
¼ cup sugar

2 tablespoons orange juice
1 cup chilled water

Combine all ingredients in a saucepan and simmer over medium heat for about 6 minutes, stirring constantly. Puree the sauce in a blender and strain if preferred. Chill for milk shake.

Note: If using frozen berries, use ½ cup water.

Milk Shake

8 ounces strawberry ice cream
1 ounce creamy peanut butter
1 ounce strawberry syrup
6 ounces whole milk

Whipped cream
½ ounce crushed honey-roasted peanuts
1 whole strawberry

Using milk shake mixer or blender, blend ice cream, peanut butter, strawberry syrup, and 4 ounces milk. While blending, add remaining milk slowly and blend until smooth. Serve in a tall glass and top with whipped cream, crushed peanuts, and a fresh strawberry for garnish. Serve immediately.

Courtesy of Christian Edwards, Co-owner of The Milk Shake Factory
by Edward Marc Chocolatier (p. 88)

Roasted Carrots, Fresh Cheese, Toasted Edamame, Little Gems Lettuce & Chili Vinaigrette

At Grit & Grace, Chef-Owner Brian Pekarcik and Chef de Cuisine Curtis Gamble have created a menu with familiar dishes, but pulled in new interesting directions. A fried bologna sandwich is reinvented with house-made mortadella and served on a steam bun, a nod to Brian's Asian-American upbringing. And the familiar breakfast combination of hot sauce on eggs has been re-created as the egg yolk hot sauce served on the crispy pig face sandwich. In this recipe, you will create a salad based upon Brian and Curtis's take on the side dish of peas and carrots.

Roasted Carrots

2 bunches mixed-color baby carrots, with tops
2 tablespoons extra-virgin olive oil

1 teaspoon ground coriander
Salt and pepper to taste

Preheat oven to 325°F. Trim the carrot tops off the mixed baby carrots and wash thoroughly under room temperature water. Place carrots in a bowl and toss with extra-virgin olive oil, coriander, salt, and pepper. Place carrots on a roasting pan and roast until the carrots are tender, turning every 10 minutes. Carrots should be tender enough to smash between your fingers.

While carrots are roasting, clean outer shell off edamame and set aside. Also, make chili vinaigrette and fresh cheese.

Chili Vinaigrette

1 tablespoon fennel seeds
1 medium shallot
2 tablespoons white miso paste
½ cup white balsamic
2 teaspoons sambal chili paste

3 tablespoons honey
1 tablespoon grated ginger
Salt to taste
1½ cups canola oil

In a saucepan over medium heat, toast fennel seeds until fragrant, about 2 minutes. Remove from heat. Place all ingredients except canola oil into a blender. Blend on low and slowly drizzle in canola oil to emulsify. Set aside.

Fresh Cheese

1 gallon whole milk	1 teaspoon citric acid
1 cup white distilled vinegar	Salt to taste

In a stockpot on low heat, combine all ingredients. Note: do not simmer. Heat until curds separate and then remove from heat. Strain mixture through a cheese cloth or kitchen towel. Discard the whey. Place curds into a bowl and season with salt to taste. Set aside.

Toasted Edamame
1 bag frozen edamame, thawed and outer shells removed

Heat a large sauté pan over medium heat until almost smoking. Add edamame and char on one side. Once charred, remove from pan and place on a plate to cool. Char edamame in batches until you have charred the entire bag.

To Serve

3 heads of little gems lettuce, cleaned and trimmed to ¼ dollar bill-size pieces	Toasted edamame
	Chili vinaigrette
	Fresh cheese curds
Mixed carrots	Salt to taste

Toss little gems lettuce, mixed carrots, and edamame with chili vinaigrette in a large bowl. Season with salt to taste. Arrange lettuce on 4 plates, showcasing the carrots and edamame on top. Crumble fresh cheese over salad and spring with a touch of sea salt on top.

Courtesy of Brian Pekarcik, Chef-Owner of Grit & Grace (p. 24)

Short Rib Pierogies

Pittsburgh's culinary scene is a mixing pot of cultures and flavors, a city where old-world dishes meet modern flavors. One such dish that we are absolutely in love with is the short rib pierogies at Braddock's Pittsburgh Brasserie. Executive Chef Jason Shaffer works to create unique dishes that are new takes on traditional Pittsburgh classics. This recipe makes enough to feed about an army, which is necessary because these little guys will disappear quickly!

Short Ribs

5 pounds bone-in short ribs, approximately 4 inches cut

Salt and pepper as needed

3 quarts beef stock

2 cups tomato paste

Parchment paper

Foil

Liberally season the short ribs with salt and pepper. Heat a medium-size roasting pan and place ribs in the pan. Quickly sear the short ribs on all sides; remove from heat. Add the stock and tomato paste; the stock should cover the ribs. Place parchment paper on top; this will keep the ribs submerged. Cover with foil or lid and place in the oven at 350°F for 1 to 1½ hours or until the ribs are tender. Remove from the oven and cool to less than 41°F. After they are thoroughly cooled, remove the fat from the top of the cooking liquid and remove the ribs. Reserve the liquid for the sauce. Pull all of the meat from the bones and place in a mixer. Mix the meat on a low speed until it is pureed.

Pierogi Dough

¾ pound cream cheese

12 eggs

9 cups all-purpose flour

Water if needed

Combine all ingredients, adding water if moisture is needed. Roll dough to a ⅛-inch thickness. You can use a rolling pin or pasta machine if you have one. Using a 3-inch ring mold, cut the pierogi rounds.

To assemble the pierogies, place approximately ½ to 1 ounce rib meat in the center of each round and fold over. Pinch edges closed with the tines of a dinner fork and parboil for 2 minutes, then cool.

Creamed Leeks

1 bunch leeks	1 pint heavy cream
Canola oil as needed	Salt and pepper as needed

Remove the green from the leeks and cut in half lengthwise. Thoroughly clean the leeks under cold running water. Cut into thin strips across the width of the leek. Place into a sauté pan over medium heat with a small amount of canola oil. Sweat the leeks for 3 to 5 minutes. Add the heavy cream and simmer for 5 to 8 minutes. Season to taste.

Pan Jus

1 cup burgundy or red wine	Salt and pepper to taste
3 cups braising liquid from the ribs	

Place the wine and braising liquid in a small saucepan and reduce by half over medium heat. Thicken slightly if needed using a cornstarch and water mixture.

Heat a sauté pan over medium heat with 3 tablespoons butter. Add the pierogies and brown slightly on both sides. Add the pan jus and continue cooking for 2 to 3 minutes. Place a small amount of leeks on the plate and arrange the pierogies around them. Finish with a drizzle of the pan jus.

Courtesy of Jason Shaffer, Executive Chef of Braddock's Pittsburgh Brasserie (p. 21)

Smoked Pork

Aramark Executive Chef Carl VanWagner cooks up thousands of meals for hungry hockey fans at every game. His goal is to offer quality, exciting cuisine in a place typically reserved for nachos and beers. A self-taught master of the kitchen, Carl has a fondness for food festivals and excellent barbecue.

CONSOL serves about 500 pounds of pork per game. Can't make it into the arena? Fire up the smoker, because this scaled-down recipe will take you to the game, and the glorious food stands, without leaving the comforts of your own kitchen.

Pork Brine

1 cup Worcestershire sauce
2 pounds brown sugar
2 cups kosher salt

1 gallon water
1 (4- to 6-pound) pork shoulder or Boston butt

Dry Rub

1 cup paprika
2 cups brown sugar
½ cup dry mustard

1 cup kosher salt
½ cup granulated garlic
½ cup onion powder

Mix pork brine ingredients and marinate the pork shoulder or Boston butt in brine for 2 days. Take pork out of brine and let dry for 2 hours.

Mix dry rub ingredients together and rub the pork with dry rub.

Preheat smoker to 220°F. Use 2 pounds apple wood chips in smoker.

Let cook for 8 to 10 hours until fork tender.

Courtesy of Carl VanWagner, Executive Chef of Aramark at CONSOL Energy Center

Spaghetti Carbonara

According to E2's Chef Kate Romane, Spaghetti Carbonara is a hearty, tasty, and easy meal to make. Her recipe here serves 2, though it could easily be doubled or quadrupled because it's sure to be a tasty meal that you will want to make for everyone in your life. Kate suggests making this meal for a cold night or a snuggle date, but we suggest you make it whenever you want. She says that this dish is also known as "the coal miner's pasta." It is very Italian but also representative of the coal mining history of Pennsylvania. Whoever you make this dish for, the fresh ground pepper and the bacon are the key ingredients.

½ pound spaghetti, uncooked
3 thick-cut strips slab bacon,
    par cooked and cubed
¾ cup heavy cream
⅓ cup green peas
Salt
Pepper

1 local egg of choice (E2 uses
    local eggs from Church-
    view Farm)
Parsley (to taste)
Grated Parmesan cheese (to
    taste)

Cook the spaghetti. When the spaghetti is almost done, sauté the bacon in just a touch of olive oil. When the bacon begins to crisp, add in heavy cream and peas. Heat until cream begins to reduce. Add salt and lots of fresh cracked pepper. When spaghetti is perfectly al dente, drain and add to sauté pan then take off the burner. Crack egg directly into pasta and toss. The heat of the pasta will lightly cook the egg and thicken sauce. Add more salt and pepper to taste. Top with parsley and Parmesan cheese and serve.

Courtesy of Kate Romane, Chef-Owner of E2 (p. 105)

Sweet Onion Sauce

Clearly, you can see from our book that there are a lot of hot dog joints we love. But the one we love the most is Franktuary. The concept of the restaurant was born out of a love affair of the New York–style frankfurter, made from quality cuts of beef enclosed in a snappy natural casing, served with sauerkraut, spicy brown mustard, and sweet red onion sauce. Franktuary cofounders Tim Tobitsch and Megan Lindsey based their initial menu around this New York street food staple and have crafted their own unique Sweet Onion Sauce. Though they say this recipe works best with Vidalia onions, you can substitute any variety of onion you have on hand, as long as you cook them low and slow until soft. The ending result of this recipe will be a sauce that is delicious not only on franks but also on burgers, salads, sandwiches, and tofu.

2 large onions (Vidalia will make the sweetest sauce, but yellow or white onions may be substituted)
2 garlic cloves
2 tablespoons oil
½ teaspoon salt
½ teaspoon cornstarch or arrowroot powder

½ cup water
1 tablespoon balsamic vinegar
1 tablespoon brown sugar
1 tablespoon tomato paste
1 teaspoon Dijon mustard
½ teaspoon dried basil
¼ teaspoon cinnamon

Peel the onions and cut in half along the line running from the root to the plant end. Place onions cut side down and slice into thin strips. Dice the garlic cloves.

Heat the oil on medium heat in a large skillet or soup pot and add onions. Sprinkle the salt over top, which will pull the water out of the onions. Cook, stirring occasionally, until the edges start to brown, but do not burn. Then add the garlic and turn the heat down to low.

Whisk together the cornstarch and water. Add remaining ingredients and whisk until smooth.

Stir onions frequently, scraping up any browned bits from the bottom of the pan. When they are uniformly softened, add the liquid.

Combine mixture thoroughly and cover pan with a lid. Simmer on low, stirring occasionally, for 45 minutes or until soft. If sauce gets too dry, add a few tablespoons of water.

Makes enough to liberally top 10 or 12 franks. Keeps in the fridge for a week, possibly more.

Serve on an all-beef natural casing frank with sauerkraut and a spicy white-wine-and-horseradish brown mustard.

Courtesy of Megan Lindsey, Owner of Franktuary (p. 24)

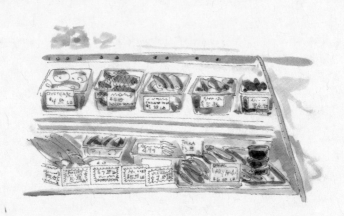

Appendices

Appendix A: Eateries by Cuisine

American

Braddock's Pittsburgh Brasserie, 21
Clifford's Restaurant, 157
Diamond Market Bar & Grill, 23
Nine on Nine, 27
Rachel's Roadhouse, 167
Six Penn Kitchen, 30
Social at Bakery Square, 132
Sonoma Grille, The, 30
Supper Club, The, 169
Ten Penny, 32
Tessaro's, 145
Union Grill, 140
Willow, 172

Asian-Fusion

Grit & Grace, 24
Tamari, 135

Barbecue

Double Wide Grill, 74
Flame BBQ, The, 160
Smoke Barbeque Taqueria, 169
Union Pig & Chicken/Harvard &
    Highland, 140

Breakfast & Lunch

Allegheny Sandwich Shoppe, 59
Bluebird Kitchen, 20
Cafe Moulin, 99
Dor-Stop Restaurant, 158
Original Gab and Eat Restaurant,
    The, 166
Square Cafe, 133
Verde Good Beans, 33
Waffles INCaffeinated, 86

Burgers

Benjamin's Western Avenue Burger
    Bar, 59
BRGR, 97
Burgatory, 155
Winghart's Whiskey & Burger
    Bar, 34

Cafeteria

Our Daily Bread, 28

Cambodian

Cambod-Ican Kitchen, 70

Appendix B: Dishes, Specialties & Specialty Food

Chicken & Waffles
Carmi Family Restaurant, 61
Meat & Potatoes, 27
Piper's Pub, 80
Savoy, 45

Cocktails
Acacia, 68
Bar Marco, 38
Butcher and the Rye, 21
Butterjoint, 98
Grit & Grace, 24
Industry Public House, 112
Kelly's Bar & Lounge, 114
Livermore, The, 117
Salt of the Earth, 128
Spoon, 133
Tender Bar + Kitchen, 136
Union Pig & Chicken/Harvard &
   Highland, 140
Verde Mexican Kitchen
   & Cantina, 141

Crepes
Cafe Moulin, 99
Crepes Parisiennes, 102
Paris 66, 120

Date Night
Alla Famiglia, 87
Casbah, 101
Crested Duck Charcuterie, 73
Dish Osteria and Bar, 73

Eleven Contemporary Kitchen, 41
Legume, 116
Lola Bistro, 63
Notion Restaurant, 119
Root 174, 126
Spoon, 133
Wild Rosemary Bistro, 171
Willow, 172

Dim Sum
Grit & Grace, 24
Everyday Noodles, 107

Fish & Chips
Piper's Pub, 80
Pub Chip Shop, The, 81

French Fries
Hello Bistro, 110
Original Hot Dog Shop, The, 144
Uncle Sam's Sandwich Bar, 146
Wings, Suds & Spuds, 172

Good Beer List
Caliente Pizza & Draft House, 101
Carson Street Deli and Craft Beer
   Bar, 72
Double Wide Grill, 74
Fat Head's Saloon, 87
Franktuary (Lawrenceville), 24
Industry Public House, 112
James Street Gastropub
   & Speakeasy, 62

Local Brews

Made to Order Mozzarella

Margaritas

Meatballs

Milk Shakes

Mollusks

Outside Seating

Index